Hands-On Excel:

Second Edition

Hands-On Excel:

Second Edition

Danny Goodman
Gordon McComb

Scott, Foresman and Company
Glenview, Illinois   London

1 2 3 4 5 6 RRC 93 92 91 90 89

ISBN 0-673-38479-9

Copyright © 1989, Danny Goodman and Gordon McComb.
All Rights Reserved.
Printed in the United States of America.

Library of Congress Cataloging-in-Publication Data

Goodman, Danny.
   Hands-on Excel / Danny Goodman, Gordon McComb.—2nd ed.
     p. cm.
   Includes index.
   ISBN 0-673-38479-9 :
   1. Microsoft Excel (Computer program)   2. Macintosh (Computer)—
   Programming.   3. Business—Data processing.   I. McComb, Gordon.
   II. Title.
   HF5548.4.M523G66   1989   89-4181
   650'.028'55369—dc19   CIP

Excel is a trademark, and Microsoft and Multiplan are registered trademarks of Microsoft Corp.
   Apple is a registered trademark, LaserWriter and ImageWriter are trademarks of Apple Computer, Inc.
   Macintosh is a trademark licensed to Apple Computer, Inc.
   MacPaint and MacDraw are trademarks of Claris (Corp.).
   SuperPaint is a trademark of Silicon Beach Software.
   IBM is a registered trademark of International Business Machines Corporation.
   Lotus and 1-2-3 are registered trademarks, and Jazz is a trademark of Lotus Development Corporation.

Notice of Liability

Scott, Foresman professional books are available for bulk sales at quantity discounts. For information, please contact Marketing Manager, Professional Books Group, Scott, Foresman and Company, 1900 East Lake Avenue, Glenview, IL 60025.

For Patricia Fluegelman

Your courage is forever a reminder
of our beloved Andrew.

ACKNOWLEDGMENTS

Without the help of several people, this book would never have seen the light of day. On the support front, I was thrilled with the outstanding cooperation I received from Microsoft, particularly Mike Slade and my programmer's connection, John Peters. On the production front, I want to thank Patricia Fluegelman for letting me turn her office upside down for a day while printing the book's illustrations. On the publishing front, special thanks go to Bill Gladstone, who brought Amy Davis and me together in the first place. Along the way, other unwitting contributors to ideas in the book included Dan Farber, Adrian Mello, and Andrew Williams. And on the home front, thank you, Linda, for being my critic and biggest supporter, no matter how surly I get near deadlines.

CONTENTS

≡ INTRODUCTION

I once told a computer book critic that I must believe in the quality and functionality of a product before I could ever write a book about it. I can't imagine encouraging owners of second-rate hardware and software to "get more out of" their albatrosses, when all it takes is a purchase of better products to cure most of their ills. With that in mind, I must say I have no reservations about leading you through Excel's nooks and crannies. Excel's popularity is well deserved. Even in the face of new challengers in the spreadsheet category, Excel's powers prevail. Excel has enormous potential energy. This book will help you harness that power and put it to practical use.

≡ How To Use This Book

This is not an accounting or finance book. In no way am I going to tell you how to run your business with a particular system customized for Excel. My job here is more like that of a music instructor. You will learn techniques that will equip you to "play" the Excel instrument like a virtuoso. After that, you can pick up any sheet music (template) that suits you or, better yet, compose your own.

≡ Prerequisites

You are expected to have at least studied the Excel tutorial to get an overview of Excel's structure and operating characteristics. I also recommend that you be acquainted with the overall content of both volumes of the manual. It's quite possible that a lot of what goes on in the *Arrays, Functions, and Macros* volume confused you at first. As you'll see, this book spends a great deal of time explaining and applying those subjects—arrays, functions, and the real power of Excel, macros.

    A term buzzing around personal computer circles these days, particularly when Excel is mentioned, is "power user." I'm not sure of its precise origin, but it has been used in the past to describe those IBM PC users who build huge worksheets in 1-2-3, complete with macros, data tables, and who knows what. Many professionals—who aren't in the least computer nerds—are proud to call themselves power users. In general, a power user is someone who works with one or two programs most of the time and who perceives himself or herself (rightly or wrongly) to be an expert on the software's powers.

You certainly don't have to be a power user to qualify as an Excel user. But by the time you go through this book the first time and start applying some of its strategies and techniques, in my eyes you will qualify as an Excel power user.

☰ What You'll Find in This Book

This book is not a substitute for the Excel manual or even for introductory and beginner's Excel books. It is, rather, an extension of the manual. In it, I'll demonstrate a large number of Excel's advanced built-in features in actual applications. I first learned about Excel's higher powers predominantly through trial and error, plus a little help from the technical folks at Microsoft. The following pages contain in-depth demonstrations of elements located throughout the Excel manual—elements that you might not have realized work together to produce sophisticated applications. I will share with you my ideas, experiences, and strategies to help you use Excel efficiently and productively.

The text of this book is divided into two parts. Part One gets right down to business with an extensive list of shortcuts and hard strategies for the four primary elements of Excel.

Chapter 1, Shortcuts, is a compendium of shortcuts valuable for day-to-day use of Excel. While a few are mentioned in the manual, the vast majority are not.

Unless you've had experience with macros on other computers, you'll find them to be a new concept for you. That's why in Chapter 2, Macro Strategies, you'll learn from the ground up about macro basics and how macros can be used effectively in your applications. You also are treated to examples of generic macros that you'll want to have handy on your disk at all times.

Chapter 3, Spreadsheet Strategies, details specific strategies to make your spreadsheets more workable and powerful. You'll uncover new ways of managing multiple documents, overlapping windows, and the contents of large spreadsheets. You'll also see several powerful macros at work.

Chapter 4, Database Strategies, shows you how to exploit the far-reaching database facilities inside Excel. You'll be introduced to Excel as a relational database and shown how to take advantage of some "secret" tips that save you a great deal of trouble and strife.

Chapter 5, Graphics Strategies, starts from the basics of selecting the right chart for the kind of message you want to send. Different charts have different requirements about how data should be arranged on the worksheet. You'll see how the organization of worksheet figures affects the outcome of your charts. You'll also see how great things can be done with Excel graphics inside MacDraw and MacPaint.

Chapter 6 discusses a feature new to release 1.5 of Excel, custom dialog boxes and menus. With the help of special macro commands, you can create your own menus and dialog boxes, making Excel look and act like a stand-alone application.

Part II applies advanced Excel techniques to a variety of real-life situations. You'll discover Excel's extensive repertoire of features and capabilities through the use of many examples: financial recordkeeping, information retrieval, decision support, sales management, forecasting, and more. Consider this section as an "ideabook" to stimulate your thinking about how you can apply these techniques to the specifics of your own business or personal life.

One final suggestion: Keep a Macintosh and a copy of Excel handy when reading this book. Make it a habit to re-create many of the models and macros described in the book. It is virtually impossible to gain expertise on a software product simply by reading about it. You'll have to scoot the mouse around a table and tap on the keyboard to try various techniques—but it's worth it.

So grab the book in one hand, the mouse in the other, and get your Hands-On Excel.

PART
1

PRINCIPLES
FOR
POWER
USERS

Chapter **1**
SHORTCUTS

Command-Key Equivalents
Opening Excel from the Desktop
Excel Menus
Data-Entry Shortcuts
Defining Names

Many software manuals and tutorial books seem to make you learn the formal way of doing things before revealing shortcuts that could have saved time had they been introduced earlier. As far as I'm concerned, you've already paid your dues with Excel. You've gone through the Excel tutorial, perhaps even tried to understand what that *Arrays, Functions, and Macros* manual is all about. It's time you got to know the shortcuts built into Excel—and there are scads of them not covered in the manual. I want you to learn them now, because you'll be using them throughout the rest of this book and, I hope, the rest of your Excel life.

≣ COMMAND-KEY EQUIVALENTS

The simplest shortcuts to identify are, of course, the Command-key equivalents listed on the various pull-down menus. For example, when you pull down the File menu, you see that five menu items—New, Open, Save, Print, and Quit—have Command-key equivalents next to them.

File	
New...	⌘N
Open...	⌘O
Links...	
Close All	
Save	⌘S
Save As...	
Delete...	
Page Setup...	
Print...	⌘P
Printer Setup...	
Quit	⌘Q

Instead of pulling down the menu with the mouse, you can simply hold down the Command ([⌘])key and press a single letter key. It's not important that you systematically learn or use every Command-key equivalent. But you should be conscious of the keyboard and mouse flow in the kinds of work you do regularly and how Command-key equivalents can improve that flow.

It's a nuisance to be busily typing away on the keyboard and find that you must reach for the mouse to pull down a menu for a single command. That kind of hand jumping gives mouse-pointing devices a bad name. Ideally, you should be able to perform a long series of actions on either the keyboard or mouse, instead of constantly hopping back and forth for single commands or keystrokes. If you find yourself leaping from keyboard to mouse and back a lot, then pay particular attention to the menu items that you select on your mouse sidetrips. With any luck, the selections you make most often will have Command-key equivalents. Gradually work these equivalents into your keyboard work. The keys associated with most menu commands in Excel are mnemonic—the Command-key letter is the first letter of the command, as in Command-Q for Quit—so they are relatively easy to remember with regular use. Excel shares a number of Command-key equivalent operations with other programs, which should help to quickly reinforce those shortcuts. It may take longer, however, to associate Command-K with Delete, especially because Command-K means different things on other programs.

Now let's get started, as we dive into the shortcuts. Most of them don't appear in the manual, while a few others that do are important enough to get a second airing.

OPENING EXCEL FROM THE DESKTOP

Every Macintosh user knows that to start Excel you need to open the Excel icon by:

- Selecting both the icon and the Open item from the File menu, or
- Double-clicking the Excel icon (I prefer the latter because there's less mouse manipulation).

You probably also know that you can start the program by opening or double-clicking documents created by Excel. That is, you can double-click the desktop icon for an Excel worksheet, macro, or chart.

Worksheet　　Macro Sheet　　Chart

There's a good chance that you'll also want to start out an Excel session at times with two or more windows open on the Excel screen. For example, if you have a macro sheet that is associated with a worksheet, both the macro sheet and worksheet must be open for you to use them together. Similarly, if you have a worksheet and graph or multiple worksheets linked together, you'll need all linked documents open to work with them. Provided the linked documents refer to each other by name, Excel allows you to open all links quickly by choosing Links from the File menu while inside Excel. But you also can open linked documents from the Mac Desktop. You'd use this technique, of course, only when you are starting Excel from the Desktop. If you are already in Excel, it's just as easy to open one document or a series, followed by the Links command.

To open multiple documents from the Desktop, you must select all related documents. One way to do this is by dragging a marquee rectangle around all contiguous documents.

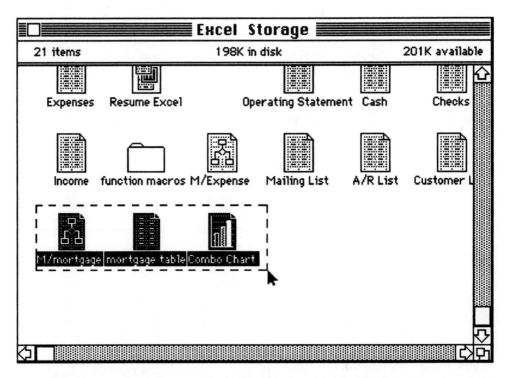

If the document icons are scattered amid a windowful of icons, hold the Shift key down and click on each icon. Shift-clicking lets you select multiple icons.

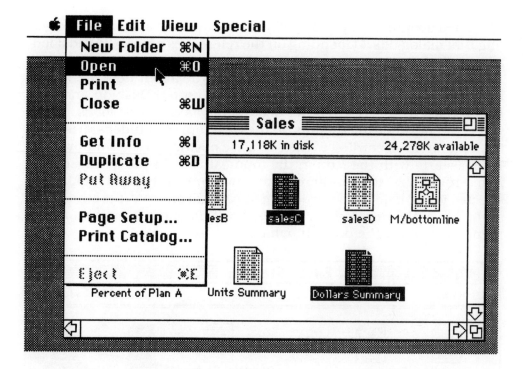

Once the desired document icons are selected, choose Open from the Desktop File menu. Excel will open, and each of the documents will be loaded into Excel.

☰ "Update References" Dialog Box

You may discover, however, that when some documents open—particularly worksheets that have linked references to other documents not yet open—the loading process halts while a dialog box asks if you want to "update references to non-resident sheets" (explained below).

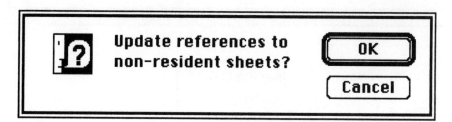

Having to click dialog boxes in the middle of what is supposed to be an automatic operation is a nuisance, especially if you intend to have all related documents open anyway. There must be a way to avoid getting that dialog box. Depending on the references among linked documents, there is.

To plan for this, you have to know a little about how the Finder looks at multiple-document icons selected on the Desktop and how Excel treats references to other documents as each one loads. When you select multiple documents on the Desktop, the Finder starts loading documents according to their relative position in the window. The Finder starts with the icon in the topmost row, in the leftmost position. From there, it scans across the row from left to right looking for selected icons. If no further icons are selected in one row, the scan starts at the left of the next lower row. The position of the document icons, then, determines the order in which they are opened.

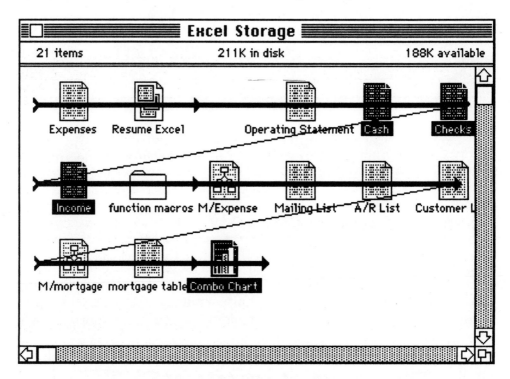

Opening Order
1. Cash
2. Checks
3. Income
4. Combo Chart

☰ Independent, Dependent, and Supporting Documents

An Excel document is one of three distinct types, depending on its relationships with other documents. A lone worksheet that is not linked to any other worksheet, does not rely on any macros, and does not have a chart drawn from its data, is called an *independent* document.

The second document type is one that fetches data from one or more other documents and even refers to other documents by name. For example, a summary worksheet that retrieves subtotals from more detailed worksheets contains references to the subtotal cells in the detailed sheets.

 File Edit Formula Format Data Options Macro Window						
E15 ☒ ☑ ='Territory2'!R78						
▤☐ ▤▤▤▤▤▤▤▤▤▤▤▤▤▤ Sales Summary ▤▤▤▤▤▤▤▤▤▤▤▤▤▤▤						
A	B	C	D	E	F	⇧

In other words, the summary sheet relies or depends on values in the detail sheets before it can perform any calculation. This document type is called a *dependent* document. An Excel chart is a dependent document because it can't display anything without help from a specific worksheet.

The third type is the opposite of the second—its data contributes to other documents. It supports the work of other documents, just like a worksheet supports a chart, even though the worksheet does not make any specific references to the chart. Such a document is called a *supporting* document.

As Excel opens a document, it does a quick check of all cell references in the document. If the program encounters a reference to another document that is not yet open, the reference update dialog box appears. At that instant, the dependent document does not have immediate access to the data it needs to update its display. The data is in one or more "non-resident" (i.e., not currently in memory) supporting worksheets. The dialog box gives you an opportunity to have Excel fetch data from the supporting documents (without opening them on the screen) or to leave the document the way it is.

If the independent document you are opening is a chart, and you elect not to update references (by choosing Cancel), the chart shows the same plotting as when you last saved it. Other dependent documents, especially worksheets containing function macros (described later) may display error messages in cells that rely on calculations from other worksheets when you elect not to update references. If you click OK in the dialog, you may have to wait a bit longer while Excel fetches current data from supporting documents. A critical point with this is that cells that support the document you're opening must contain simple values and not formulas. If the cells contain formulas, the document on the screen may display the #REF! error message in cells pointing to the supporting document. There's nothing to worry about, however. As soon as you open the supporting documents, the messages will disappear (with automatic calculation turned on).

≡ Avoiding the "Update References" Dialog Box

Fortunately, you can reduce the likelihood of seeing that dialog box. To avoid the dialog box when opening linked documents from the Desktop, position the icons on the Desktop so that all supporting documents open first and all dependent documents open last. If you are opening linked worksheets, supporting worksheets should be opened first.

Inevitably, you will design a worksheet that is both dependent and supporting. If that happens, the update reference dialog box will show up. Click OK to update the references, even though it slows down the load, because if you cancel, the references will not necessarily update themselves once all the documents are loaded (if manual calculation is selected).

≡ Folder Organization

To facilitate opening a series of linked documents from the Desktop, I recommend keeping all related icons in a single folder. In that way, they'll be easy to locate, easy to select, and easy to keep in the physical order necessary for unattended loading once you start the works going.

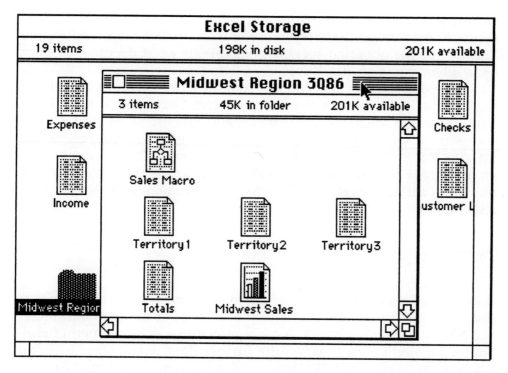

For example, three supporting spreadsheets, each with figures from a specific sales territory, supply their data for a dependent summary spreadsheet, labeled "Totals." Figures from the Totals worksheet are used to generate a graph of overall performance. Icons for these documents are positioned for opening in order from the Desktop.

The fastest way to start Excel with multiple documents in a folder is to open the folder, type Command-A (select All from the Edit menu), and then select Open from the File menu. The Finder will first open Excel, then load each of the selected files, starting with the top macro, proceeding next to the row of worksheets, starting with the leftmost file and working to the right, and then finishing up by opening the chart file.

Using Resume Excel

Another valuable shortcut for opening multiple Excel documents from either the Desktop or from within Excel is to set up suites of Excel documents in a Resume Excel file. To create one of these files, open all documents that you'd like to have open at once. Then, without closing any windows or documents, choose Quit from the Excel File menu. Excel saves into the System Folder a small file named Resume Excel. This file contains specifications about what documents were open when you last quit Excel.

The good news is that you can rename this Rename Excel file on the Desktop and place it in any folder you like. For example, if you have a couple linked sales forecast worksheets, a macro sheet, and a chart that you work with on a regular basis, you might wish to rename the Resume Excel file something like "Sales Forecast." By double-clicking on the Sales Forecast file in the Desktop or opening the Sales Forecast file from within Excel, all documents will open with one simple command.

EXCEL MENUS

Now let's take a close look at various menu items to see how you can save time and unnecessary mouse movement in issuing commands and answering dialog boxes. A high percentage of Excel menu items produce dialog boxes that require further details and specifications before any action occurs. While a few of these menu items can be called with Command-key equivalents, most cannot. You may be wondering, therefore, why you should bother to learn keyboard shortcuts for dialog boxes that appear in response to mouse commands. After all, isn't that against the principles of consistent keyboard and/or mouse flow? On the surface, it is. But as you'll see later in this book, many of these dialog boxes can be summoned from the keyboard with the help of macros. Therefore, dialog shortcuts you learn now will come in handy later. They are revealed here because we may as well cover all menu item–related shortcuts at once, especially because their behaviors often are very similar. In fact, you're bound to see several behavorial patterns as we proceed. I'll summarize these at the end.

The File Menu

Items in the File menu control Excel's link with the "outer world." All connections to disks and printers are handled with these commands.

```
┌─────────────────────────┐
│ File                    │
├─────────────────────────┤
│ New...            ⌘N     │
│ Open...           ⌘O     │
│ Links...                 │
│ Close All               │
│ Save              ⌘S     │
│ Save As...              │
│ Delete...               │
│ ....................... │
│ Page Setup...           │
│ Print...          ⌘P     │
│ Printer Setup...        │
│ ....................... │
│ Quit              ⌘Q     │
└─────────────────────────┘
```

New

Starting at the top of the File menu, the New item has a Command-key equivalent, the mnemonic Command-N. Unlike many other Mac programs, in which the New selection simply brings up a blank sheet of whatever it is the program works on (a MacWrite blank page, a Mac-Draw blank grid sheet, and so on), Excel produces a dialog box with three choices, depending on what kind of blank you want to work on: Worksheet, Chart, or Macro Sheet.

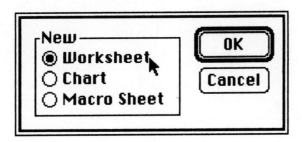

To let Excel know what you want to do next, you must reply to the dialog box.

When you see "radio buttons" next to a batch of answers, it means that only one of the selections can be chosen at a time. Selecting Chart, for example, highlights the Chart radio button, while turning off the Worksheet button, if it had been highlighted previously. You're probably accustomed to using radio buttons from other Mac programs and quickly aim the mouse pointer to the desired button. What you might not have realized is that when you see a radio button or checkbox control, you don't have to be too precise with the location of the pointer when you click. As long as the pointer is on the control or the descriptive text next to it, the click will register. In Excel, there's a keyboard shortcut, too.

Select New from the File menu, either with the mouse, or better yet, with Command-N. Now type the first letter of the three choices, W, C, and M, at random. When you type M, the radio button next to the Macro Sheet selection becomes highlighted. Type W and Worksheet is selected. If you look in the fine print of the Excel reference manual, you'll find instructions about double-clicking any one of these radio buttons to not only select the desired sheet, but also perform the equivalent of clicking the OK button. The same is true if you double-type the selection. For example, type two Cs in rapid succession. Voilà, you have a new blank chart.

With the New dialog box on the screen, you also can type N, which returns the dialog box display to the setting it had when you opened the box, the *default setting*, as it's called. Like W, C, and M, the N is mnemonic, but for the title word of the dialog box, New. The default setting changes, depending on what kind of window is the active window when you select New. For example, if you have a chart window as the active window and type Command-N, the Chart radio button is automatically selected in the New dialog box; but if a worksheet is the active window, then the Worksheet radio button is highlighted in the dialog box. In other words, typing N into the dialog box selects the radio button of the most recent default setting.

At first, this might not seem too important, but you can put this knowledge to use if you have multiple, nonoverlapping windows on the screen. When you select the New command, all window activity stops, and you might not know which window is the active window.

** File** Edit Gallery Chart Format Macro Window

Operating Statement '84

	A	I	J	K	L
3		August	September	October	November
17	Utiliti	.01		$39.80	$40.79
18	Teleph	.60		$111.82	$104.87
19	Insur	.00		$0.00	$0.00
20	Cost o	.00		$391.92	$0.00
21	Trave	.00		$71.00	$721.80
22	Vehicl	.00		$254.46	$271.19

New
- ○ Worksheet
- ◉ Chart
- ○ Macro Sheet

OK **Cancel**

Macro1

	A
1	boldface macro
2	=SELECT(SELECTION())
3	=STYLE(1,0)
4	=RETURN()
5	
6	
7	
8	
9	
10	

Chart1

Telephone

Bar chart with values ranging $0.00 to $200.00, categories 1-12.

There's more to this little box. By now, you probably know that the dark border around the OK button indicates that it has been preselected for you by the program. To activate the OK button from the keyboard, all you need to do is press Return or Enter. In this case, however, because you can perform both a selection and confirmation by double-typing one of the mnemonic letters, you'll use the OK button only if you need another blank of the same variety as the active window. For example, if you are in a worksheet and need a blank one, simply type Command-N and quickly press Return. The dialog box will not appear fully, nor do you have to wait for all the text in the dialog box to appear before issuing further commands (this applies to double-typing mnemonic selection, as well).

But what if you want to cancel the dialog box from the keyboard? To the credit of the Excel designers, the program follows an all-too-infrequently upheld Macintosh convention of canceling actions with the keyboard sequence, Command-period, as many programs' printing routines demonstrate. To cancel the New dialog box, simple type Command-. and the box goes away, having made no new selection.

Open

If you thought that the New dialog box has a lot of hidden keyboard gold, you ain't seen nothin' yet. I'm so impressed by the attention to design detail of the often-used Open dialog box, that I believe it should serve as a prototype for all Mac programmers (the techniques have been used in previous Microsoft products). Select Open from the File menu (Command-O) and let's investigate the treasures.

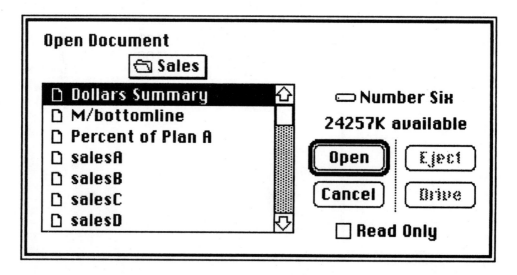

First, you can narrow your search for a specific file by taking advantage of Excel's sorting of file names in the scrollable window. The sort is largely according to the ASCII values of the characters comprising the file name. An ASCII value is a number that was assigned to every character of the English alphabet plus numerals and punctuation by an industry standards group years ago (ASCII stands for American Standard Committee for Information Interchange). In the chart in Table 1, you'll notice that letters are alphabetical.

To help further in locating a particular file, Excel allows you to type the file name's first several letters. Doing so causes the first file name starting with those letters to be selected in the box. If no file name starts with the letter you type, then the first file name higher on the value table is selected (e.g., "Monthly Report" would be selected if you type L and no other file name begins with L).

You also can "click" the buttons at the right of the Open dialog box with the keyboard. Of course, the Open button is preselected for you and can be activated by pressing Return or Enter. The other three

Table 1.1

ASCII No.	Character	ASCII No.	Character	ASCII No.	Character
32	SP	65	A	98	b
33	!	66	B	99	c
34	"	67	C	100	d
35	#	68	D	101	e
36	$	69	E	102	f
37	%	70	F	103	g
38	&	71	G	104	h
39	'	72	H	105	i
40	(	73	I	106	j
41	)	74	J	107	k
42	*	75	K	108	l
43	+	76	L	109	m
44	,	77	M	110	n
45	-	78	N	111	o
46	.	79	O	112	p
47	/	80	P	113	q
48	0	81	Q	114	r
49	1	82	R	115	s
50	2	83	S	116	t
51	3	84	T	117	u
52	4	85	U	118	v
53	5	86	V	119	w
54	6	87	W	120	x
55	7	88	X	121	y
56	8	89	Y	122	z
57	9	90	Z	123	{
58	:	91	[	124		
59	;	92	/	125	}
60	<	93	]	126	~
61	=	94	∧		
62	>	95	__		
63	?	96	'		
64	@	97	a		

buttons, Cancel, Eject, and Drive, also can be pressed from the keyboard, but not with single letters—if you typed E by itself, the program would select the first file name starting with the letter e. To let Excel know that you mean to click the buttons, you have to hold down the

Command key while typing period (.) for Cancel, E for Eject, and D for Drive.

As with most other keyboard-activated dialog boxes, you can chain commands quickly, even before the box appears on the screen. Therefore, if you know that the file you want to open is on a disk not in one of the disk drives, you can type Command-O, Command-E in rapid succession to Open a file and eject the disk in the drive Excel recognizes as the current drive (click the Drive button or press Command-D to change the current drive).

Links

Because the Links menu item does not have a Command-key equivalent to get it going, it is assumed that you will have your hand on the mouse when the dialog box appears. Moreover, if you summon this command from within a macro, you will likely instruct the macro to go right ahead and open specific linked files, rather than have the macro present this dialog box for you to select various files: Making yourself open individual, linked files is counterproductive to the spirit of macros. Other than selecting a single file with the Up and Down Arrow keys, you don't have much keyboard help in this dialog box. Of course the Return or Enter keys are the same as clicking the OK button once you've selected one or more links to open, or you can type Command-. to cancel.

Keep in mind, however, that you can select more than one file at a time in this dialog box. Either drag the pointer down a contiguous list of linked files to open them all or Command-click to select only those files you want opened at once.

Close All

The Close All menu command presents a dialog box only if one or more of the windows about to close has been changed but not saved.

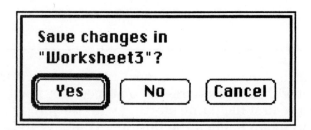

For each such window, you'll have to confirm or deny that you wish to close the window without saving the changes. Fortunately, the program preselects the Yes button. If you want to close the window and save your changes, simply press Enter or Return. To click the No button from the keyboard, type N. And our old friend, Command-period, cancels the whole operation. This same dialog box appears with the issuance of the Quit command. The same keyboard commands apply to it as well.

Close

"What's going on here?" you're probably asking. "There's no Close item on the menu." That's true. In many other popular Mac programs, however, the Close option closes the active window. Under mouse control, you can do that quite effectively in Excel by clicking the Close Box on the window.

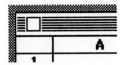

You also have a keyboard substitute for the Close Box: Command-W. If you have made changes to the window, you'll get the same dialog box mentioned above under Close All. Similarly, you can respond using the keyboard.

Save and Save As

I combine the discussions of Save and Save As together because they are somewhat interrelated. First of all, the Command-S keyboard equivalent of the Save command should be the one you use most often and regularly, like every 15 minutes. Any experienced personal computer user will tell you that periodically saving your work can save you the nightmare of lost work.

If you've never enjoyed the power going out on you or having some system error stop you cold after typing in an hour's work, I know you won't heed my warnings. I didn't when I first started using computers years ago. All it took was once, when two hours of my work went blooey because I hadn't saved to disk before disaster struck. When it happens to you, you'll humbly admit that I told you so.

Fortunately, Excel, like many Mac programs, gives you the Command-S keyboard shortcut to saving work in progress.

Use Command-S to save often!

Any time you have to turn from the computer for a few seconds—to answer the phone, to reply to someone coming into your office, to shuffle the papers you're working from, to think of what you're to do next—type Command-S. I can't stress this enough.

The first time you proceed to save a document, Command-S is a shortcut to the Save As menu item, which does not have a Command-key equivalent of its own. When the windows are labeled "Worksheet," "Macro," or "Chart" (with a serial number after the words), and you invoke a Save, the Save As dialog box appears.

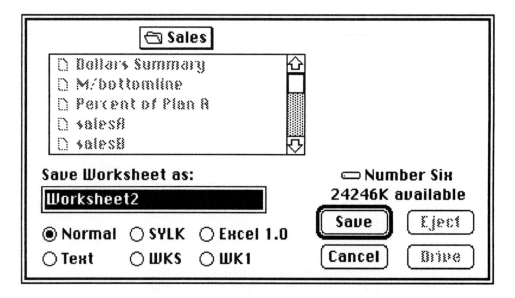

Note that when the box first appears, the temporary name for the document is selected in the one-line edit window. If you touch just about any key, the temporary name disappears, and the new characters take their place, following editing conventions common to MacWrite, Microsoft Word, and dozens of other Mac programs. It also is possible to adjust the dialog's radio buttons (when saving a worksheet or macro) or the text buttons with the help of the Command key.

Try it now. With either a new worksheet or new macro sheet as the active window, type Command-S to bring up the Save As dialog box. Now type Command-T, and the radio button next to Text is selected. To activate any radio button, type the Command-key sequence with the mnemonic for the selection:

Command-N	Normal
Command-T	Text
Command-S	SYLK
Command-E	Excel 1.0
Command-W	WKS

Note that WK1 can't be selected directly from the keyboard, because Command-W is intercepted by the WKS selection. Also, if you have an ejectable disk active (e.g., a floppy disk), Command-E invokes the disk Eject button instead of the Excel 1.0 format radio button.

Cancel, Eject, and Drive are activated the same way as in the Open dialog box, and you can save the file to the name you type in by pressing Enter or Return to signal the preselected Save button.

Delete
The Delete dialog box shares the same shortcuts as the Open dialog box, above. Note, however, that every file in the current folder level on the disk—including non-Excel documents—is listed in the box.

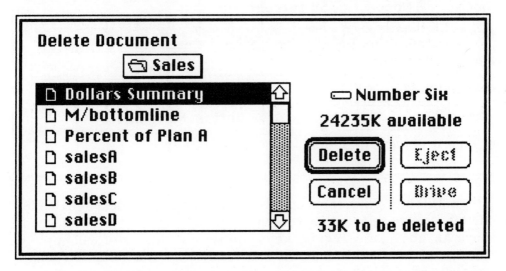

Incidentally, this menu item is, in itself, a shortcut compared to the operation of most programs. If it weren't for this command, you'd have to return to the Desktop to physically drag a document icon to the Trash. From inside Excel, however, you can delete unneeded files to make room on a disk for new files.

Page Setup

Select Page Setup from the File menu. The large dialog box you see as a result allows you to set a number of important parameters that affect the way your printed Excel output will appear. By a little experimentation in this box, you'll also see a pattern in the way keyboard shortcuts work. Note that the exact appearance of the Page Setup box will vary depending on the type of printer you are using (Laserwriter or ImageWriter), and the version of the system software you currently are using in your Macintosh.

ImageWriter (Standard or Wide)   [**OK**]

Paper: ◉ US Letter   ○ A4 Letter
              ○ US Legal   ○ International Fanfold   [Cancel]
              ○ Computer Paper

Orientation: ◉ Tall   ○ Tall Adjusted   ○ Wide

Pagination: ◉ Normal pages ○ No breaks between pages

Reduction: ◉ None   ○ 50 percent

Page Header: | &f |

Page Footer: | Page &p |

Left Margin: | 0.75 | **Right Margin:** | 0.75 |

Top Margin: | 1 | **Bottom Margin:** | 1 |

☒ **Print Row & Column Headings**   ☒ **Print Gridlines**

In this box, you see six editable fields, including one, Page Header, that is already selected for you when the box appears. As you saw in Save As, above, any regular keys you type at this point will apply to the text in the selected field. As you tab through the fields, the default text settings are selected so you can type in the settings you want or leave them as they are.

But now, type some Command-key combinations that you might use to adjust the radio buttons and checkboxes in this dialog. For example, try Command-C. The Computer Paper radio button in Paper selections goes on. Now press Command-U, and the US Letter selection is highlighted.

How can you get to the US Legal from the keyboard? Sorry, you can't. It appears that the routine inside the program that lets you do this Command-key stuff with radio buttons and the like simply looks for the first occurrence of the Command-key letter and applies it to the first selection. Therefore, you can use the keyboard to select any of the paper choices other than US Legal because the "U" is already claimed by US Letter, which is higher up in the box, and the first selection the program encounters as a match.

Similarly, you can select Wide orientation on the ImageWriter by typing Command-W and back to Tall with Command-T, but there's no keyboard way to select Tall Adjusted. Type Command-5 to select 50 percent reduction; press it again to cancel and return to normal 100 percent printing. And, finally, Command-P simply turns on and off the Print Row & Column Headings checkbox at the bottom of the dialog. If you don't want to print gridlines, you'll have to grab the mouse and uncheck the box.

It's unfortunate that you cannot access every selection from the keyboard here, but the alternative for the program designer was to change the wording of many of the selections—something easily done except for the break from comfortable standardization. Because this dialog box appears in many different programs, the decision was to maintain compatibility with other programs rather than go it alone to accommodate rarely made selections.

Print

There are few keyboard shortcuts in the dialog box presented when you select Print from the File menu or press Command-P (you'll see a different dialog box if you print on a Laserwriter or are using a different version of the Macintosh Finder/System software).

ImageWriter (Standard or Wide) — **OK**

Quality:	○ High ◉ Standard ○ Draft	
Page Range:	◉ All ○ From: [ ] To: [ ]	Cancel
Copies:	[1]	
Paper Feed:	◉ Continuous ○ Cut Sheet	
☐ Preview		

Chances are, however, that you will be doing the bulk of your printing on the same printer with the same settings most of the time. If so, you can quickly press Command-P and Return to get printing started. The outline of the dialog box will appear, but none of the text will show up. This is a shortcut I use in many Mac programs.

Printer Setup

The Printer Setup command is one you'll probably never use, particularly if the printer you're using is a Laserwriter, Imagewriter, or a printer with a print driver that modifies the Imagewriter print driver (Softstyle, for example, makes Macintosh compatible printer drivers for the Epson FX-80, Texas Instruments TI-855/865, Hewlett-Packard ThinkJet, HP LaserJet, and other printers).

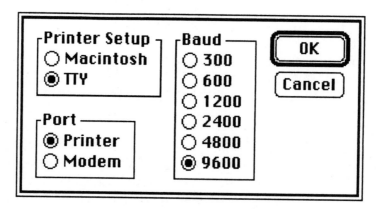

But if you need to adjust the data in this box, you can use the mnemonic keyboard shortcut to activate TTY and Printer port radio buttons, as well as any one of the baud rate selections (each starts with a different number, as in 9 for 9600 baud).

Quit

The dialog box that appears when you quit Excel with unsaved documents is the same box as detailed in Close All, above. All shortcuts apply.

≣ The Edit Menu

Edit menu choices give you the power to copy and move data around the worksheet. Most of the commands should be familiar to you, except those near the bottom of the menu that edit the makeup of the worksheet and perform multiple copy operations in one stroke.

```
┌─────────────────────────┐
│ █Edit███                │
├─────────────────────────┤
│ Undo            ⌘Z      │
│ Cut             ⌘H      │
│ Copy            ⌘C      │
│ Paste           ⌘U      │
│ Clear...        ⌘B      │
│ Paste Special...        │
│ ........................ │
│ Delete...       ⌘K      │
│ Insert...       ⌘I      │
│ ........................ │
│ Fill Right      ⌘R      │
│ Fill Down       ⌘D      │
└─────────────────────────┘
```

Undo, Cut, Copy, and Paste

All four common edit functions—Undo, Cut, Copy, and Paste—summon no further dialog boxes. The Command-key equivalents for these four selections have been standardized among Macintosh applications. Because all four are easily keyboarded with the left hand, you can get into a habit of using the mouse with your right hand to point to and select the desired cell or text and then issue the desired command with the left hand (this surely causes ergonomic problems for left-handed users).

The only caution here is that Cut, Command-X, works differently in Excel than you might be accustomed to in other applications. In other programs, when you select a chunk of text and Cut it, the text disappears from the screen and goes into the Clipboard until you copy or cut something else into the Clipboard. Cutting Excel cells, however, is different. If you point to a cell and Cut it, the data and formatting in the cell stays put until you select another cell and issue a Paste command. At that time, the original material is removed from its starting location and shifts to the new one. That single paste action, by the way, also removes the cut data from the Clipboard.

In other words, cutting and pasting in Excel is a one-time-only operation. If you need to copy data from one cell into several other cells,
then you should use the Copy command to put the data securely in
the Clipboard and then paste as needed.

If you expect to use the Cut command to remove data from a cell
entirely, you should direct your attention, instead, to the Clear
command.

Clear

Excel's Clear command is the one you use to remove data and/or formatting from a cell when you no longer need it. Of course, removing
data from a single cell may be easier by selecting the cell and simply
pressing the Backspace key. This action erases the data from the formula bar. The action is not "official" until you either select another
cell, click the Enter icon on the formula bar, or press Return, Enter,
or Tab.

Clear is most useful when you need to erase data in one or more
blocks of cells. Simply select the cells you need, including noncontig-
uous blocks (by pointing to and dragging the cells with the Command
key pressed), and invoke the Clear command from the File menu. When
you select the item from the menu, you are presented with a small dialog box.

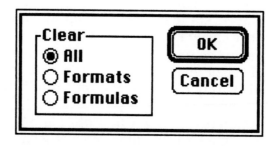

You have access to some mnemonic keyboard control for this box.
The letter A selects "All," while F selects "Formats." Because Formats
is higher in the dialog box than Formulas, the keyboard letter F will
match only Formats. Pressing C, the mnemonic for the Clear command,
returns the selection to the default setting, Formulas. Command-period
cancels and either Return or Enter sets the command in motion. As
with other dialog boxes of this type, if you double-type a selection, it
is the same as selecting an item and pressing Enter.

Interestingly enough, the Command-key equivalent for Clear, Command-B, offers a shortcut around the dialog box. By using this keyboard equivalent, you're telling the program to clear the selected cells of both formulas only (as if selecting Formulas from the dialog box). This is handy, if most of the clearing you'll be doing will be of everything in the selected cells—the Command-key equivalent short circuits the dialog box before it ever appears. But beware that any formatting you have assigned to the selected cell—dollars-and-cents number format, for example—will not be cleared along with the data when you press Command-B.

Paste Special
You won't be able to choose Paste Special from the Edit menu unless you select a cell range and copy it into the Clipboard. Then you can see the Paste Special dialog box, which presents nine radio buttons.

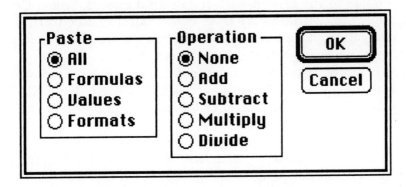

Unfortunately, the first letters of several words are shared by other words. But because you'll be using the mouse to select this menu item anyway, you'll be ready to click the appropriate buttons, including the Cancel or OK buttons (although the dialog can be canceled with Command-period).

Delete
Strange things sometimes happen in the dialog box presented by the Delete command in the File menu. The keyboard shortcuts available to you vary depending on the pattern of cells selected for deletion and how Excel second-guesses your intentions.

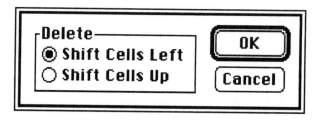

When you look at the first letters of the two radio button choices, you would by now expect the letter S to be matched with only the first one, Shift Cells Left, with no way to access Shift Cells Up. Instead, when you type S, it applies to the lower choice. To choose the upper one, type D, which is the mnemonic for the Delete function.

What's strange is that this works only if Excel anticipates that you want a Shift Left (based on the proportions of your selection and its relationships to nearby cells). If Excel anticipates a Shift Up, the dialog box comes to the screen with the second choice, Select Cells Up, already selected, with no way to select the first choice from the keyboard, even though you can click that button with the mouse and, indeed, may want to shift those cells left. Weird.

In either case, if you want the second choice, you can double-type S, which is the same as clicking both the Shift Cells Up radio button and the OK button. Command-period cancels the box.

Insert

Not surprisingly, the Insert dialog box behaves with the same quirks as does the Delete dialog box.

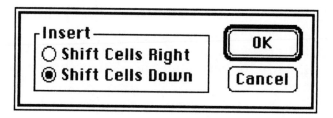

As long as Excel anticipates a Shift Right, you have keyboard access to both choices.

There is, moreover, an extra shortcut that makes a lot of sense, but this time, it's a combination keyboard and mouse shortcut. To see how this works, first fill up several cells in a column with any kind of data, even gibberish. Then hold down the Option key while you click one of the cells you just filled. Suddenly, the Insert dialog box appears for your selection of shift direction.

You also can insert a block of cells this way. Simply keep the Option key pressed while you drag the block of cells representing the number of cells you wish to insert. The instant you release the mouse button, the Insert dialog box appears.

Similarly, you can insert complete rows or columns by selecting the appropriate row and column headings. For example, if you want to insert two entire rows between the data in rows 3 and 4, hold down the Option key, click and drag the pointer over the row headings 4 and 5, and then release the mouse button. Because you are inserting complete rows here, Excel knows how to shift cells, so it skips the dialog box.

Remember this Option-click insert shortcut when you're in a real hurry. You can always Undo (Command-Z) it if you make a mistake.

The Formula Menu

In the Formula menu are a variety of commands largely responsible for creating and retrieving functions that eventually appear in cell formulas. Also here are four commands that help you locate specific spots in a large worksheet.

```
 Formula 
 Paste Name...
 Paste Function...
 Reference          ⌘T
 ..................................
 Define Name...     ⌘L
 Create Names...
 ..................................
 Goto...       ▶     ⌘G
 Find...             ⌘H
 Select Last Cell
 Show Active Cell
```

Paste Name
You have the same control over the Paste Name dialog as you do in the Open File dialog. The Up and Down arrow keys move the selection

bar through the list of defined names. You may also type the first one to three letters of a defined name to select it.

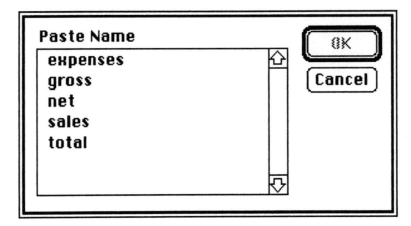

You can also cancel the box with Command-period and accept the selected name with Return or Enter.

Paste Function

Used quite often during the creation stage of a worksheet or macro, this menu item lets you narrow down your choice of function by allowing you to type up to the first four letters of the function (in upper- or lowercase.)

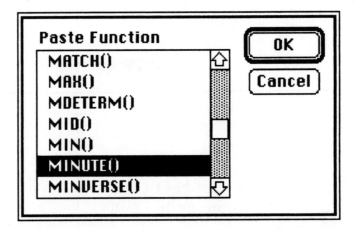

Therefore, if you type "m," the first function beginning with m, MATCH(), is selected. If you type "mi," then the first function matching those letters, MID( ), is selected. Typing "min" brings the selection down to the function MIN( ). And typing "minu" lands you on the

MINUTE( ) function. In all fairness, you have to be pretty fast to get the program to acknowledge a four-letter selector. Three letters probably is more realistic for most users, although even then you'll need some practice to get the feel for the cadence needed to register all letters. Note that the multiple-key repeat feature (in Keyboard Control Panel desk accessory) is turned off.

Once you have made the appropriate function selection, press Return or Enter or type Command-period to cancel the whole thing.

Reference

As far as I am concerned, there is no way to use this command effectively except with the Command-T keyboard equivalent. By repeatedly pressing Command-T with the text pointer in a cell reference on the formula bar, you can cycle through the possible combinations of relative and absolute references. Just keep on cycling through the styles until you find the one you want, then proceed with the rest of the formula.

Define Name

In the dialog box displayed from the Define Name command, Excel often fills in the name and always fills in the cell reference of the selected cell.

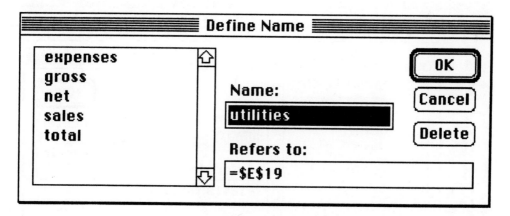

Knowing how the automatic name feature works can save you a little work. When you select a cell to be defined by a name, Excel checks one cell to the left and one cell up to see if either one contains a text label. If only one of them does, then Excel proposes that name in the Define Name dialog box. If both cells have text, Excel nominates the label to the left. When you select a range of cells, Excel proposes the name of the title above the top of the column or the left edge of the row.

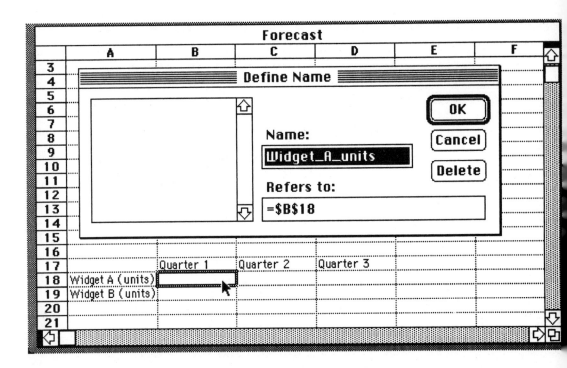

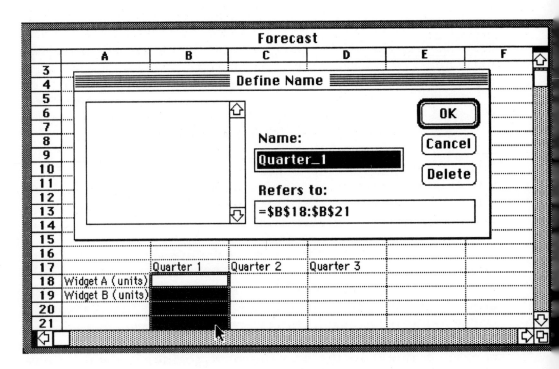

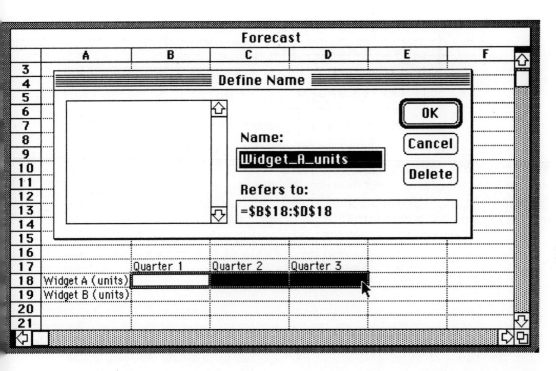

You can change a proposed name, of course, but generally speaking, a named reference will be easier to work with later if you correlate defined names with the column or row titles on the worksheet. Because the information in the Define Name dialog box usually is complete when the box appears, you can confirm by pressing Return or Enter in place of clicking the OK button. Command-D simulates clicking the Delete button, which you'd probably only do after selecting a name from the scrollable list with the Up and Down Arrow keys.

Create Names

The Create Names function is quite a shortcut in itself. With it, you can define many names at one time along either or both the top row and left column of a selected range.

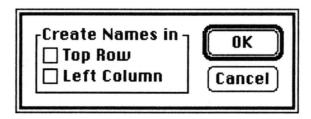

For example, instead of defining individual names for the labels down the left column of an operating statement, you can select the entire range of label cells and value cells to the right, invoke Create Names from the Formula menu, check the Left Column box, and confirm OK. You have the option of pressing T and L to toggle the checkboxes in front of the two choices in the dialog box (a toggle checks and unchecks the box each time you press the key). Command-period cancels the operation, and a press of either the Return or Enter key is like clicking the OK button.

Find

Built into the Find function are several shortcuts. The most obvious ones are those that let you select various radio buttons by typing the mnemonics for each of the choices.

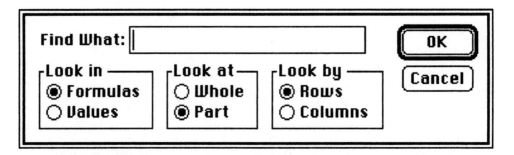

Note that because there is a data entry field in this dialog box, the radio button keys are Command-key sequences (e.g., Command-V to look in Values).

Another important shortcut comes when you need to issue the equivalent of a Find Again command, that is, have the program continue the search for the string because the program stopped on an instance other than the one you want to find. If you select Find from the Formula menu, you'll get the dialog box again. But to do a fast Find Again, simply issue the Command-H keyboard equivalent of the Find command. This is a two-edged shortcut, however. If, later in the same session, you wish to find a different string, you'll have to invoke Find from the pull-down menu in order to get the dialog box to type in the new string to search.

≡ The Format Menu

While none of the items in the Format menu have Command-key equivalents to set them in motion from the keyboard, several items have subsequent dialog boxes with numerous keyboard shortcuts.

```
┌─────────────────────────┐
│ Format                  │
├─────────────────────────┤
│ Number...               │
│ Alignment...            │
│ Style...                │
│ Border...               │
│ Cell Protection...      │
│ ....................... │
│ Column Width...         │
└─────────────────────────┘
```

The importance of these shortcuts will become more apparent later on when I demonstrate an application of macros that just about every Excel user will find to be a time saver. Productive use of several of these macros ultimately will involve keyboard shortcuts available in the Format menu.

Alignment
Selections in the Alignment dialog box determine how the contents of the selected cells are to be aligned with respect to the left and right edges of their cells.

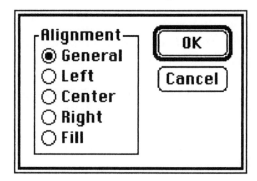

With this dialog box on display, you can select any one radio button by typing the mnemonic letter for the choice: G for General, L for Left, C for Center, R for Right, and F for Fill.

The last option, Fill, is perfect for those instances when you wish to fill a series of cells with a character for the purposes of making a border around a section of a worksheet. For example, enter a slash into a cell and select Fill in the Alignment dialog. Slashes instantly fill the cell. Even if you resize the column width, the cell remains filled with the characters.

Style

In the Style dialog box, you have two choices, Bold and Italic.

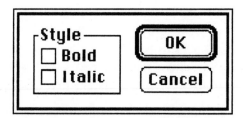

Because the control in front of each choice is a checkbox, instead of a radio button, you can select both choices at once, if you desire. With the dialog box in view, you can toggle either choice by pressing the respective mnemonic key, B for Bold and I for Italic. Because Excel does not let you mix fonts or font sizes on one worksheet, I heartily recommend you use these style adjustments whenever possible to provide needed emphasis, as you'll often see in examples later on.

Border

The Border dialog box works like the Style dialog box, but with a longer list of checkboxes.

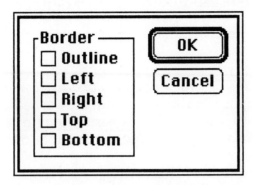

You should realize that checking Outline (type the letter O) is a shortcut for checking the other four boxes together. Checking Outline and the other four border sides does not make for a bolder border. As you'll see, borders come in handy, particularly in database applications of Excel, as well as in printing worksheets when you print without the gridlines.

Cell Protection

The small dialog box of the Cell Protection function behaves just like the two-option Style dialog box noted above, but with the choices of L for toggling Locked and H for toggling Hidden.

Column Width

To adjust the width of selected columns, the Column Width command presents a dialog box with a field in which you type the number of spaces wide the columns should be, plus a checkbox that lets you reset the column to the default setting, 10 spaces.

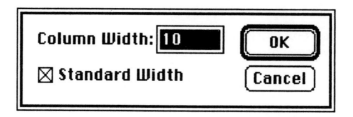

You can quickly reset to the default by either clicking the checkbox with the mouse—at which point the text in the field instantly turns into a 10—or by typing Command-S from the keyboard. When the standard width number is in the field, it is selected (inversed). Therefore, to change the number, simply type the number of spaces you'd like to change the columns to.

You also should know that when you view a macro sheet, the column width setting in the dialog box is doubled on the screen. In other words, a setting of 10 spaces actually produces a macro column width of 20 spaces. When you start writing macros, you'll appreciate the extra space that comes to you by default, but don't be concerned about the apparent dialog box error.

☰ The Data Menu

As its name indicates, the Data menu's commands are largely used for database applications. Yet some commands are quite practical in number-oriented spreadsheets.

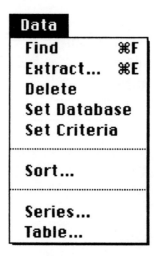

Find

When you have database and criteria ranges set and proceed to perform a search for a particular group of records, use the Find command. While you're in the Find mode, the thumb of the vertical scroll bar (that's what programmers call the white box in a scroll bar) takes on a striped pattern. If you find what you're looking for, and the striped thumb indicates that there are more records matching your criteria, you can exit the Find mode most quickly by clicking the mouse pointer in any cell outside of the database range.

	A	B	C	D	E
53	3/5/84	overhead	$600	Wheelin's Gas Co.	
54	3/5/84	overhead	$200	Ralph J Cook Garbage	
55	3/5/84	overhead	$440	City of Franklin	
56	3/5/84	overhead	$560	City of Franklin	
57	3/6/84	inventory	$20,000	SW Wholesale	
58	3/5/84	salary	$2,000	Mary Fuller	
59	3/5/84	salary	$2,540	Carol Stansen	
60	3/5/84	salary	$1,890	Jim Parsons	
61	3/5/84	salary	$1,400	Karen Bush	
62	3/5/84	salary	$2,000	James Gregory	

This, to me, is much faster than going to pull down a menu command, which also stops the Find mode.

Sort

When the Sort command's dialog box comes on the screen, there are many selections that cannot be accessed from the keyboard.

Sort

Sort by
- ● Rows
- ○ Columns

OK

Cancel

1st Key
$G$20
- ● Ascending
- ○ Descending

2nd Key
- ● Ascending
- ○ Descending

3rd Key
- ● Ascending
- ○ Descending

Those that can be controlled—Rows, Columns, and Ascending or Descending for the 1st key only—must be done so in concert with the Command key. Otherwise, the mnemonic letters you type would appear in the text entry fields for the search keys.

But because the Ascending and Descending choices for the second and third keys have the same first letters as those of the first key, you can't control them from the keyboard. Fortunately, most sorting is performed in ascending order, so these choices may be rarely adjusted by most users.

Series

The dialog box that comes up from the Series command at first appears to have a double mnemonic—the Command-D for Date and Command-D for Day.

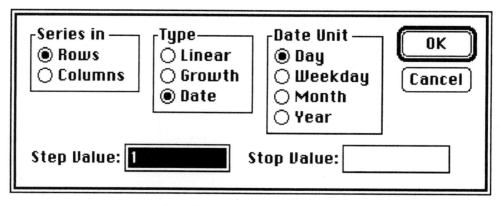

But in practice, this does not present a problem for keyboarders. Here's why:

When you first get this dialog box, the top radio buttons in all three categories are preselected. That means that because Linear is selected in the Type grouping, all choices in the Date grouping are inactive (they are shaded). If you then proceed to type Command-D to activate the Date grouping, the top one of that group, Date, already is selected. If that is the date unit you want, then go ahead and set the variable values for interval and maximum value, if any. Otherwise, type the Command-key mnemonic for any of the other three date units you wish.

☰ The Options Menu

Commands in the Options menu affect a number of important functions for printing, display characteristics, and calculation. There is only one regular Command-key equivalent—Calculate Now—but an important one when your worksheets get so big you need to select manual calculation to speed data entry.

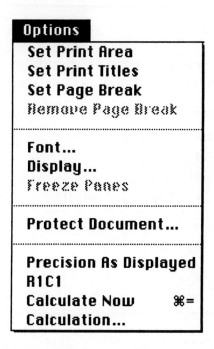

Font

I don't have a shortcut per se for the Font command, but I do want to point out something that may not be obvious. If you are printing on a LaserWriter, you can type in any whole number font size you wish in the text entry field in the Font dialog box.

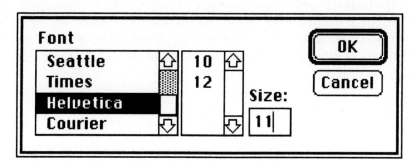

You are not restricted to the sizes displayed in the scrollable box. Those sizes are for the fonts in the System File. They represent the sizes that the Mac can display on your screen without scaling (scaling usually results in distortion on the screen and in printing on the ImageWriter). The LaserWriter, however, can interpret virtually any font size you'd want on a spreadsheet (from 4 to 127 points), even if the font on the screen is scaled and distorted.

Display

Three checkboxes in the Display dialog box allow you to select a variety of ways for the spreadsheet and its contents to appear on the screen. Additional checkboxes allow you to set gridline and heading color if you are using a Macintosh capable of color display.

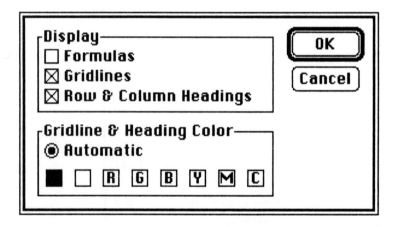

Mnemonic keyboard commands toggle Formulas, Gridlines, and Row & Column Headings display on the worksheet. You must use the mouse to select the color choices, however.

Freeze Panes

The Freeze Panes command invokes no dialog box and offers no keyboard shortcuts. It removes the split screens created by the horizontal and vertical window-splitter handles (located on the far top and left of the scroll bars) and forms two or four scrollable "panes" that contain selected portions of the worksheet. Cancel the panes by reselecting the command.

Calculation

When the Calculation dialog box first appears (provided it has not been altered before), the Automatic calculation method is the choice selected.

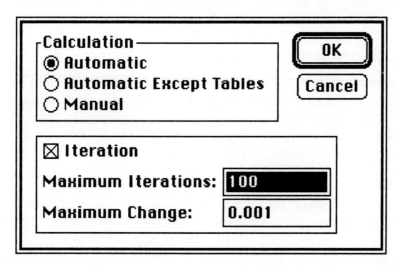

From keyboard commands, you can choose only Manual, for the A, for Automatic Except Tables, is already taken for the first Automatic selection.

If you type I, the Iteration box is checked, and the two fields in the lower portion of the dialog box come to life. When these fields are active, you must use Command-key keyboard shortcuts to control the radio buttons or the typed letters will appear in the currently selected field. But you can turn off the fields by typing Command-I, thereby toggling the checkbox back to "off."

≡ ## The Window Menu

While it's not obvious from the Window menu, there is a shortcut to replace the mouse work required to bring one of the open windows to the foreground and make it active. The documented command is Command-M. By pressing Command-M repeatedly, you cycle through all open windows, bringing each one to the forefront and making it active until you type Command-M again.

If you have many windows open at once, this may not be so fast as selecting the precise window you want from the Window menu, but chances are you'll find it ergonomically easier to use the keyboard equivalent than to reach for the mouse.

≣ The Gallery Menu

The Gallery Menu is visible only when creating or editing a chart. While none of the Gallery menu items can be called directly from the keyboard, an individual graph type can be specified from the keyboard once the gallery is on display (as is possible with the help of macros, discussed later). Just press the corresponding number of the graph type you want to use.

Press the Next or Previous buttons to cycle through the various graph types. These buttons can't be activated from the keyboard.

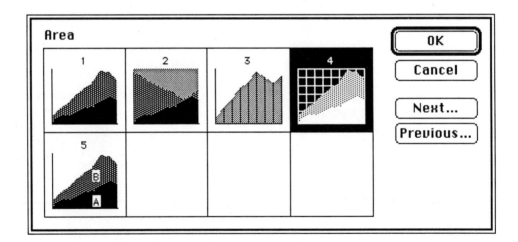

≣ The Chart Menu

The Chart Menu is visible only when creating or editing a chart. About the only worthwhile shortcuts under the Chart menu are for the Main Chart Type and Overlay Chart Type menu items. For each of these selections, you see a dialog box with a list of chart types and their respective radio buttons.

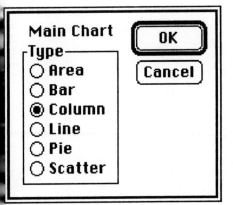
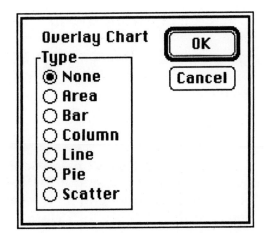

Luckily, the names for the chart types begin with different letters, so the mnemonic scheme of typing the first letter of the chart type selects the corresponding radio button. Both dialog boxes are the same except for the added selection of None in the Overlay Chart dialog box.

Dialog boxes for two other selections, Axes and Attach Text, have one or more collisions of mnemonic keyboard commands. The Axes dialog is the worst, because it has two identical lists of checkboxed choices, one for Category Axis, the other for Value Axis.

Any keyboard command you issue will be intercepted by the left-most list. Even then, that list contains three selections beginning with the letter M, so you have toggle control only over the first two selections, Category Axis and Major Grid Lines. Because you must call this menu item with the mouse, you may as well continue using the mouse to make your selections. And there is little likelihood that you'd put this menu item in a macro, unless you already know exactly what selections you want to make and can insert them into the macro, thus bypassing the dialog box altogether.

☰ The Chart Format Menu

The Format menu is different when creating or editing charts than when you are working with an Excel worksheet. You can achieve some keyboard shortcuts on the dialog boxes presented in response to just about every item on the Format menu.

```
┌─────────────────────────┐
│ Format                  │
├─────────────────────────┤
│ Patterns...             │
│·························│
│ Main Chart...           │
│ Overlay Chart...        │
│ Axis...                 │
│ Legend...               │
│ Text...                 │
└─────────────────────────┘
```

But as it turns out, the actions in this menu are better handled with the mouse. As you might expect with graphics-oriented functions, the mouse plays a key role in simplifying adjustments to the chart. In these cases, use the mouse, for that's where the work flow leads. These functions are intended as fine-tuning controls to your charts.

☰ Menu Shortcut Summary

I'm sure that by now you've detected several patterns when it comes to using shortcuts in menu selection dialog boxes. Many common threads run through these aids. The best part about this commonality is that once you understand how these shortcuts work, you don't have to remember specific ones, but rather can apply the knowledge of how they work to each as you need it.

Here, then, is a list of rules governing menu shortcuts:

1   In dialog boxes without text entry fields, the mnemonic commands can be typed from the keyboard as single letters.
2   In dialog boxes containing text fields, the mnemonic commands must be typed as Command-key sequences, as in Command-A.

3   When options preceded by radio buttons are grouped together inside a border box, you can choose only one of the options at a time with a mnemonic command.

4   When options in a dialog box have checkboxes before them, the keyboard command toggles the checkbox on and off each time you type it.

5   When two or more options begin with the same letter, in nearly every case the topmost option will be controlled by the keyboard command and any below it will not be available from the keyboard.

DATA-ENTRY SHORTCUTS

Because data entry is largely a keyboard-intensive task, there is no small incentive to learn as many keyboard tricks as possible to facilitate the entry of your values into cells. I'm not talking about the worksheet creation stage here, but rather the stage after that—when you begin plugging in the numbers to be summed, percentaged, and otherwise massaged by the formulas you entered during the creation stage.

Cursor Exercises

To become a true Excel virtuoso, it is important to be totally comfortable with the method of moving the active cell cursor around the screen. It is a waste of energy to shift to the mouse to move the cursor a few cells down and three to the right, when the whole thing can be done with a few keystrokes. A few minutes of exercises should help ingrain the dynamics of cursor movement into your mind.

As the manual details, you have four-way movement of the cursor with keys other than the arrow cursor keys:

Keystroke	*Direction*
Tab	Right
Shift-Tab	Left
Return	Down
Shift-Return	Up

I found the best way for me to get used to this cursor arrangement was to practice moving the cursor diagonally from one corner to the opposite one. For example, with the cursor in cell A1, I'd set cell F19 as my target and then work my way back again, sometimes stopping in the middle of the screen and heading for corners A19 or F1.

   To go from A1 to F19, you need to move down three for every one to the right. Start by pressing the Enter key three times, followed by one press of the Tab key. Continue this sequence until the cursor is at F19. Now reverse the procedure by holding down the Shift key while pressing Return three times, Table once, and so on. You don't have to release the Shift key between movements—keep it nailed to the floor. I feel most comfortable holding down the right hand Shift key while moving the cursor, but do what feels the most comfortable for you.

   Now mix up the pattern by trying to go from the center of the screen to cells A19 and F1. Moving in the bottom-left to top-right direction (and back again) takes a combination of shifted and unshifted commands. Practice this several times, and you'll begin to feel more at home with this somewhat unorthodox method of cursor movement. I doubt these exercises will become as popular as an aerobics videocassette class, but at least Excel's cursor movement during data entry may become more automatic for you.

☰ Numeric Keypad

If your keyboard doesn't already have a numeric keypad, you'll want to invest in one. Entering numerical data is far easier with the keypad than using the number keys along the top row.

☰ Option-key Cursor Movement

Excel provides yet another option in the cursor movement department. This one, however, is much more of a shortcut and applies primarily to moving a group of selected cells, rather than a single cell cursor. With a group of cells selected on the screen, if you hold down the Option key before issuing any one of the four directional cursor commands detailed above, the entire selection moves in the direction you type in. Let's look at a practical example that shows how this can be a productive shortcut.

 File Edit Formula Format Data Options Macro Window

B15		12.5

	Operating Statement				
	A	**B**	**C**	**D**	**E**
3		January	February	March	April
15	Postage	$12.50			
16	Rent	$350.00			
17	Utilities	$35.43			
18	Telephone	$40.56			
19	Insurance	$120.00			
20	Cost of Sales	$0.00			
21	Travel/Entertainm.	$200.75			
22	Vehicle*	$45.00			
23	Legal/Accounting	$0.00			
24	Office Expense	$23.00			
25	Dues/Subscripts.	$11.95			
26	Publications	$2.50			
27	Equipment	$275.00			
28	Bank Service Charge	$10.00			
29	Moving Expense	$0.00			
30	Miscellaneous 3	$0.00			
31					

In the above worksheet, I want to enter values into each column of the 12 months. I could scroll around the worksheet and select all cells in the block from B15, the first figure in January, to M30, the last figure in December, but that seems like extra mouse work if I can avoid it. Because I'll be entering the figures by month, I select the cells in the first month column. While those cells are selected in a block, I can press the Tab, Enter, or Return keys to enter a value in one cell and advance the cursor to the cell below. When I reach the bottom of the column, the cursor jumps back to the top of the column of selected cells.

Instead of moving to the mouse to select the same bank of cells in the February column, though, I can hold down the Option key and press the Tab key once. This action moves the selected cells in the direction of the Tab cursor movement.

```
 ‖   🍎  File   Edit   Formula   Format   Data   Options   Macro   Window
        C15       |           |
```

	A	B	C	D	E
3		January	February	March	April
15	Postage	$12.50			
16	Rent	$350.00			
17	Utilities	$35.43			
18	Telephone	$40.56			
19	Insurance	$120.00			
20	Cost of Sales	$0.00			
21	Travel/Entertainm.	$200.75			
22	Vehicle*	$45.00			
23	Legal/Accounting	$0.00			
24	Office Expense	$23.00			
25	Dues/Subscripts.	$11.95			
26	Publications	$2.50			
27	Equipment	$275.00			
28	Bank Service Charge	$10.00			
29	Moving Expense	$0.00			
30	Miscellaneous 3	$0.00			
31					

The window title bar reads **Operating Statement**.

Similarly, I can type Option-Shift-Tab to move the selected cells to the left or Option-Return to move the selection down, and so on. When the selected cells are in column F, and I press Option-Tab, the screen scrolls to show column G, with all desired cells already selected. Yet no matter in which direction I move the selected cells, I still retain the ability to move the active cursor inside that block of cells with the Tab, Return, or Enter keys (adding the Shift key before any one of them to move the cursor up the column).

☰ Formula Bar Icons

To the left of the formula bar at the top of the Excel screen appear two icons whenever you are entering or editing the contents of a cell.

```
 ‖   🍎  File   Edit   Formula   Format   Data   Options   Macro   Window
        C17    ☒ ☑   =SUM(B24:B26)
```

These two icons, the cancel box and the enter box, are practical shortcuts when used correctly. Of the two, however, I find the enter box far more useful, while I rarely use the cancel box, preferring a more functional keyboard command instead.

The enter box is a mouse-activated equivalent of pressing the Enter key. When you have only a single cell selected, pressing the Enter key enters a formula or value into the cell without advancing the cursor in any direction. That's exactly how the cursor behaves when you click the enter box with the mouse pointer.

Now just because the enter box does what the Enter key does is no reason to reach for the mouse every time you type in a value or formula. If your hands are on the keyboard, use the keys. But if your hand is already on the mouse, use it and click the enter box.

I don't care too much for the cancel box. It functions like a crippled Undo operation—crippled in that it undoes typing, yet offers no way to recover what it just erased. When I'm mousing around entering formulas or editing existing text, I always have one hand available to hit Command-Z for Undo. At least Undo allows you to toggle back and forth between undoing your mistake and un-undoing it.

DEFINING NAMES

The deeper you get into Excel, the more you appreciate the ability to assign names to various parts of your spreadsheets and macros. It greatly simplifies the creation of formulas in linked worksheets because you can assemble the elements from more familiar names rather than the gibberish of cell references. Additionally, once you assign a name to a selection of cells, you can move the selection, insert cells, delete cells, and otherwise destroy the integrity of the original worksheet, and yet any formula with reference to that name will find the appropriate cells. You don't have to worry about how moving cells around the spreadsheet will affect other parts of the system you're building.

Therefore, even though it may take some extra time during the worksheet and macro sheet creation stage, I strongly recommend that you assign names to those parts of the sheets that interact with other areas of your system. Excel makes it about as easy as possible to name cells (Define Name and Create Names commands from the Formula menu) as well as recall those names for entry into formulas (Paste Name). The names will become valuable shortcuts as you fine-tune your system later on.

Now that you're an Excel shortcut wizard, it's time to get down to some strategy sessions. The first one, in the next chapter, is dedicated to macros.

Chapter 2
MACRO STRATEGIES

Macro Fundamentals
Keep Macro and Sheet Names Short
Use Mnemonic Columns for Command Macros
Beware Multiple Macro Sheets
Create Generic Macro Libraries
Approach Macros as a Language

There's no question that you can do a lot with Excel without the aid of macros. But using Excel while ignoring macros is like using the Louvre solely as shelter from an afternoon Parisian downpour. You'll miss the treasures inside.

This discussion of macro strategies is intentionally early in the book. I want you to be comfortable enough with macros to work them into your daily Excel use. Right now, I want you to start looking for ways macros can make your Excel models more automatic and more powerful. In fact, macros will play key roles in demonstrating other basic strategies in the next few chapters. But because most Excel users will be new to macros, let's take one step back for a moment and examine what a macro is.

MACRO FUNDAMENTALS

The term "macro" is a convenient abbreviation for "macroinstruction." Very simply, a macroinstruction is a single command that takes the place of several other commands normally executed in sequence. For example, when you first teach a newcomer to start MacPaint on a Macintosh, you detail the individual steps of turning on the Mac, inserting the disk, double-clicking the disk icon, and so on. These are the *micro*instructions or smallest practical steps involved in the process. Once the newcomer has those instructions down, you can thereafter simply give the instruction, "Start MacPaint." That two-word *macro*-instruction, or macro for short, triggers a long sequence of precise steps every time you say it. A macro saves time because one instruction takes the place of several. A macro also extends the instruction language, because later you can use a macro as a part of a still more encompassing macro. Let's see how all this applies to Excel.

If you perform a menu operation in Excel, such as making the contents of a cell boldface, you normally have to pull down the Format menu, choose Style, and then check the Bold box in the subsequent dialog box. These steps are microinstructions. But if you find that you are often performing the same series of steps, you will save time and energy by combining those steps into a macro—one command that does the whole series of steps in a flash. In Excel, this kind of macro—one that substitutes a single command for a sequence of mouse and keyboard maneuvers—is aptly called a *command macro*.

Even if you've never programmed an Excel macro yet, you surely have used something that resembles a macro—one of Excel's built-in functions, which you enter into cell formulas (often with the aid of the Paste Function menu choice). The built-in function for present value, for example, is a simplified way of entering what would otherwise be a horribly long math formula, one that everyone would probably mess up at one time or another. But by reducing that series of math steps to a single, two letter function (PV), Excel makes life simpler and calculation more accurate.

Excel lets you extend the power of functions significantly, because you can build your own functions that take the place of specialized formulas not built into Excel. You build these functions into "function macros," whose names can appear in the same list of functions you see in the Paste Function dialog box. Other kinds of function macros can be inserted into worksheet cells, taking the place of extensive calculations that would otherwise damage the visual integrity of a worksheet.

When an Excel macro starts to work, the program stops whatever it may be doing on a worksheet or chart and jumps to the macro's listing of instructions on the macro sheet. Depending on what kind of macro it is and what you've instructed the macro to do, Excel performs the commands in order, down the column beginning with the first cell of the macro. Some macro instructions jump further to other macros on the same or other macro sheet, while other instructions do things to the worksheet, such as select specified ranges and any one of the dozens of equivalent menu and dialog box commands. At the end of the macro is a single command (RETURN), which returns control of the program to the original worksheet, in the precise location from which it had departed for the macro.

Several strategies apply to virtually every application, making macros easier to edit and more powerful.

KEEP MACRO AND SHEET NAMES SHORT

One of the fabulous advantages of the Macintosh over computers such as the IBM PC and others that have command-oriented operating systems is that you can give extraordinarily long names to files.

In the IBM PC world, for example, you are limited to a name consisting of no more than eight letters, followed by a period and a three-letter extension—a total of 11 letters with no spaces in between. Often, this is not enough to identify the contents of the file a week later when you forget what COMPMUS.LTR means.

On the Mac, however, you can go wild with explanatory file names up to 31 characters long, including spaces and just about every number and punctuation symbol except the colon. That freedom, however, occasionally leads to problems if unrestrained. A case in point is the name you might give to a macro sheet.

Because a macro sheet is a separate file, you could give it a very long name, and the Mac wouldn't mind. But when you try to find a particular command macro in the Run dialog box, you'll have a problem. The scrollable list in this dialog displays the Option-Command-key equivalent for the command (if any), the name of the macro sheet, and the name of the macro.

That's a lot of information to cram into a short line in the dialog, and if the names for your macro sheet and macros are very long, you won't be able to distinguish one macro in the listing from the next.

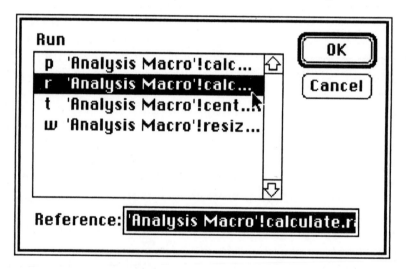

As a guideline, try to keep macro sheet names to under ten characters. Because all macros have a unique icon on the Mac desktop, you don't need the word "macro" in the file name. But you will need some distinguishing mark if you open most of your macro sheets with Excel's Open command. Consider, then, starting the name of the macro sheet with an identifying prefix, such as "M/", so that a file name would read "M/Analyze."

Command macro names, too, should be kept as short as possible, but hopefully a short macro sheet name will leave plenty of room for descriptive macro names. Still, there are a couple tips that can make macro naming easier and more space efficient.

As often illustrated in the Excel manual, it is a good idea to type in the name of the macro as the first cell of the macro listing (Excel does this automatically for you when you are creating macros with the Macro Recorder).

Not only will it help you identify the macro later if you need to edit it, but Excel automatically places the name from the top cell of a selected macro into the edit field of the Define Name dialog box that asks for the name of the macro to be defined (note: the defining process is automatic when using the Macro Recorder). Thus, putting the name in the top macro cell does double duty for you.

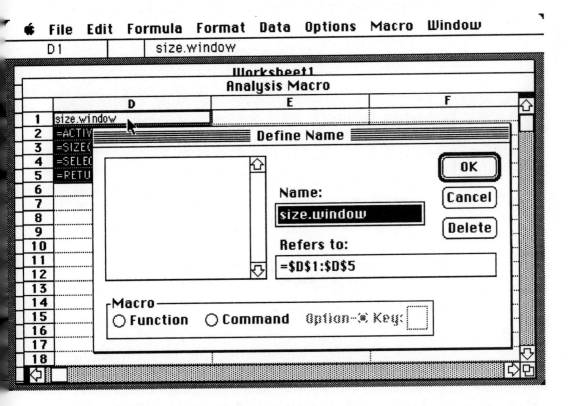

There's no problem creating macro names that have two or more words. In fact, sometimes it's the only way to properly identify a series of similar macros, as you'll see in Chapter 3.

Don't, however, type spaces between words in command macro names. If you do, Excel places underlines in the names (in the Define Name dialog box) to hold the places left by the spaces. While nothing bad will happen if you do this, the underlines take up a lot of room on a line in the Run dialog box. If you type a period between words, however, you'll be using the space most efficiently.

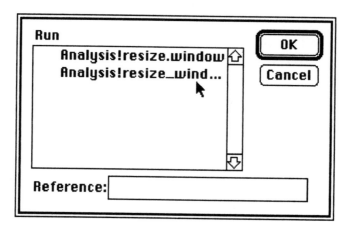

Also, if the macro name is more than one word and if there is a series of similar macros, be sure to place the distinguishing words at the beginning of the macro name. For example, instead of naming two macros "align.right" and "align.left," name them "right.align" and "left.align." The reason for this is that if the macro sheet names or macro names get too long, the last characters of the macro name may be truncated, or cut off, in the Run dialog box. It might look like you have two macros called "align." But if you can see the distinguishing name, there's a better chance you'll know what it is.

USE MNEMONIC COLUMNS FOR COMMAND MACROS

I would wager that the majority of the command macros you will be writing for your worksheets will be the type that have Option-Command-key equivalents. Keyboard-driven macros are much faster to execute than having to pull down the Run dialog box every time. Of course, if you forget a keyboard equivalent, you always have the dialog box to fall back on.

When you are starting to write macros for the first time or when you are assembling a substantial collection of macros on a single macro sheet, assign names to the macro routines that begin with different letters of the alphabet. Then type the macros in the macro sheet column with those letters. For example, a macro that boldfaces the contents of the current cell might be called "boldface" and assigned the keyboard equivalent, Option-Command-B. That macro should be typed on the macro sheet in column B.

This scheme does a couple things for you. First, it reinforces in your mind the mnemonic command that you will issue later to invoke the macro. Second, if you have lots of macros on the sheet, you'll know exactly where to look for a macro listing when it comes time to edit it.

As a rule, when following this procedure, I place all macros with lowercase-letter keyboard commands in the first 26 columns, A through Z. I place uppercase-letter keyboard command macros in the next 26, AA through AZ. By having both uppercase and lowercase letters available for macros, you can have two macro names that begin with the same letter.

As to which macros to give uppercase and which lowercase letters, I look upon the two series quite differently. Lowercase commands are those that I tend to call most frequently—procedures for which I need instant action and with which I don't want to be bogged down having to hold down four keys at once.

Uppercase commands, on the other hand, are those that are more "deliberate." Typically they are ones that either call menu dialog boxes for further data input or perform procedures that might overwrite existing data if executed without care—there's no automatic undoing the damage done by a macro.

When you write your first several macro sheets, you probably will forget that you cannot assign keyboard commands to four lowercase letters: e, u, i, or n. To remember these letters to avoid, think of either the South Pacific island of Niue or the French-derived word, ennui (less one of the "n"s). This is an unfortunate nuisance, but something we must all live with, because the Macintosh must reserve these letters to create accented characters. The uppercase versions of these letters, luckily, are in the clear.

You might consider creating a blank macro template that has the top row of columns N, I, U, and E filled with some symbol to remind you that these letters are off-limits. To use such a template, you would open the blank template macro sheet instead of creating a new macro sheet with the New item in the File menu. If you find yourself mistakenly planning macros in these four columns often, then try this template idea.

I suggest that this mnemonic macro column technique be used only by beginners or in the creation stages of macro writing because there is a penalty for writing macros in their mnemonic column locations: memory and disk space. Recall that the size of any worksheet is an area measured by the greatest number of used cells in the horizontal times the vertical direction. If you have macros placed in several cells along the first 52 cells (A through AZ) and one macro is ten cells deep, Excel reserves disk and memory space for a macro 520 cells, even though your macros may not fill more than 50 cells.

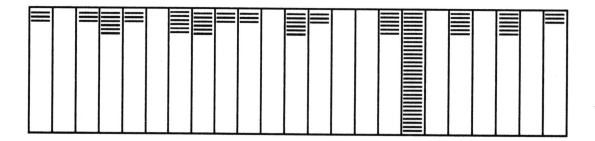

This space penalty won't be much of a problem unless you start building power-user Excel environments consisting of huge worksheets or many windows. At that time, you'll appreciate having a few more kilobytes free in memory.

To conserve macro sheet space, you can stack macros in one or two columns, even if it means cutting and pasting them from their mnemonic structure to the compacted structure once the macros are debugged.

All macros—command and function—are constructed in such a way that macro execution stops the instant it encounters a RETURN (or HALT) instruction. Therefore, if you define Macro "B" below a RETURN instruction of Macro "A," Macro "A" will not run into Macro "B."

BEWARE MULTIPLE MACRO SHEETS

Building a library of macros can be a bit tricky, it turns out, if you like to have several command macro sheets open at the same time. If you are prone to assigning keyboard command equivalents to most of your command macros, be prepared for possible conflicts between two macros on different macro sheets, both of which run from the same command key. Excel can distinguish between the two macros in the Run dialog box—each macro name consists of the macro sheet name plus the name of the macro itself.

While you may assign the same name to different macros on different sheets, it is very unlikely that you would ever have a completely identical macro name (including macro sheet name) open at the same time. Therefore, you can easily select the proper macro from the Run dialog box.

But if two macros have the same keyboard equivalent, the macro higher up on the list in the Run dialog box will execute.

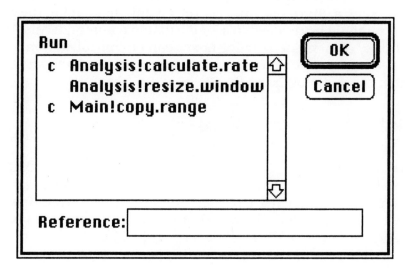

Depending on the macro, particularly if the macro simply applies to any active worksheet rather than to one with a specific name, the inadvertent macro instructions could really mess up your worksheet.

In sum, avoid having more than one macro sheet with command macros open at a time. If you must have multiple sheets open, then design the sheets so that there are no overlaps or conflicts of keyboard command equivalents. Or safest of all in those cases, use the Run dialog box to run your macros.

CREATE GENERIC MACRO LIBRARIES

After you use Excel for a while, you undoubtedly will notice that you perform a number of menu commands repeatedly at specific times during the worksheet and chart creation, data entry, and analysis stages. If you can recognize such patterns, then build command macros that do those chores for you. In all likelihood, the macros will bear a striking resemblance across several worksheets.

I discovered, for example, that I continually issue the same menu commands during the worksheet creation stage. Many of those commands, I recognized, could be more easily carried out if they were command macros with keyboard equivalent commands. I also found that many of my worksheets were of the financial record variety, complete with a row of headings listing the months of the year and a totals column. Such a chore—typing, centering, and boldfacing the column headings—could be reduced to a single macro command. And because the majority of menu item dialog boxes can be controlled from the keyboard (as demonstrated in Chapter 1), why not have keyboard macros summon those dialog boxes?

Worksheet Creation Macros

The result is a set of 27 macros on one macro sheet that I call "M/Create." Whenever I am about to start work creating a new worksheet, I make sure M/Create is open and in the background (with the worksheet as the active window). In its mnemonic column layout (as I will show it here), M/Create takes up 14K; in a compacted format, however, it is only 6K. Lowercase and uppercase keyboard commands are arranged so that most immediate actions are in the simpler, lowercase commands. More deliberate actions, like displaying a menu item dialog box, are uppercase keyboard commands.

To show you what is in my M/Create macro (yours may have more or fewer macros, as your worksheets may dictate), I will work my way from left to right across the macro sheet. Many of the macros are only a couple lines long, but they save much mouse manipulation. As I describe each macro, pay close attention to the way I treat arguments to many of the macro commands.

Bold Currently Selected Cells

The first, in column B, boldfaces the contents of the currently selected cell(s) in the main worksheet.

	B
1	boldface
2	=STYLE(1,0)
3	=RETURN()
4	
5	
6	
7	
8	
9	

M/Create

The STYLE command here is a substitute for pulling down the Style dialog box (on the Format menu) and checking one or both boxes for bold and italic font style. Arguments for this macro command refer to the conditions of the checkboxes if you were looking at the dialog box—the first argument controls bold, the second italic. While the manual suggests you state these conditions as TRUE or FALSE, you also can substitute the accepted values of one (or any nonzero value) for TRUE and zero for FALSE. As with all command macros, no values are returned directly from the macro to the worksheet, so no arguments follow the RETURN command.

Incidentally, I chose the keyboard command "b" not only because it is mnemonic to the boldface function, but it is the same mnemonic command as the boldface option in MacWrite (Command-B) and Microsoft Word (Shift-Command-B). The more you can keep your keyboard macro commands in line with other programs you use, the easier it will be for you to remember the commands.

Dollars-and-Cents Format

In column C is the number format that turns the values into the dollars-and-cents figures.

```
≣▢▤▦▦▦▦▦ M/Create ▦▦▦▦
                        C
1 │ dollars.cents
2 │ =FORMAT.NUMBER("$#,##0.00;($#,##0.00)")
3 │ =RETURN()
4 │
5 │
6 │
7 │
8 │
9 │
```

I chose column C because D was reserved for the format that turns values into dollars only. At least the C stands for the cents to help me remember it. The arguments for the FORMAT.NUMBER command were copied from the listing of prewritten number formats in the Number dialog box. This format displays the dollar sign, commas every three digits, two digits to the right of the decimal, and a minimum display of $0.00. Negative amounts are displayed in parentheses, according to accounting principles. It is important to note that the argument for the FORMAT.NUMBER command must be in quotation marks—making it a "string" in computer lingo.

Dollars Format

Because some worksheets deal strictly in whole dollars, I created the dollars macro in column D.

```
▤□▦▦▦▦▦▦ M/Create ▦▦▦▦▦▦
                    D
1   dollars
2   =FORMAT.NUMBER("$#,##0;($#,##0)")
3   =RETURN()
4
5
6
7
8
9
```

This macro is identical to dollars.cents, above, except for the details of the number format argument string. This format displays no figures to the right of the decimal.

Return to Cell A1

Dorothy was right when she wished, "There's no place like home." In a worksheet, "home" is where the cell A1 is, and during the worksheet creation process it often is handy to return to the starting point and begin a survey of your work so far. The macro in column G carries you back to cell A1 faster than you can click the heels of your red shoes.

```
▤□▦▦▦▦▦▦ M/Create ▦▦▦▦▦▦
                    G
1   goto.a1
2   =SELECT(!A1)
3   =RETURN()
4
5
6
7
8
9
```

Notice that the cell reference in the SELECT command does not contain a reference to a specific worksheet name but rather to any active worksheet (denoted by the exclamation mark without a worksheet name before it). With this reference, the macro will be usable with any worksheet you're creating, both before and after you've named it. This is where the macro sheet gets its "generic" designation.

Select Last Cell

Next to column G, and also next to the keyboard command "g," is the macro in column H that selects the last cell in the worksheet.

	H
1	last.cell
2	=SELECT.LAST.CELL()
3	=RETURN()
4	
5	
6	
7	
8	
9	

M/Create

I often find it informative to see what the coordinates of the last cell of a worksheet are, especially when I am constructing it. Of course, be aware that if you delete cells or clear data in cells at the extremities of the worksheet, the last cell won't be adjusted inward until you save the worksheet. To get a true picture of the last cell's location, you might want to add a SAVE() command before the SELECT.LAST.CELL command in this macro.

Fill Down or Right

In columns J and K are a pair of commands that allow you to perform rather powerful entry of copied (filled) formulas across or down a spreadsheet directly from the keyboard. These macros also demonstrate for the first time in this book the command that displays an input dialog box. In column J is the macro that fills down.

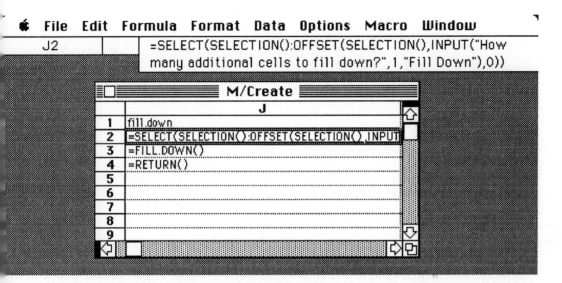

I think it is important to tear apart the first formula, because it contains quite a few functions.

First of all, the purpose of this macro is to ask you to type in the number of cells below the current cell you wish to fill. This assumes, as does the menu Fill Down command, that you have already entered some value or formula into the selected cell. As with the menu version of this command, the Fill Down macro command expects that the range of cells to be filled has already been selected. This macro, then, preselects the appropriate range for you and then issues the equivalent of the Fill Down command.

Excel's macros not only allow you to nest commands, but they often insist on it as a way to accomplish an otherwise complex task. You often have to look at macro functions as equivalents of other operations.

For example, the basic macro command in cell J2 is SELECT. If you were selecting a simple cell range, say A1:A5 on the main worksheet, the macro formula to do that would be =SELECT(!A1:A5), with the arguments referring to that range on the current worksheet.

In the case of the fill.down macro, however, I can't be specific about the range because until I tell it how many cells down I want to fill, the SELECT command will have no valid arguments to act on. I must, therefore, substitute other functions that furnish valid values—cell references in this case—to the SELECT function.

Look at the arguments in the SELECT function in cell J2. Notice that despite all the commands lumped into the argument, the basic form still holds: a cell range reference consisting of the beginning cell, followed by a colon, followed by what should be the reference to the ending cell of the selection. The beginning cell reference is listed as SELECTION( ). This function furnishes, or "returns," to the SELECT function the equivalent of the current cell's reference.

If the currently selected cell is B5 when the macro is run, then "B5" is substituted for SELECTION( ) in this formula at the time it is run. At another time, if cell Y503 is the current cell, then "Y503" is plugged in that place. In other words, whenever I need to plug in the currently selected cell into a macro formula (and that cell may change depending on when I run the macro), I can enter the SELECTION( ) function instead.

To tell the macro formula where the end of the selected range is, I chose to use the OFFSET function, which also returns a cell reference. The OFFSET function allows me to cite as the end cell one that is a certain number of cells distant from the first cell. Arguments for the OFFSET command consist of the anchor cell, or starting point for the offset counter to work from, and the number of rows and columns to be counted from the anchor cell.

The cell reference returned from this function is the cell pointed to as the result of the offset counting from the anchor cell. Because, in this case, I want to count down from the currently selected cell, I supply SELECTION( ) as the location of the anchor cell, just like I used it earlier to stand in for the beginning cell of the overall selection to be filled down.

Next, the OFFSET command will be expecting some kind of number to indicate how many rows down (or up with a negative number) the offset counter should count. This is where the INPUT command comes in.

Because I don't know how many rows will be filled down until I issue the macro, I need some way to communicate to the macro how many rows I want filled. By inserting the INPUT command at this juncture of the macro, I can type in a number and have that number passed to the OFFSET command just as if it had been typed into the formula when it was created.

The INPUT function's arguments are, simply enough, the text of the prompting message in the dialog box, the type of data that will be entered into the box and returned by the function, and the text, if any, of the title bar of the dialog box.

 **  File Edit Formula Format Data Options Macro Window**

| F4 | | =SUM(B4:E4) |

Worksheet1

	A	B	C	D	E	F
1						
2		Quarter 1	Quarter 2	Quarter 3	Quarter 4	Total
3	Item No.					
4	1001	12	3	44	3	62
5	1002	66	54	78	48	
6	1003	86	55	19	41	
7	1004	88	84	27	51	
8	100					
9	100					
10	100					
11	100					
12	100					
13	101					
14						
15						
16						
17						
18						
19						

Fill Down

How many additional cells to fill down?

[OK]

[Cancel]

9

Because the data that OFFSET expects here is a number, the data type for the INPUT function is 1. Other possibilities (and their type numbers) for this function include formula (0), text (2), logical TRUE or FALSE (4), cell reference (8), an error message (16), or an array (64).

The last entry of the OFFSET function is the number of columns to the right (or left with a negative number) the offset counter is to count. Because I want the counter to count down in the same column only, the column offset value is zero. A summary of how these various nested function pieces supply data to functions one level closer to the outside level is illustrated below.

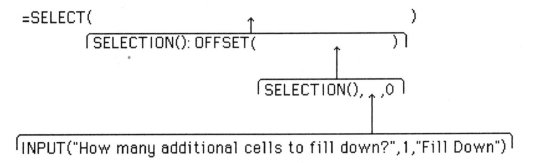

```
=SELECT(                                          )
        SELECTION(): OFFSET(                  )

                    SELECTION(),    ,0

INPUT("How many additional cells to fill down?",1,"Fill Down")
```

As a side note, substituting functions for numbers, cell references, and text is the way to make macros function most efficiently and powerfully. Unless you've had some experience programming a computer in a language, this concept may take a bit of practice to sink in. Wherever I can, I'll explain the application of nested macro forms throughout this book.

Once the desired cell range is selected, the fill.down macro then executes the macro equivalent of the Fill Down command from the Edit menu.

File	Edit	Formula	Format	Data	Options	Macro	Window

| | F4 | | | =SUM(B4:E4) | | | | |

Worksheet1

	A	B	C	D	E	F
1						
2		Quarter 1	Quarter 2	Quarter 3	Quarter 4	Total
3	Item No.					
4	1001	12	3	44	3	62
5	1002	66	54	78	48	246
6	1003	86	55	19	41	201
7	1004	88	84	27	51	250
8	1005	81	32	11	57	181
9	1006	48	69	50	30	197
10	1007	63	72	85	24	244
11	1008	55	36	78	31	200
12	1009	48	83	10	50	191
13	1010	58	73	33	55	219
14						
15						
16						
17						
18						
19						

While you can supply a negative number in response to the input dialog box requesting the number of cells to fill down, the FILL.DOWN function, like its menu equivalent, does not know how to fill up. Therefore, supplying a negative number will cause the SELECT function in cell J2 to select a range of cells going up from the anchor cell. The succeeding FILL.DOWN function won't see any cells into which it can fill down and appears to do nothing. Your worksheet won't be harmed, but you won't get the results you expected.

The fill.right macro in column K is the same as the fill.down macro except for some fine details of the nested OFFSET function.

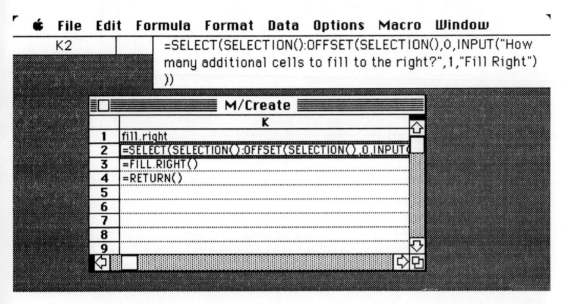

```
 ❤  File   Edit   Formula   Format   Data   Options   Macro   Window
     K2    |         |  =SELECT(SELECTION():OFFSET(SELECTION(),0,INPUT("How
                        many additional cells to fill to the right?",1,"Fill Right")
                        ))
```

```
   ▭▤▤▤▤▤▤▤▤▤▤▤▤▤▤ M/Create ▤▤▤▤▤▤▤▤▤▤
                          K
   1  fill.right
   2  =SELECT(SELECTION():OFFSET(SELECTION(),0,INPUT(
   3  =FILL.RIGHT()
   4  =RETURN()
   5
   6
   7
   8
   9
```

The most important difference is that because this macro needs to count columns to the right in the same row, the argument controlling the row offset is zero, while the column offset is defined by the number typed into the INPUT dialog box. The other differences are simply the wording of the two text strings in the input dialog and the use of the FILL.RIGHT function.

You can use these two macros together in series if you need to both fill down and right, as often happens in financial spreadsheet formulas. When you issue the fill.down macro, for instance, the entire filled cell range remains selected after the cells have been filled. Without touching the mouse, you can then issue the fill.right macro command, which fills to the right the entire columnar range of cells, thus completing the filling of the grid. In both cases, relative cell addresses make the proper adjustments in formulas for a very fast and mousefree way to set up a large number of formulas in a worksheet.

Cell Alignment
Columns L, M, and R contain three important alignment commands. Each replicates the Alignment choice from the Format menu and the selection of either Left, Center (M or middle, here), or Right.

```
▤□▤▤▤▤▤▤▤▤▤▤ M/Create ▤▤▤▤▤▤▤▤▤
          L               M               R
  1  left.align       middle.align    right.align
  2  =ALIGNMENT(2)    =ALIGNMENT(3)   =ALIGNMENT(4)
  3  =RETURN()        =RETURN()       =RETURN()
  4
  5
  6
  7
  8
  9
```

I could have added alignment macros to replicate the General and Fill alignment options (represented by ALIGNMENT arguments 1 and 5, respectively), but because I rarely use them, I kept it simple. Notice, too, that the mnemonics are the same as the command-key equivalents in MacWrite, MacPaint, and other programs for left, middle, and right alignment of text. That makes these a snap to remember.

Cell Borders

The outline macro in column O is a simple one that performs the same command as if checking Outline in the Border dialog box.

```
▤□▤▤▤▤▤ M/Create ▤▤▤▤▤
              O
  1  outline
  2  =BORDER(1,0,0,0,0)
  3  =RETURN()
  4
  5
  6
  7
  8
  9
```

Like the STYLE macro command, BORDER expects logical values for the conditions of each of the possible outline selections, as shown in the menu command's dialog box. Again, I find it easier to type in ones and zeros instead of TRUE and FALSE logical values as arguments for this command.

Percent Format

Another number format, percentage, is specified in the macro in column P.

```
┌──────────────────────────────────────┐
│ ▤▢▤▤▤▤▤  M/Create  ▤▤▤▤▤▤▤▤         │
├─────┬─────────────────────────┬──────┤
│     │           P             │  ⬆  │
├─────┼─────────────────────────┼──────┤
│  1  │ percent                 │  ▯  │
│  2  │ =FORMAT.NUMBER("0.00%") │      │
│  3  │ =RETURN()               │      │
│  4  │                         │ ░░░ │
│  5  │                         │ ░░░ │
│  6  │                         │ ░░░ │
│  7  │                         │ ░░░ │
│  8  │                         │ ░░░ │
│  9  │                         │  ⬇  │
├──┬──┴─────────────────────────┴──┬───┤
│◁ │░░░░░░░░░░░░░░░░░░░░░░░░░░░░│ ▷ ▣│
└──┴────────────────────────────┴───┘
```

While I elected to make my percentage values with two digits to the right of the decimal, you can enter "0⁶" as an argument if your worksheet percentages are typically whole numbers. Similarly, you could create a second macro on this sheet to accommodate whole number percentages if your worksheets frequently use both formats. Remember, too, that you're in charge of the format to the extent that you can specify even custom formats in a macro as you would in the Number dialog box when working from the menu (including color for color monitors).

Enter Current Date

Over the years, I've discovered that it's a good idea to "time-stamp" worksheets with the current date. That way, when you print the worksheet, you know precisely how current the information is. In other kinds of worksheets, such as those used as forms for invoices or other database purposes, the current date is almost always one of the fields.

To simplify the entry of the current data formula in a cell of a new worksheet, I added the today macro in column T.

```
┌──────────────────────────────────────────┐
│ ▤▢▤▤▤▤▤ M/Create ▤▤▤▤▤▤▤▤ │
├────┬───────────────────────────────────┬─┤
│    │                T                  │▲│
├────┼───────────────────────────────────┼─┤
│ 1  │ today                             │ │
│ 2  │ =FORMAT.NUMBER("mmm-dd-yy")       │ │
│ 3  │ =FORMULA("=now()")                │▓│
│ 4  │ =RETURN()                         │▓│
│ 5  │                                   │▓│
│ 6  │                                   │ │
│ 7  │                                   │ │
│ 8  │                                   │ │
│ 9  │                                   │▼│
├────┴───────────────────────────────────┴─┤
│ ◁▓▓ ▢ ▓▓▓▓▓▓▓▓▓▓▓▓▓▓▓▓▓▓▓▓▓▓▓ ▷ ▣│
└──────────────────────────────────────────┘
```

The first order of business in this macro is to format the current cell in a recognizable date format. I chose the mm-dd-yy format, but your can use any one you like. Then comes the FORMULA function, which may be difficult to grasp. If I had typed the NOW function in macro cell T3, Excel would have recognized it as a formula applying to that cell and placed the date in cell T3.

What I needed to do was instruct Excel to place that NOW formula in the current cell on the active worksheet. The FORMULA function tells Excel to copy the contents of the macro's argument to the current cell on the active worksheet. The argument is in quotation marks, because I want Excel to essentially type the string "=now()" into the appropriate worksheet cell. Try to remember, therefore, that the FORMULA function passes its argument to the current cell, just as if you were typing it into the worksheet cell yourself.

There is no requirement for formatting the cell as a date before placing the NOW function in it. If I had reversed the order of those two macro formulas each time I run the macro, I would see the raw date number for an instant before it was formatted into mm-dd-yy. In case this macro reaches the hands of an inexperienced computer user, it is much cleaner to simply have the properly formatted date appear in the cell.

Note that this macro places a formula in a cell that always updates the date each time you open the file. Keyboard shortcuts Command- : and Command- - insert the time and date, respectively, at the instant of those commands.

☰ Macros That Call Dialog Boxes

A majority of macros in cells AA through AT—those invoked by upper-case keyboard commands—are simple ones that bring to the screen the dialog boxes associated with many menu choices.

I put these here for a couple reasons.

- By limiting the predefined dialog box selections to a few macros in the lowercase group (such as boldface from the Style dialog), there won't be too many little macros to get mixed up in my mind.
- Because most of the selections in those dialog boxes can be made from the keyboard (see Chapter 1 for details on these shortcuts), it would be a smooth procedure to call up the dialog box and make any selections all from the keyboard.

You probably noticed in the Excel manual's macro function directory that virtually every menu command that produces a dialog box can be called in a macro by placing a question mark between the command word and the parentheses. For example, in M/Create macro column AA, the macro calls the Alignment dialog box.

	M/Create
	AA
1	align.box
2	=ALIGNMENT?()
3	=RETURN()
4	
5	
6	
7	
8	
9	

Once the dialog box appears on the screen, I can type the mnemonic letter of the appropriate selection and press Enter or Return (or Command-period to cancel). Now the entire procedure can be handled without reaching for the mouse.

Similar dialog boxes are called by the following macros:

Keyboard Command	Macro	Dialog Box
B	=BORDER?( )	Border
C	=CALCULATION?( )	Calculation
D	=DISPLAY?( )	Display
F	=FONT?( )	Font
I	=STYLE?( )	Style
N	=FORMAT.NUMBER?( )	Number
P	=CELL.PROTECTION?( )	Cell Protection
R	=RUN?( )	Run
S	=SORT?( )	Sort
T	=DATA.SERIES?( )	Series

Make New Line Chart

Column AH contains a macro that automatically creates a line chart from the data that is selected on the worksheet.

	AH
1	new.chart
2	=NEW(2)
3	=GALLERY.LINE(1)
4	=LEGEND(TRUE)
5	=RETURN()
6	
7	
8	
9	

The steps are quite simple. First it performs the equivalent of selecting Chart from the New dialog box (at this point, Excel draws the chart with the preferred chart type—the column chart, unless you've changed it). Then the macro selects line chart type number 1 from the Gallery menu. Finally, it adds a legend by passing the TRUE parameter (or any nonzero number in its place) as if selecting Add Legend from the Chart menu. If my worksheets often created more than one chart type, I would make up a separate macro for each chart type.

Format Months Heading
I come, at last, to the longest macro on this macro sheet, called months.

```
╔══════════════════════ M/Create ═══════════════════╗
║ ▣□▦▦▦▦▦▦▦▦▦▦▦▦▦▦▦                             ▦▦▦ ║
║                          AM                      ⬆ ║
║  1  │months                                      │ ║
║  2  │=DEFINE.NAME("here",SELECTION())            │ ║
║  3  │=SELECT(SELECTION():OFFSET(SELECTION(),0,13))│ ║
║  4  │=FORMULA("January")                         │ ║
║  5  │=SELECT(,"RC[1]")                           │ ║
║  6  │=FORMULA("February")                        │ ║
║  7  │=SELECT(,"RC[1]")                           │ ║
║  8  │=FORMULA("March")                           │ ║
║  9  │=SELECT(,"RC[1]")                           │ ║
║ 10  │=FORMULA("April")                           │ ║
║ 11  │=SELECT(,"RC[1]")                           │ ║
║ 12  │=FORMULA("May")                             │ ║
║ 13  │=SELECT(,"RC[1]")                           │ ║
║ 14  │=FORMULA("June")                            │ ║
║ 15  │=SELECT(,"RC[1]")                           │ ║
║ 16  │=FORMULA("July")                            │ ║
║ 17  │=SELECT(,"RC[1]")                           │ ║
║ 18  │=FORMULA("August")                          │ ║
║ 19  │=SELECT(,"RC[1]")                           │ ║
║ 20  │=FORMULA("September")                       │ ║
║ 21  │=SELECT(,"RC[1]")                           │ ║
║ 22  │=FORMULA("October")                         │ ║
║ 23  │=SELECT(,"RC[1]")                           │ ║
║ 24  │=FORMULA("November")                        │ ║
║ 25  │=SELECT(,"RC[1]")                           │ ║
║ 26  │=FORMULA("December")                        │ ║
║ 27  │=SELECT(,"RC[2]")                           │ ║
║ 28  │=FORMULA("Total")                           │ ║
║ 29  │=ALIGNMENT(3)                               │ ║
║ 30  │=SELECT(!here)                              │ ║
║ 31  │=RETURN()                                   │ ║
║ 32  │                                            │ ║
║ 33  │                                            │ ║
║ 34  │                                            │ ║
║ 35  │                                          ⬇ │ ║
╚═════════════════════════════════════════════════╝
```

The actions programmed into this macro are:

1   Select a horizontal range of cells extending 13 cells to the right of the selected cell.
2   Place the name of a month into each cell, leaving a blank column between December and Total.
3   Center the titles in their respective cells.
4   Return the cell cursor to the original cell without the rest of the title cells selected so the user can continue moving the cursor by itself around the worksheet with the keyboard.

The first line of macro instructions defines the currently selected cell in the worksheet as the name "here." This definition is required for the end of the macro, when I need to "deselect" the rest of the row by selecting this cell only. Only two of the four possible arguments apply to the DEFINE.NAME command when the command affects a worksheet (instead of a macro sheet). The two are the name you wish to assign to the cell or cell range and the cell reference to which that name is to apply. Although I assigned the name "here," it could be any string. The cell reference is the SELECTION( ) command, which returns the reference to the currently selected cell in the active worksheet.

Next, the macro needs to select the range into which the labels will be placed. By selecting the range at the outset, I can use the simple method of advancing the cursor through the selection (shown below), rather than specifying a specific offset for each cell. The SELECT formula in cell AM3 is similar to the one used in the fill.right and fill.down macros, except I know ahead of time that I want 13 cells selected in addition to the current cells, so there is no need for an INPUT command. The range to be selected begins with the currently selected cell (handled by the SELECTION( ) function) and ends with a cell offset from that anchor cell 13 columns to the right in the same row.

For the next 16 formulas in the months macro, I alternate between inserting the text string of the month (with the FORMULA command) and advancing the cursor to the next cell with a special SELECT formula construction.

When a range of cells is selected, you can control the movement of the cursor in the range with a macro by specifying which cell in the range should be the active cell. When you omit the first argument in a SELECT function (the argument that specifies the cell range reference), the function assumes you mean the current cell range, whatever it is. Then you can indicate which cell within the range is to be the active one without deselecting the range.

Specifying which cell in the range is to be the active cell is done with a row-and-column measure relative to the currently active cell. Therefore, in months macro cell AM5, the SELECT function selects the cell in the same row (no number next to the "R") and one column to the right (indicated by the 1 in brackets after the "C").

While technically this command simply activates a different cell, I see it more as the equivalent of pressing the Tab key in a selection, moving the cell cursor to the right one cell. With this method, you can move the cursor inside a selected range in any of four directions, "x" number of cells:

Formula	Direction	Key Equivalent
SELECT(,"RC[x]")	RIGHT	TAB
SELECT(,"RC[-x]")	LEFT	SHIFT-TAB
SELECT(,"R[x]C")	DOWN	RETURN
SELECT(,"R[-x]C")	UP	SHIFT-RETURN

It so happens that because the selection made by this macro is a single row, pressing the Return key also moves the cursor one cell to the right, so either of the two SELECT formulas (equivalent to Tab or Return) would work without any problem.

In months macro cell AM27, the cursor is advanced two cells to the right to leave a space between the December and Totals columns. Not everyone likes this format, but I find it much clearer to read both on the screen and in printouts.

While all cells in the range are still selected, the macro gives the ALIGNMENT(3) command in cell AM29 to center the monthly labels. Finally, the original cell is selected, thus deselecting the rest of the range.

Note that the cell reference for this SELECT command is simply the name as defined in cell AM2, above. Note, too, that the reference is preceded by an exclamation mark. This is absolutely necessary. Without that exclamation mark, the macro will look for a cell in the macro that has been defined with the name "here" rather than in the worksheet. The DEFINE.NAME command in cell AM2, however, assigned that name to a cell in the worksheet.

While this macro might be useful as is for many Excel users, it is quite possible that your worksheets frequently have other kinds of title series, either across the top row or down the left column of a spreadsheet. If so, then customize this macro to fit those applications. Always be on the lookout for command macros that can eliminate the repetitive typing that you do while creating worksheets and charts.

≣ ## Other Generic Macros

Generic macro sheets aren't restricted to worksheet creation. If you carefully name items in various worksheets, you can develop a macro sheet that helps you perform data entry and analyses or print distinct elements of a variety of worksheets.

As an example of the last possibility, let's say you link several similar worksheets together, such as budget forecasts for each territory, into a summary worksheet. It's quite possible that each of those worksheets has more than one spreadsheet on it, such as manpower forecasts, equipment forecasts, and operating expense forecasts. To print out these worksheet segments, you normally would select each segment on the screen, choose Set Print Area from the Options menu, and then choose Print from the File menu. That could get rather tedious for worksheet after worksheet.

To turn over the work to a macro, you could assign a name to each of those segments in the worksheets, such that the manpower segment, for example, has the same name in every worksheet. You then can make one generic macro that prints each of the segments of the active window. The macro would select the named cell reference (preceded by an exclamation mark, not the name of a specific worksheet), print it, select the next named reference, print that one, and so on.

Moreover, you could develop a generic printing macro that selects each of the windows in turn so that the complete printing job is managed by the macro. Then, when you're through entering values into the spreadsheets, you could invoke the generic multiwindow printing macro. Here's how it would be structured.

A1	print.loop	
A2	=ACTIVATE("Macro.sheet")	By activating the macro sheet, first you'll be able to cycle through the other windows without the risk of running the macro on its own window.
A3	=SET.VALUE(A7,1)	Sets the counter in A7 initially to 1.
A4	begin	The name of the macro section that activates succeeding windows and the print routines. This cell must be defined with the same name as called in the GOTO command below.

A5	=ACTIVATE.NEXT( )	The same as pressing Command-M to cycle through the windows.
A6	=print.man( )	Subroutine to another macro that selects the manpower area of the current window and prints it.
A7	=A7+1	Increments the counter by 1.
A8	=IF(A7=4,,GOTO(begin)	Checks to see if the counter indicates whether all three manpower worksheets have been printed. If so, execution continues to the next cell, otherwise, it loops back to the part of the macro named "begin."
A9	=RETURN( )	End the macro.

In the rest of this book, I'll demonstrate other instances of useful macros that can be made into generic macros with careful planning on your part. It's really not that difficult, and it can simplify the management of your library of macros by reducing the number of macro files cluttering up your disk.

APPROACH MACROS AS A LANGUAGE

To really master Excel macros, you must become comfortable with the commands listed in both the function and macro directories in the Excel manual. These commands are actually the words of a language, just like vocabulary words of modern spoken languages. If you ever hope to converse fully in French, for example, you must learn the vocabulary and the grammar rules that influence how those words go together into intelligible sentences. Excel's macro language also has vocabulary and rules.

One major difference between a programming language and a spoken language, though, is that you can often get by in a spoken language even if you make several mistakes along the way. The listener usually can make out what you're trying to say, even if you're not exactly on target with your pronunciation and grammar.

Computers, however, are not so forgiving, at least not yet. Programming languages require extreme precision, and the machines "listening" to you are quick to tell you when you've gone wrong ("Error, Error!"). But at the same time, computers are forever patient with you and won't ridicule you if you make mistakes all day. So don't be concerned when an error message appears on the screen in response to something you programmed. Look on it not as a criticism of your work but as a pointer to a solution.

And, finally, have patience while learning the vocabulary and rules. If you recall any language training you've had, the term "vocabulary building" was prevalent. That's the key: Learn a few commands, then slowly build on that knowledge, using those commands you've learned with a couple of new commands. It won't take long before you'll have a working knowledge of "conversational Excel macro programming." You may not become the William Safire of the Excel language, but then no one has to be such an expert to program sophisticated macros.

Chapter **3**
SPREADSHEET STRATEGIES

A blank spreadsheet to someone with a math task is not unlike a blank sheet of paper to a writer. Sit two writers down with a piece of paper and pencil in front of each, give them both the same assignment, and you'll wind up with two distinctly different results.

The same happens if you give the same number of crunching tasks to two Excel users. Yes, there would be some commonality, particularly if there was only one function that would allow them to arrive at the answer. But there would be many other points of diversity. Each would have a different way of labeling columns and rows, placing the work on the enormous empty worksheet, and so on. The answers may be (nay, should be) the same, but there are no hard-and-fast rules that every spreadsheet user must follow to achieve that answer.

With that in mind, I tread carefully in the realm of suggesting strategies for using the Excel worksheet. Not all of my suggestions will work for everyone in every application of Excel. Rather, I will furnish you with the methodologies that I follow in most of my Excel spreadsheet work. Look on them not as rules but as ideas that you might find helpful in your work. They may even spark new thoughts for you.

THINK SMALL

You might think that because Excel provides a blank spreadsheet of enormous proportions—more than 4,000,000 cells—that I'd advocate utilizing that space to build huge megamodels. After all, there's room to gang up several related spreadsheets together on one gigantic sheet, a sheet that, if printed out and pasted together, would paper one wall of your office. No way! In fact, I advocate just the opposite: Make your worksheet files as small as possible.

Over the years, especially when I've written about the IBM Personal Computer, I have encountered self-proclaimed spreadsheet "power users" who complained that the 640 Kilobyte memory of their PC was too small for them to get their models in memory. There must be a lot of these kinds of folks, or at least enough of them for chip maker, Intel, and PC power spreadsheet developer, Lotus Development, to work together on an expanded PC memory standard for expanded spreadsheets. Today, you can build a four-megabyte Symphony spreadsheet model.

One big question hangs in my mind, though, when I hear that someone is even exceeding a more realistic 512K or 1 megabyte RAM capacity: How do you find your way around a spreadsheet of that size?

Now I readily admit that there are instances when there is no alternative but one giant spreadsheet, that is, just one model that has tons of data. But more often than not, a memory-gobbling file in 1-2-3 or Symphony consists of several models combined into one file. There might be good reason for this, as when individual models depend on one another—in a spreadsheet program such as 1-2-3 Release 2, multiple spreadsheets cannot be dynamically linked, and combining data from one file to another is not a particularly easy task. Fortunately, in Excel you don't have to worry about keeping all related models on a single worksheet. In fact, it can sometimes work against you.

To illustrate my point, I'll work with a relatively simple application both as a single worksheet with four models on it and as four separate files. This example system, incidentally, is representative of business financial records that a self-employed professional might keep.

The four models are:

1   A record of each income source and the amount received from that source each month;
2   A record of expenses paid by check each month, detailed by expense category;
3   A record of expenses paid in cash each month, detailed by expense category; and
4   A summary of income and expenses, resembling an operating statement.

The operating statement model draws income and expense data from the other three models and calculates profit and loss figures for each month and on a year-to-date basis.

I originally set up the four models on one worksheet organized as diagrammed below.

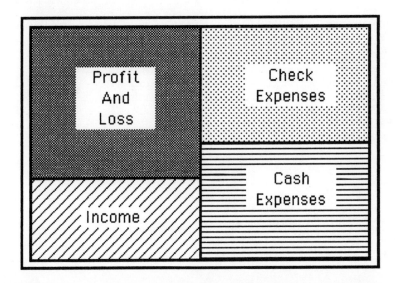

To help me recognize the boundaries of each model, I filled surrounding cells with greater-than and less-than symbols. Doing this makes the model a bit more memory- and disk-space hungry than storing the models separately, but clear boundaries make it easier to navigate the worksheet.

The problem I had working with the four models on one worksheet was that it was difficult to see exactly where I was in the worksheet unless I was lucky enough to have one of the upper-left corners of a model showing: In those corners I had placed identifying words, such as "Cash" or "Checks." And finding a particular cell, such as the one that would let me record a cash payout in October for vehicle parking, was no picnic. It took a bit of hunting and scrolling until I found it.

When checking for the time required to recalculate the worksheet after making a change in a single cell, the average was about five seconds (on a Macintosh Plus), regardless of which model I entered a new value into.

As a comparison, I next set up the four models in four separate files, each of which has its own window on the screen. I found several advantages to this arrangement.

File   Edit   Formula   Format   Data   Options   Macro   Window

K8

Operating Statement

Cash

Checks

Income

	A	B	C	D	E	F
1		January	February	March	April	May
2	Source:					
3	Ace Manufacturing	$800.00			$450.00	
4	Zebra Tech.		$7,500.00			
5	Bear Gulch Coop			$400.00		$8
6	Anderson Tool Co.			$623.00		
7	Icons East & Co.		$125.00		$125.00	
8	Graphics Plus				$2,250.00	
9	Dennis Kaplan					
10	DD&C Advertising					
11						
12						
13						
14						
15						
16						
17						

First of all, it is a snap to find the particular model into which I wish to enter data.

If all models are open, all I have to do is keep typing Command-M until the window with the plain language title, such as "Checks" or "Income," comes to the top of the pile.

Second, with each of the models in a separate window, it is possible to tile each window in such way that the titles are frozen along the top row and left column. To freeze titles, first open the document. Next, scroll the spreadsheet so that the top row labels are in the topmost row of the window and the left column of labels are along the left edge of the window.

** File   Edit   Formula   Format   Data   Options   Macro   Window**

A1

Operating Statement

Cash

Checks

	A	B	C	D	E	F
1		January	February	March	April	May
2	Checks:					
3	Rent					
4	Postage	$34.70	$1.45	$12.50	$12.50	$12.
5	Utilities	$120.75	$254.33	$244.66	$244.66	$244.
6	Telephone	$90.08	$76.34	$120.00	$120.00	$120.
7	Subscriptions	$20.00		$13.50	$13.50	$13.
8	Publications	$45.80	$33.90	$12.95	$12.95	$12.
9	Vehicle	$55.00	$76.30	$60.00	$60.00	$60.
10	Insurance	$120.00				
11	Depreciation					
12	Office Expense	$56.25	$56.25	$56.25	$56.25	$56.
13	Equipment	$356.21	$2,200.00	$39.67	$39.67	$39.
14	Legal/Acctg.					
15						
16	Total Checks	$898.79	$2,698.57	$559.53	$559.53	$559.
17						

Drag the split bar from the upper-right corner of the window down so that it is even with the bottom border of the top row labels. Drag the split bar from the lower-left corner of the window to the right so that it is even with the right border of the left column labels.

Horizontal
Split Bar

Vertical
Split Bar

 File   Edit   Formula   Format   Data   Options   Macro   Window

A1

Operating Statement

Cash

Checks

	A	A	B	C	D	E
1			January	February	March	April
1			January	February	March	April
2	Checks:	Checks:				
3	Rent	Rent				
4	Postage	Postage	$34.70	$1.45	$12.50	$12
5	Utilities	Utilities	$120.75	$254.33	$244.66	$244
6	Telephone	Telephone	$90.08	$76.34	$120.00	$120
7	Subscriptions	Subscriptions	$20.00		$13.50	$13
8	Publications	Publications	$45.80	$33.90	$12.95	$12
9	Vehicle	Vehicle	$55.00	$76.30	$60.00	$60
10	Insurance	Insurance	$120.00			
11	Depreciation	Depreciation				
12	Office Expense	Office Expense	$56.25	$56.25	$56.25	$56
13	Equipment	Equipment	$356.21	$2,200.00	$39.67	$39
14	Legal/Acctg.	Legal/Acctg.				
15						
16	Total Checks	Total Checks	$898.79	$2,698.57	$559.53	$559

At this point, you have what looks like a kind of a mess: Cell A1 is displayed in four different tiles. To straighten things out, choose Freeze Panes from the Options menu. This command (new with Excel 1.5) eliminates all the extra scroll bars of the tiled windows. Single vertical and horizontal scroll bars control scrolling of only the lower right pane. A single-thickness line separates the frozen panes from the scrolling one.

←	File	Edit	Formula	Format	Data	Options	Macro	Window

F16	=SUM(F3:F14)

Operating Statement
Cash
Checks

	A	B	C	D	E	F
1		January	February	March	April	May
3	Rent					
4	Postage	$34.70	$1.45	$12.50	$12.50	$12
5	Utilities	$120.75	$254.33	$244.66	$244.66	$244
6	Telephone	$90.08	$76.34	$120.00	$120.00	$120
7	Subscriptions	$20.00		$13.50	$13.50	$13
8	Publications	$45.80	$33.90	$12.95	$12.95	$12
9	Vehicle	$55.00	$76.30	$60.00	$60.00	$60
10	Insurance	$120.00				
11	Depreciation					
12	Office Expense	$56.25	$56.25	$56.25	$56.25	$56
13	Equipment	$356.21	$2,200.00	$39.67	$39.67	$39
14	Legal/Acctg.					
15						
16	Total Checks	$898.79	$2,698.57	$559.53	$559.53	$559
17						
18						

From now on, as you scroll, the labels along the top and left scroll in synchronization with the big tile. Leave the tile arrangement the way it is: It will be saved with the worksheet and will return to this format each time you open it from the disk.

A third advantage of breaking this large model into smaller ones is that if If have some income to add to the records (a rare occurrence, indeed), I need only open the Income file, which is smaller and faster to load than if I had to open the four-model giant. Because the Operating Statement file is merely a recap and summary sheet based on the original data in the Income, Cash, and Checks files, there really is no need to open it at all until I need to print out or inspect the bottom-line figures.

With four separate models, the system is actually the equivalent of a three-dimensional spreadsheet.

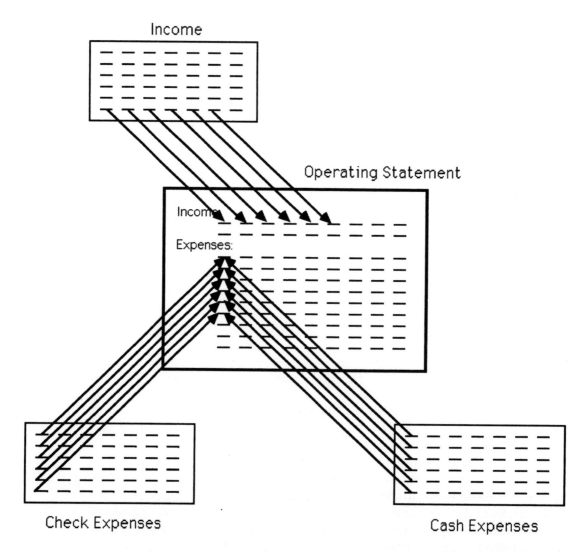

Because the four models share a lot in the way of labels, I was able to set up all four inside of two minutes, including all the formulas that link the four models together. Some special cautions prevail when doing the linking formulas, however. For details on how to set up a three-dimensional spreadsheet with linked formulas, see the step-by-step example in Chapter 6.

Having these four models as separate files has a potential draw-back when opening the models from within Excel. When you open the dependent document of this link, in this case the Operating Statement, it looks for references from worksheets not yet open and attempts to fill the cells containing references to those other models. Because the references are not available, the cells with such references become filled with the #REF! error indicator.

	File	**Edit**	**Formula**	**Format**	**Data**	**Options**	**Macro**	**Window**	

A1

Operating Statement

	A	B	C	D	E	F
1						
2						
3		January	February	March	April	May
4	Income	#REF!	#REF!	#REF!	#REF!	#REF!
5	Commissions					
6	Cost of Goods					
7						
8	Gross Income	#REF!	#REF!	#REF!	#REF!	#REF!
9						
10						
11	Expenses:					
12	Rent	#REF!	#REF!	#REF!	#REF!	#REF!
13	Postage	#REF!	#REF!	#REF!	#REF!	#REF!
14	Utilities	#REF!	#REF!	#REF!	#REF!	#REF!
15	Telephone	#REF!	#REF!	#REF!	#REF!	#REF!
16	Subscriptions	#REF!	#REF!	#REF!	#REF!	#REF!
17	Publications	#REF!	#REF!	#REF!	#REF!	#REF!
18	Vehicle	#REF!	#REF!	#REF!	#REF!	#REF!
19	Insurance	#REF!	#REF!	#REF!	#REF!	#REF!

There's nothing wrong with this as far as the integrity of the spreadsheet goes, but it holds you up for about ten seconds as the sheet goes through many unsuccessful calculations. You then can select Links from the File menu. In the dialog box are listed the names of the other three files referred to in the dependent document. Fortunately, you can select all three by dragging the pointer down the list and click-ing the Open button.

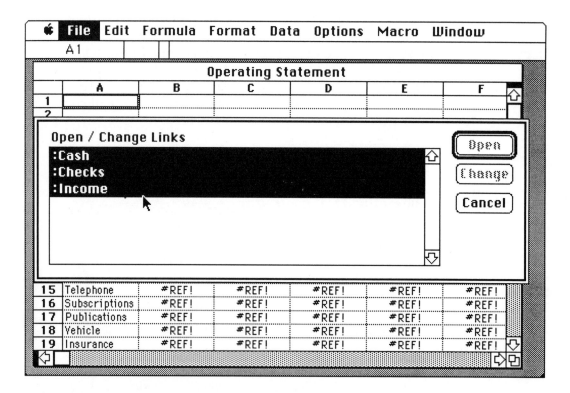

Each one is loaded in turn.

The alternative way of loading linked documents from within Excel is none too appealing. It entails opening each of the supporting documents one-by-one before opening the dependent document. I don't recommend this method to anyone except the most dedicated Macsochists.

From the desktop, however, just remember the shortcut detailed in the first chapter. Store all four files in one folder so you can find them quickly. Arrange the icons in the folder so that the dependent document, the Operating Statement here, is the last one to be opened.

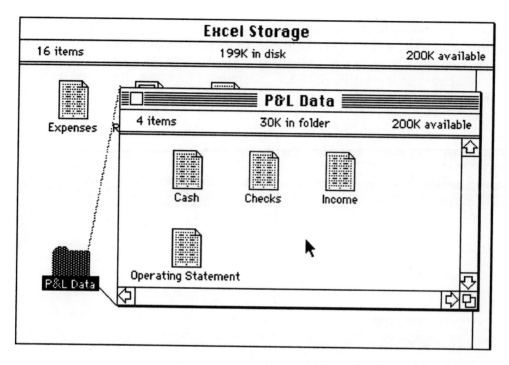

Then select all four icons and Open from the File menu. They'll all be loaded in proper sequence, with the Operating Statement window coming to the screen on top. Excel gives everything a first-time calculation to test that all the links are working properly. Now you're ready to enter data, play what-if, or whatever. Also, if you open this combination of files frequently, consider creating a Resume Excel version, as detailed in Chapter 1.

USE NAMES IN LINKED WORKSHEETS

In Chapter 1, I indicated that defining names for cells and cell ranges can prove to be a shortcut over the long run, even though it takes a bit more time to set up while creating a spreadsheet. Now I'm going to demonstrate why this is such a wise spreadsheet strategy. I encourage you to follow along on your Mac and try further experimentation after I've told my side of the story.

The example is a simple but effective one. I'll set up two worksheets on the screen so I can see both of them and switch quickly between the two (by clicking the pointer on the desired window). Worksheet 1 is labeled as the DEPENDENT Worksheet (the one that expects data from another worksheet) and Worksheet 2 is labeled as the SUPPORTING Worksheet.

⬦ File Edit Formula Format Data Options Macro Window

K6

Worksheet1

	A	B	C	D	E
1		DEPENDENT Worksheet			
2					
3					
4		The Answer Is-->			
5					
6					
7					

Worksheet2

	A	B	C	D	E
1		SUPPORTING Worksheet			
2					
3					
4		Supporting Data-->			
5					
6					
7					
8					

The goal of this exercise is to import a value from the "Supporting Data" cell (located to the right of this label) into the cell in Worksheet1 to the right of the "The answer is" cell.

The formula in Worksheet1 cell C4 multiplies the supporting data value by pi (3.14159...). To enter the formula, I select cell Worksheet1!C4 and then choose PI() from the Paste Function dialog box. I type an asterisk into the formula for the multiplication symbol. Now comes the critical part. I point to cell C4 in Worksheet2. This cell reference automatically is entered into the formula as an absolute cell reference.

🍎 File Edit Formula Format Data Options Macro Window

| C4 | ☒ ☑ | =PI()*Worksheet2!$C$4 |

Worksheet1

	A	B	C	D	E
1		DEPENDENT Worksheet			
2					
3					
4		The Answer Is-->	rksheet2!$C$4		
5					
6					
7					
8					

Worksheet2

	A	B	C	D	E
1		SUPPORTING Worksheet			
2					
3					
4		Supporting Data-->	✛		
5					
6					
7					

When I click the enter box (or press Return or Enter), I now can enter a value in Worksheet2 cell C4 and watch it multiplied by pi in Worksheet1 cell C4.

 File Edit Formula Format Data Options Macro Window

| C4 | | 10 | | |

Worksheet1				
	A	**B**	**C**	**D**	**E**
1		DEPENDENT Worksheet			
2					
3					
4		The Answer Is-->	31.4159265		
5					
6					
7					
8					

Worksheet2				
	A	**B**	**C**	**D**	**E**
1		SUPPORTING Worksheet			
2					
3					
4		Supporting Data-->	10		
5					
6					
7					

If I later decide that I don't like where the cell is located in Worksheet2 and need to cut it and paste it elsewhere on the sheet, I get myself into trouble. When I do the cut and paste, the cell reference in the pi formula still looks to cell Worksheet2!$C$4. Finding no value in that cell, it multiplies pi by zero.

 File   Edit   Formula   Format   Data   Options   Macro   Window

| B7 | | Supporting Data--> |

Worksheet1

	A	B	C	D	E
1		DEPENDENT Worksheet			
2					
3					
4		The Answer Is-->	0		
5					
6					
7					
8					

Worksheet2

	A	B	C	D	E
1		SUPPORTING Worksheet			
2					
3					
4					
5					
6					
7		Supporting Data-->	10		

Even if I had changed the reference to a relative reference (by cycling through the Command-T Reference command) when I entered the formula, it wouldn't matter: The minute I move the supporting cell in a supporting worksheet, the dependent worksheet loses track of it— unless, that is, I define the supporting cell by a name.

Starting over with two new worksheets, I now can define Worksheet2 cell C4 with the name "Supporting-Date," which Excel suggests (this is a default setting because Excel figures that the value cell probably is related to the adjacent label cell).

Back in Worksheet1, I enter the formula in cell C4 the same way as before except for the reference to the supporting cell. Instead of pointing to the cell C4 in Worksheet2 while entering the formula, I make Worksheet2 the active window, select Paste Name from the Formula menu, and then select "Supporting-Data" from the list of defined names (there's only one name listed here now).

	File	**Edit**	**Formula**	**Format**	**Data**	**Options**	**Macro**	**Window**

C4   ☒ ☑   =PI()*Worksheet2!Supporting_Data

Worksheet1

	A	B	C	D	E
1		DEPENDENT Worksheet			
2					
3					
4		The Answer Is-->	31.4159265		
5					
6					
7					

Worksheet2

	A	B	C	D	E
1		SUPPORTING Worksheet			
2					
3					
4		Supporting Data-->	10		
5					
6					
7					
8					

After clicking the enter box on the formula bar, I'm again ready to try values in the supporting data cell.

But now, I also can cut and paste the supporting cell anywhere on Worksheet2, and the formula in cell C4 of Worksheet1 will know where to find that supporting data.

& **File** **Edit** **Formula** **Format** **Data** **Options** **Macro** **Window**

| B6 | | Supporting Data--> |

Worksheet1

	A	B	C	D	E
1		DEPENDENT Worksheet			
2					
3					
4		The Answer Is-->	31.4159265		
5					
6					
7					
8					

Worksheet2

	A	B	C	D	E
1		SUPPORTING Worksheet			
2					
3					
4					
5					
6		Supporting Data-->	10		
7					

You'll never have to worry about linked cells before cutting and pasting cells in a supporting document.

While this example is not a real-life application, I can think of many instances in which you'll be moving cells in a supporting worksheet all the time.

Take, for example, a supporting document that acts like an ever-growing journal of financial records, such as a log of individual daily sales or cash payouts (totals are then fetched by a dependent summary spreadsheet). The most efficient use of RAM and disk space would suggest you keep moving the "totals" figure at the bottom of the sheet down one row each time a new entry is made (a macro is ideal for this). If the formula in the dependent document refers to the totals cell by cell number, the link will be lost the instant a new entry shifts the totals cell down one row. But by naming that totals cell and inserting its name into the dependent document's formulas, you shift the cell all over the worksheet, and the link will remain intact.

I hope this little exercise has shown you the importance of defining names and using them in your worksheet formulas. They can be a real headache-saver later on.

INCORPORATE FUNCTION MACROS

Not every worksheet can make use of function macros, but many of them can and still more should. I suspect that many Excel users who have studied the manual still have a fuzzy picture about the differences between command macros and function macros and perhaps no picture about how to make function macros run automatically from within a spreadsheet. A function macro is a particularly powerful worksheet feature of Excel and with a knowledge of how it works, you may find opportunities to simplify some of your spreadsheets and turn them into rather intelligent creatures, doing most of the work for you.

Function Versus Command Macros

The distinction between function and command macros perhaps is best learned in the context of the way in which they are initiated while you have a worksheet displayed.

Command Macros

The easier of the two macros to comprehend is the command macro, because you can start it either by selecting its name from the Macro menu's Run dialog box or by typing an Option-Command-key combination you assign to the macro on the macro sheet (you always can go back later and add the Option-Command-key command if you find you use a particular macro much more than you expected originally). In other words, a command macro is one that you deliberately initiate to perform a predetermined series of operations, just like a command on a pull-down menu. In fact, command macros can even emulate pull-down menus and commands, as you'll see more completely in Chapter 6.

Function Macros

A function macro, on the other hand, executes more automatically, behaving very much like functions you see listed in the Paste Function dialog box. If the function is given a value to work with, then off it goes to perform its complex calculation, returning an instant later with the result. In fact, Excel's built-in functions are essentially function macros that don't need macro sheets. Let's follow one through a calculation.

Take, for example, the built-in function that calculates present value (PV). This simple-looking function actually is the result of a hefty calculation based on the following formula:

$$pv * (1 + rate)^{nper} + pmt * (1 + rate * type) * \frac{(1 + rate)^{nper} - 1}{rate} + fv = 0$$

pv = present value
rate = interest rate
nper = number of payment periods
type = ordinary annuity (0) or annuity due (1)
fv = future value

When you ask Excel to perform the PV function inside a formula, the program knows to take the factors for the interest rate, number of periods, payment amount, and future value of the loan. After plugging those values into the formula, Excel crunches away and instantaneously produces the answer.

In line with the user programmability built into many parts of Excel, you can name your function macros so that they, too, appear in the list of scrollable functions when you select Paste Function from the Formula menu. Here's what the box looks like with a function macro named "Secret.Function" stored on a macro sheet with the short file name "M/".

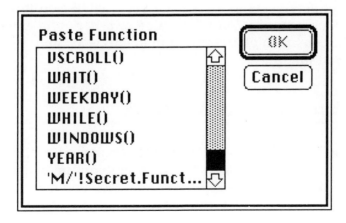

Once you design a function macro, you can import it into spreadsheet formulas just as easily as you import Excel's built-in functions.

You design function macros in cells on macro sheets just like entering formulas into spreadsheet columns. At first glance, function macros resemble command macros, but there are some significant differences in the way they behave and the kinds of things you should expect each to do.

A Comparison of Power and Flexibility

Perhaps the most important operational difference between the two kinds of macros is that function macros do not perform as many of the macro operations as command macros do. For example, you can write a command macro that selects a range of cells on your worksheet and fills them with a linear series of numbers. You don't have such power from a function macro. Function macros are intended primarily for added number-crunching powers behind the scenes, while command macros are capable of many of those same hidden number-crunching powers plus a lot of on-screen worksheet action.

At the same time, function macros have a power that command macros do not have. A function macro can pass arguments to formulas on a macro sheet for further calculation. An argument is programmer's talk for any text or number value that you want to carry over to the macro's calculations behind the scenes.

As an example, most of Excel's built-in functions require arguments. Present Value, as noted above, requires that four other values are passed to the function before it can calculate the result. A function macro takes its arguments from specific cells in the worksheet, massages those numbers inside the macro, and then returns some kind of value or other answer to the worksheet. Just like built-in functions, function macros want to return a value or other entry into the worksheet at the cell in which the function macro is located. We'll see how this works in just a bit.

☰ Putting Function Macros to Work

Some of the best applications of function macros are those that perform automatic computations for you quietly in the background (i.e., on the macro sheet beneath the worksheet) as you merrily enter data into the worksheet. I have just such an example, which I will explain in significant detail. It utilizes some features and techniques that I discovered through trial and error, because much of what the Excel manual tried to teach me about function macros went right over my head.

As I go through this example, pay particular attention to the way I define the problem, plan the solution, and execute same. You don't have to follow this methodology all the time, but it is one way to organize the work involved in creating function macros for your worksheets.

Define the Task

For this particular job, I want a one-screen form that I will use to enter orders that come into a small mail-order company. The form on the screen will be used to gather information about the customer, details of the order, and automatic calculation of the totals, including the pesky sales tax.

Sales tax is a special nuisance in this case, because the company is located in California, which has two state sales tax rates (when this model was first created), depending on the county the customer lives in. For much of the state, the tax rate is six percent; for many counties around major metropolitan areas such as Los Angeles and San Francisco, the tax rate is six-and-a-half percent, the extra one-half percent usually going to public-transit districts. Fortunately, the state prints a schedule of cities and zip codes that fall under the higher tax rate. Normally, I would have to look up the customer's zip code to make sure the proper tax was added to the order. What's more, no sales tax is collected on out-of-state orders, so the order form must know that if the customer is not from California, the sales tax is zero.

The Plan

The form I designed will play many roles because it will be printed out on a multiple-part form.

- One copy goes immediately to the customer as an order confirmation.
- The second is a special copy with the pricing information blanked out, and will be used as a packing slip when the merchandise is shipped.
- Another copy will be used for invoicing if the customer didn't send money up front.
- The last copy will be used for the company files.

In a real business form, especially one that generates an invoice, there would be additional fields for entry of ship dates, routing instructions, and other data, depending on the kind of business you're running. The one in this example is simplified for demonstration purposes, but could be expanded easily to fit an actual business.

Here is the layout of the form.

```
┌─────────────────────── order confirm ──────────────────────┐
│ Today's Date:   22-Jul-85                                 ⬆ │
│                                                             │
│ Name        ┌────────────────────────────────┐           ▢ │
│ Street      └────────────────────────────────┘             │
│ City                                                        │
│ State                                                       │
│ Zip                                                         │
│                                                             │
│   Quantity          Description        Cost Each    Total   │
│                                                     $0.00    │
│                                                     $0.00    │
│                                                     $0.00    │
│                                                     $0.00    │
│                                                     $0.00    │
│                                                   _____   │
│                                                             │
│                                   SubTotal          $0.00   │
│                                   Sales Tax         $0.00   │
│                                                   _____   │
│                                   Total Order       $0.00  ⬇ │
└─────────────────────────────────────────────────────────────┘
```

I've adjusted the width of column B to allow for long names for both customers and item descriptions. After I set up my titles and formulas, I also turned off the gridlines with the Display option in the Option menu. Follow along as I recount the creation of the form in a blank Excel worksheet.

Forms Creation

My first steps were to type the titles for the date and customer data. Because the title cells are all in one column, I simply started with cell A1, entered the title, and pressed Enter twice to skip down to cell A3. From there, I just typed each title and pressed Return to proceed down the list to cell A7.

Next, I typed the titles in row 9 by first selecting the range A9:D9. With these cells selected, I could type each title and proceed to the cell to the right by pressing Return after each entry. While the cells were still selected, I chose Alignment from the Format menu; in this command's dialog box I selected Centered. With the cells still selected, I chose Border from the Format menu and selected Underline from that command's dialog box.

At the top of column B, I needed to insert the formula that automatically displays today's date (as determined by the Mac's internal clock). The built-in function that does that job is the NOW( ) function, which I pasted in with the help of the Paste Function menu (although I could have just as easily typed it in). When I put that function in the cell, however, the display comes back as the serial number Excel uses to keep track of the date (as detailed in the manual). Because that number doesn't mean anything to me, I changed the number format to the d-mmm-yy format through the Number command in the Format menu.

If I enter some sample data in the customer information section, everything looks fine until I enter the ZIP code. That's because Excel recognizes the entry as a value, rather than a chunk of text, like the rest of the customer data. Excel, therefore, aligns the value right-justified in the wide B cell. After selecting cell B7, I selected Alignment from the Format menu and instructed Excel to left-align any information in this cell, so all customer data is aligned the same.

Next, I set up the rows and columns that will hold information about the order. Because my customers usually order very few items at a time, I limited the available entries to five, although I could have gone much longer and scrolled the form down as needed.

As far as the formulas go, they are pretty straightforward. The cell D10 is merely the product of A10 multiplied by C10, quantity multiplied by cost each. The formula in cell D10, therefore, is =A10*C10. The fastest way to get the corresponding formulas entered in cells D11 through D14 was to select the range of cells D10:D14 and issue the Fill Down command. Because all the references in the D10 formula were relative cell references, the formulas filled down from it were converted to calculate the products of columns A and C in their own rows. Next, I selected cell D14 by itself and gave it a bottom border, which ends up resembling a line drawn under the columns of numbers to be added.

For the subtotal, tax, and total area, I first placed the respective titles in cells C16, C17, and C19. Cell D16 is the total of all the extensions above, so its formula is =SUM(D10:D14). The cell for the sales tax was to hold a macro, so I left it blank for a moment, except that I gave it an underline border. Finally, in the last cell, the formula is simply the sum of the two cells above it, =D16+D17.

Two more housekeeping chores remained. First, I wanted the quantity figures to be centered in the column uner the Quantity title. I selected the range A10:A14 and centered them through the Alignment command. Second, the cells in C10:C14 and D10:D19 all will be dollars-and-cents cells. After selecting those ranges at once (selecting each with the Command key pressed), I chose the proper dollar format through the Number command.

Macro Design

Then came the fun part: designing the function macros that perform all my automatic sales tax calculations for me. The first thing, therefore, was to call up a blank macro sheet with the New command.

Planning these macros was no more difficult than tracking the non-computing steps involved and then converting those steps into Excel commands. To recap the steps:

1   If the customer is from California, charge some kind of sales tax, otherwise charge nothing.
2   If the California customer is from the special transit-district counties, charge 6.5%, otherwise charge 6%.
3   Calculate the total tax by multiplying the amount of the order by the tax rate.

I set up three macros that perform these three steps. The first one, which I labeled state.check, is in column A of the macro sheet.

	A
order macro	
1	state.check
2	=ARGUMENT("state",2)
3	=IF(state="CA",SET.NAME("tax",1),SET.NAME("tax",0))
4	=RETURN("")
5	
6	
7	

With the aid of a special, hidden formula in the worksheet, which I'll describe in a moment, this macro will look at worksheet cell B6 and determine whether the state is entered as CA. Depending on the outcome of that test, the macro will assign a kind of "yes/no" label to a word. This label will act like a light switch inside the macro: If the state is California, the switch will be turned on, otherwise it will be turned to the off position. One of the other macros will later look at that switch to see which way it is set and make further decisions based on that setting.

The part that probably loses most Excel macro beginners is how to transfer the value of a cell in the main worksheet into the macro— in this case, how to convey the contents of worksheet cell B6 to the macro so it can test to see if I typed CA in it or not. The answer lies in the function macro ARGUMENT. Let's pause for a minute to define what an argument is, for it has nothing to do with the type of heated conversation you might have with a boss or spouse.

Function Arguments

The kind of argument that Excel macros use has its origin in mathematics. In math, an argument is a value supplied to a function so the function can be calculated. It's as if the function is there all the time waiting for someone to fill in the missing value. The same can be said for arguments in computer-talk. In this case, however, an argument is a value you give to a program or other procedure so it may continue.

For example, when you select New from the Excel File menu, you are presented with a dialog box and three choices, Worksheet, Chart, and Macro sheet. When you click the Worksheet button, you actually are sending an argument to the program that tells it, "OK, go ahead and give me a blank worksheet." Programmers talk not of sending arguments but of "passing" arguments. Passing an argument is like handing a value to a program for it to munch on.

In an Excel function macro, an argument is passed from the calling formula on a worksheet (or from another macro on the macro sheet). The links between the worksheet and the macro are not as mysterious as the manual may lead you to ponder. A function macro called from a worksheet must have a formula in the worksheet that not only calls the macro (i.e., specifies the name of the macro to be run) but also cites the locations of any cells that contain values to be passed as arguments (if any). Let's see how this works with the first macro in my example, state.check.

The formula in the spreadsheet that runs this macro is located in cell C6.

	File	Edit	Formula	Format	Data	Options	Macro	Window

C6   ='order macro'!state.check(B6)

order confirm

	A	B	C	D
1	Today's Date:	22-Jul-85		
2				
3	Name	Steve Simkins		
4	Street	334 Main Street		
5	City	San Jose		
6	State	CA		
7	Zip	95102		
8				
9	Quantity	Description	Cost Each	Total
10	2	Model 122 Semiconductive Tape (300' roll)	$5.00	$10.00
11	9	Model 200 26 gauge wire (1000' spool)	$10.00	$90.00
12				$0.00
13				$0.00
14				$0.00
15				
16			SubTotal	$100.00
17			Sales Tax	$6.50
18				
19			Total Order	$106.50

You don't see anything in the cell, because I've designed the macro so that it does not display any distracting values. I could have placed this formula in any unused cell on the worksheet, including outside the view of the window as shown. But because the cells in columns C and D to the right of the customer data aren't being used, I put them to work. Placing these formulas within the bounds of the worksheet won't make the overall worksheet any larger than is necessary, thus conserving a bit of computer memory and disk space.

The formula in cell C6 that runs this macro is

='order macro'!state.check(B6)

Let's dissect the formula:

- The first reference, 'order macro'!, is the reference to the macro sheet I've titled "order macro."
- The exclamation point indicates that the name to its left is of another worksheet or macro sheet. In this case, it happens to be a macro sheet.
- After the exclamation point is the name of the macro, state.check. When I was building this formula in C6, I pasted in the name of the macro from the 'order macro' macro sheet. I had previously defined the macro as state.check.
- The last portion is the reference to the cell that contains the value to be passed as an argument. In this case, it is cell B6, the cell that holds the state abbreviation.

Over on the state.check macro itself, you'll notice that the first line of the macro is =ARGUMENT("state",2). This formula is the one that does the translation of the data specified by the calling formula in cell 'order confirm'!C6. The ARGUMENT function takes the value from the worksheet cell and assigns it to the word "state." This is the same as saying, "From now on in this macro sheet, the word 'state' has the same meaning as whatever is typed in cell B6 on the main worksheet" (if you've ever programmed in BASIC, this is like assigning a value to a variable or, more specifically, a string to a string variable). The numeral, 2, after the name specifies the type of data coming from the worksheet cell, text in this case (other data types and their numbers are listed in Chapter 9 of the Excel *Arrays, Functions, and Macros* manual under the direct listing for ARGUMENT).

The relationships among worksheet cell, argument, and macro are diagrammed below:

1.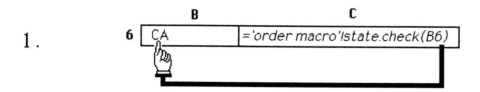

2.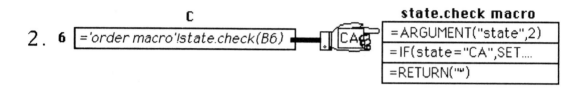

3.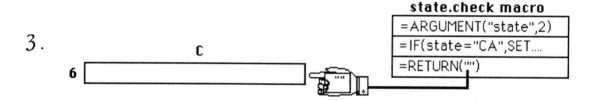

Now that you understand how data is passed to a macro, let's continue the explanation of the state.check macro. We left off in macro cell A2, where the text of the state from the worksheet is assigned to the argument name "state."

In macro cell A3, we use the name right away to test if the text in the worksheet cell is CA or not. The core of the formula is a standard IF function. The results of the test of whether state equals "CA" is either TRUE or FALSE (internally, Excel treats all text as uppercase letters, so even if I type "ca," Excel sees it as "CA").

- If the outcome of the IF test is TRUE, then the SET.NAME function assigns the value 1 to the name "tax," which means that later on, the macro will be able to check whether the customer should be taxed.
- If the outcome of the IF test is FALSE, then the name, tax, is assigned the value zero, which will serve as an indicator to a later macro that the customer should not be taxed.

The last line of the macro is a RETURN function. All macros—function and command macros alike—must end with a RETURN function, which returns control to the main worksheet. Notice, however, that I have added two quotation marks in the parentheses. The reason for this is that, as I mentioned earlier, a function macro always wants to display some sort of outcome in its cell after the macro runs. In other words, the function macro cell on the worksheet, C6, must have something displayed at the end of running the macro.

If I placed nothing in the parentheses of the =RETURN( ) formula, the macro would send back its logical answer, #N/A, the "error value" that tells you no value is available to display. Error is really too harsh a term for what this answer means, because you've done nothing wrong, and the macro or worksheet won't "bomb" on you for this reason. It simply means that it would like to display something, but there's nothing handy for it to display.

To prevent #N/A from showing in cell C6, I typed the two quotation marks in the macro's RETURN formula. These two marks are sending what programmers call a "null string," that is, a value with no actual characters in it. I'll bet that if you have no programming experience that this sounds crazy, but it's true, and in this instance, it works fine, for it keeps cell C6 blank and takes up not one extra byte of memory (as a blank space between two necessary quotation marks would do).

In macro column B is the macro that ultimately looks up the zip code typed into worksheet cell B7 to see if it falls in an area that gets the 6.5[6] tax. The worksheet formula that passes the zip code to the macro is in cell C7 and reads

=‘order macro’!zip.compare(B7)

In other words, this formula maintains a constant watch on cell B7. The instant a new value is entered into B7, the formula copies that value and hands it off to the macro named zip.compare.

	order macro
	B
1	zip.compare
2	=ARGUMENT("zip",1)
3	=IF(tax=0,RETURN(""))
4	=IF(ISNA(MATCH(zip,percenters,0)),SET.VALUE(rate,0.06),SET.VALUE(rate,0.065))
5	=RETURN("")
6	
7	

The macro assigns the actual zip code number to the name "zip." The numeral, 1, after the name in the formula is another one of those argument-type identifiers. This time, because the content of the argument is a number, type 1 is specified.

A test in macro cell B3 heads off any arguments that fall outside of California. After all, it's no use wasting time by having the macro check a Texas zip code against a select few in California. Therefore, the formula calls the name (tax) that was given a value in the state.check macro in the previous column. If the value of "tax" is zero (meaning that the customer is not to be taxed), then the formula returns to the main worksheet immediately, plugging a null string (two quotation marks in the RETURN parameters) into the cell that called the macro.

Notice that I placed no third argument in the B3 IF formula—the argument that executes if the test produces a FALSE result. When no argument is present, macro execution proceeds to the next cell down the column when the IF test proves FALSE. Therefore, if the state is CA, the macro continues to plod its way through the rest of the macro and proceeds to the next cell down the column, B4.

In this cell is the heart of the entire series of macros. This is where the zip in the worksheet (now an argument with the name "zip") is compared against the 6.5% zip code list, which begins at cell B16.

I structured this formula so it does several things in one cell. Starting with the inmost (most-nested) function, I have the macro see if there is a MATCH between the value assigned to zip and all the numbers in a range of cells named "percenters." That range of cells begins at cell B16 and contains all the zip codes in 6.5% sales tax area. The MATCH function has as its three parameters:

1   The name of the values it is testing (zip).
2   The name of the range of cells it is to compare zip against (percenters).

3   Type zero, which means that during the lookup process, there must be an absolute match for the function to signify that there is, indeed, a match.

Now it happens that the MATCH function does not encounter an absolute match in the range of cells, it generates an [5]N/A error signal (if there is a match, it generates the number of the item down the column it matches—a number we won't be using at all in this macro). One of Excel's functions, ISNA, tests for the presence of that #N/A error value. Therefore, it would be TRUE if the ISNA function found the #[5]N/A value as the result of the MATCH function. In other words (and this gets somewhat confusing because everything is turned around), ISNA says TRUE when the MATCH function does *not* find a match (as in, "YES, we have no bananas").

When I put an ISNA function inside an IF function, the answer to the IF test will show TRUE when there is no match of zip codes and FALSE when there is a match in the 6.5% category. When the condition is TRUE, SET.VALUE (rate,0.06) assigns the value 0.06 to a cell I have yet to define, but one called "rate," which will contain the sales tax rate to be applied to the subtotal. When the condition is FALSE, the second SET.VALUE function assigns the value 0.065 to the rate cell. After all the matching and value setting are done, the macro returns to the main worksheet, placing a null string in the cell that called the macro.

The final macro in this series, macro sheet column C, is relatively simple.

	C
1	tax.compute
2	=IF(tax=0,RETURN(0))
3	=RETURN(rate*'order confirm'!SubTotal)
4	
5	
6	
7	

order macro

The formula that calls this macro is located in the cell on the worksheet where the sales tax value is to appear, cell C7.

The structure of the formula that calls the sales tax computation macro is in a slightly different form than those in cells C6 and C7. In cell D17, it looks like this:

    ='order macro'!tax.compute(D16,B6,B7)

The three cell references are to the subtotal, state, and zip cells. If the macro were looking for arguments to manipulate, this would be one way to pass three arguments to it (providing the macro has three separate ARGUMENT functions in a row at the top of the macro).

But because no arguments are going to be passed here, the three references are simply places where the macro comes to life whenever data is entered into any one of those cells. That means that if I change the zip code in cell B7 from a 6% to 6.5% code, the tax will be recalculated immediately. Similarly, as I enter additional merchandise in the order form, the tax is calculated each time the subtotal changes, which it will as long as automatic calculation remains turned on.

In this macro, there is little need for an argument to be imported from the main worksheet, because there is one straightforward calculation to be performed on one value from the worksheet, the subtotal. Macro cell C2 bypasses the tax computation altogether by returning a zero to the sales tax cell if tax is zero (meaning that the state is other than CA).

The actual tax computation takes place in cell C3, where the value of the cell rate (which I decided for no apparent reason would be cell C11) is multiplied by the subtotal cell in the worksheet (I had defined the name of the subtotal cell, D16, as "SubTotal").

Notice that I have combined the calculation of the tax with the RETURN function in the formula. The result of the calculation in parentheses will be returned to the sales tax cell on the worksheet.

This is a very compact way of accomplishing the desired result. Perhaps it reveals my heritage as a programming hobbyist in the days when a 4K RAM computer was high-tech. On second thought, perhaps it's that I'm lazy and prefer to enter as few macro cells as possible.

Admittedly, this order form does not store the information typed into the cells unless I save each form under a different name. It would be of much more use if I could extract this data and store it in an Excel database. In Part II of this book, I'll show you ways of creating a database from a form such as this using command macros.

Function Macro Summary

This is only one way to use the powerful abilities of Excel function macros. Because they allow you to branch automatically from your worksheet into a wide array of calculations in a macro worksheet, you should look for ways to include them in your worksheets when you need that kind of power. As you can see from the example, function macros can be programmed to do drudgery work for you, such as looking up a sales tax table. Like most useful information sources on a computer, however, they take some time and care when setting up. But once they're debugged and running smoothly, you'll probably forget they're even there. Whenever possible, make the program do your dirty work.

VIEWING MORE CELLS

Excel allows you to change the number of cells you can see at one time. Three factors control how many cells fit on the screen. One is the size of the window. Now this may seem overly obvious, but you actually have two standard sizes of window at your disposal. One is the default window size, which you get when you select a new worksheet. But by double-clicking on the title bar of that window or clicking the zoom box at the right edge of the title bar, you can have the window fill up every available millimeter of viewing space on the screen. When you do that in the default font and font size, you gain another row of cells, increasing the viewing area from 19 to 20 rows deep on a 9-inch Macintosh screen.

The other two factors affecting the viewing area are font and font size, both of which are controllable for each window. While you cannot adjust individual cells to different fonts, you can have different windows in different fonts, if you like. For example, you might want to have a data-entry window, which several other people in your office use, in a large, 12-point Chicago size, while the data is stored on another worksheet in the default font, Geneva-10 (you'll see an example of this in Part II).

If you would be more comfortable seeing more cells of your worksheet at a time, you can adjust the font and font size downward to squeeze a few more cells into the window. Conversely, if you have trouble reading the smaller sizes, then by all means select a larger font, even if it means you'll be doing more scrolling through the worksheet.

As a convenience, I've listed the number of rows and columns you can see for a number of popular fonts and font sizes in Table 3.1. In all cases, the number of columns listed represents the number of full-width columns you can see. Partial columns don't count, because when you move the active cell cursor to a cell in a partial column, the screen automatically scrolls over to bring the entire cell into view, thus destroying the integrity of your full-screen view. I've also listed the available cells according to the two default window sizes on a MacPlus or SE screen: new window and full-screen window. An asterisk next to a column value indicates that by resizing the New Window a bit wider, you can get an additional column without any problem.

Table 3.1

Font	Size	Full Window			New Window		
		Rows	Columns	Total	Rows	Columns	Total
Chicago	12	15	5	75	16	5	80
New York	9	19	6*	114	20	7	140
New York	10	19	6*	114	20	7	140
New York	12	15	5	75	16	5	80
New York	14	13	4	52	14	4	56
Geneva	9	19	6*	114	20	7	140
Geneva	10	19	6	114	20	6	120
Geneva	12	15	5	75	16	5	80
Monaco	9	20	7	140	21	7	147
Monaco	12	15	6	90	16	6	96
Helvetica	9	22	8	176	23	8	184
Helvetica	12	17	6	102	18	6	108
Times	9	22	8	176	23	8	184
Times	12	19	6	114	20	6	120

*Last column partial

As you can see, if you really want to cram cells into the window, then Times-9 and Helvetica-9 are about the best you can do with a standard font. I don't recommend using font sizes on the screen other than the sizes that appear in the scrollable box in the Font dialog box. The reason is that any other size you choose will scale the fonts that are stored on the System Disk. While there's nothing dangerous about doing this, the results on the screen aren't too appealing. Characters often will be distorted and difficult to read. If you plan to print out such a worksheet on an ImageWriter, the printer will re-create on paper the same distorted figures you have on screen.

It's a different story, though, when you print out your work on a LaserWriter using the so-called laser fonts (Helvetica, Times, and Courier). The LaserWriter can interpret virtually any size of those fonts you give to it and performs the needed sizing of the font so that it looks perfect, regardless of how it looks on the screen. In the Times-10 laser font, you can fit 8 columns across by 21 full rows down in the Full Window mode.

	A	B	C	D	E	F	G	H	I
1									
2		January	February	March	April	May	June	July	Augu
3									
4									
5									
6									
7									
8									
9									
10									
11									
12									
13									
14									
15									
16									
17									
18									
19									
20									
21									
22									

That's enough columns to view an entire half-year of monthly figures plus totals. The font has been "tuned" so that it is readable on the Mac screen, although it might strain the eyes to work at that size all day. Still, it is a convenience to view 168 cells at one glance.

"WHAT-IF"
WITH DATA TABLES

One feature of a spreadsheet that has attracted many a believer is the ability to quickly plug in values to see how the bottom line is affected by changing one or more factors in a complex calculation. I suspect that many managers have used this ability to fudge forecasts by tweaking the forecasts of salespeople until the total comes up to the entire region's expectations.

I've seen many spreadsheet models in which the designer has fashioned one or two cells as input cells for a calculation, with the results appearing somewhere at the bottom of the screen. The user then can insert a variety of values and see what the final figures look like in each case.

	B	C	D	E
1				
2		Mortgage Loan Calculation		
3				
4				
5		Present Value	$150,000	
6		Rate (per mo.)	1.03%	
7		No. of Months	360	
8				
9		Payment:	$1,584.61	
10				
11				

This ends up being more of a trial-and-error method of achieving the desired results. A drawback to this method of model design is that once you cover one value with another input attempt, you've lost record of your trials, unless you bothered to write them down (which seems antithetical to what the computer is all about). You see snippets, but can't get the "big picture" of your calculations and trial values.

A better way to structure such an application is to take advantage of Excel's data table function. At its most powerful, a data table allows you to set up a chart consisting of final results based on a series of trial values for up to two variables in the calculation. An example would be the monthly payment based on a range of house prices and interest rates. If you had the results in a grid, you could see much more quickly how your payments are affected by going for a house $10,000 more at the same interest rate, for a less-expensive house at a higher interest rate, and so on. Let's set up such a data table to demonstrate its powers. Because I can't resist applying macros to a worksheet. I'll also throw in some extra features that will make it easier to change the ranges of trial values.

Two-Input Table

The example worksheet is titled "Mortgage Loan Analysis." Its purpose is to present an array of monthly payments based on a range of house prices and interest rates, taking into account the amount or down payment and length of the loan.

mortgage table

	A	B	C	D	E	F
1			*Mortage Loan Analysis*			
2						
3		Down Payment:	10%	No. of Years:	30	
4						
5	0	12.00%	12.25%	12.50%	12.75%	13.00%
6	$137,500	1,272.91	1,296.77	1,320.73	1,344.78	1,368.92
7	$140,000	1,296.05	1,320.35	1,344.74	1,369.23	1,393.81
8	$142,500	1,319.20	1,343.93	1,368.76	1,393.68	1,418.70
9	$145,000	1,342.34	1,367.50	1,392.77	1,418.13	1,443.59
10	$147,500	1,365.48	1,391.08	1,416.78	1,442.59	1,468.48
11	$150,000	1,388.63	1,414.66	1,440.80	1,467.04	1,493.37
12	$152,500	1,411.77	1,438.24	1,464.81	1,491.49	1,518.26
13	$155,000	1,434.91	1,461.82	1,488.82	1,515.94	1,543.15
14	$157,500	1,458.06	1,485.39	1,512.84	1,540.39	1,568.04
15	$160,000	1,481.20	1,508.97	1,536.85	1,564.84	1,592.93
16	$162,500	1,504.35	1,532.55	1,560.86	1,589.29	1,617.82
17	$165,000	1,527.49	1,556.13	1,584.88	1,613.74	1,642.71
18	$167,500	1,550.63	1,579.70	1,608.89	1,638.19	1,667.60
19	^Home Price^					

Because the home price and interest rate are the most variable factors in typical mortgage calculations, they are the ones that are presented over a range of values. You can change the percentage of down payment or length of the loan as you see fit. Of course, you also may want to see home prices and interest rates that are beyond the range listed in the spreadsheet or more finely detailed, such as 11.43 percent interest. That's where the macros will come in later. For now, however, let's concentrate on the worksheet.

First, a few words about the way some of the cells are formatted and named. The title, Mortgage Loan Analysis, is entered solely in cell C1, for text can run longer than its cell without any penalty.

To highlight the title against the rest of the worksheet, I selected bold and italic from the Style dialog box. Titles for Down Payment and

No. of Years were entered as text and then aligned-right so they will be close to the numbers in the adjacent cells (which are left-aligned). Although the Down Payment title filled cell B3, I still selected right alignment in case I adjust the column width later. Cells C3 and E3 also have outline borders around them, as selected from the Border dialog box.

Because cell C3 deals with a percentage, it was troublesome to handle with standard Number formats. If I had selected the built-in percent number format (0%), percentages would have to be entered as decimals each time I want to test a new value. In other words, if I were to enter 10 in cell C3 with the regular percent format, the value would be displayed in the cell as 1000%. Because I'm the lazy type, I'd rather just type in percentages as I'm accustomed to calling them, and let the computer figure out how to deal with the number. It was definitely time to design a custom number format.

The resulting format is rather simple, but it demonstrates that Excel has the flexibility to accommodate even the laziest users, like me. The new format I entered into the Format dialog box was

    #0"%"

which, in retrospect, looks like something Sergeant Snorkel would call Beetle Bailey in the comic strip.

- The pound sign (#) and zero are place holders, meaning that any number can go there.
- The zero has a special meaning in that if no number is entered into the cell, a zero is plainly displayed.
- The percent sign inside the quotation marks means that the percent sign always will be displayed. The sign is strictly a piece of text and has no mathematical significance to the numbers before it. This means that the number stored in cell C3 will be an integer, such as 10 or 20.

Later, when the worksheet calculates the loan amount (home value minus the down payment), there will have to be a formula that properly converts the figure into a percentage. But that's even easier than it sounds, as you'll see.

As a further help later in the spreadsheet, when I would need the values from the down payment and number of years cells, I defined names for each: "down" and "years," respectively.

To set up my initial interest-rate trial values, I decided to use the standard percentage number format, for it would mean one less calculation that would have to be performed for each calculation in the Data Table, thus speeding up recalculation. While I could have entered any values I wanted into the top row of table cells (B5:F5), I had the Series command automatically put in a range of values with even increments.

To do this, I first entered the value 0.12 in cell B5 in the proper decimal so that the percent number format would interpret it correctly as 12%. Then I selected the range B5:F5 and invoked the Series command (from the Data menu). In the dialog box, I merely typed in the interval step of .0025, which, in the percent format's way of looking at numbers, was .25% increments.

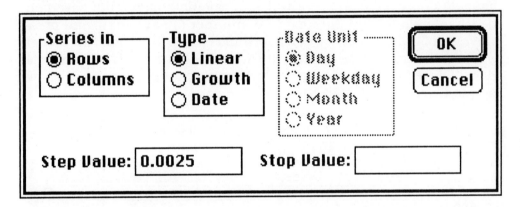

While the range was still selected, I called the Border command to put bottom borders across the range, and then I called the Style command to boldface the cells for emphasis.

I did a similar Series operation to load the home prices down the column range A6:A18. The only differences are that the number format was the one for whole dollars, and the border selected was the right, instead of bottom. As an extra reminder that the column lists the home price, and not the value of the loan (which is home price minus down payment), I stuck the title in cell A19 surrounded by circumflexes that point upward. That cell I gave an outline border.

I'll have more to say later about the contents of cell A5 at the top left corner of the table, but for now, suffice it to say that I simply gave it a right and bottom border as extensions of the borders I had already specified. The rest of the table cells, however, needed some kind of number formatting. I decided against a dollar format because the table would look too cluttered with columns of dollar signs. Instead, I settled for a simple two-decimal number format.

As an alternative, I could have selected the top row of payment cells and given them the dollar sign format, but in the end I thought it unnecessary for this application.

≣ Payment Formula

To perform the payment calculations, I selected the PMT function that is built into Excel. It's quite possible that professional financial managers may have other formulas to calculate payments based on the three main factors (interest rate, number of payments, and present value of the property). Such a formula can be built into this model as a function macro, as described earlier in this chapter. The actual calculation of all the payments is done, simply enough, in one cell below the main screen, cell C25.

⚫ File   Edit   Formula   Format   Data   Options   Macro   Window

| C25 | =ABS(PMT(C22,C23,C24)) |

mortgage table

	A	B	C	D	E	F
17	$165,000	1,527.49	1,556.13	1,584.88	1,613.74	1,642.71
18	$167,500	1,550.63	1,579.70	1,608.89	1,638.19	1,667.60
19	^Home Price^					
20						
21						
22		Rate	0			
23		No. of Months	360			
24		Present Value	$0.00			
25		Payment:	$0.00			
26						
27						
28						
29						
30						
31						
32						
33						
34						
35						

Because the PMT function requires three arguments (the interest rate, number of payments, and present value), I've set up three cells above the PMT function as the holding position for those values. The formula in C25, therefore, is

=ABS(PMT(C22,C23,C24))

The ABS function at the head of the formula turns the results of the PMT operation into a positive number. If you look in the Excel reference manual for the PMT function, you'll see that this and other financial functions return negative numbers for moneys that are paid out. I figured that such notation would only serve to confuse the table of payment figures—I don't need an accountant to know that these payments will be going OUT. The references to cells C22, C23, and C24 in the formula are the same as telling the PMT function to look in those cells for the values (arguments) it needs to perform its calculation.

Before I tell you about the formulas in cells C22:C24, we need to review some details about Data Tables. While they are a powerful feature of Excel, they also place some demands on the way you structure the worksheet in which they are used. In the case of this two-input data table (two varying ranges of data: interest rates and home prices), you must have two cells elsewhere on the worksheet into which the values from each range will be plugged in. It's just as if you were manually plugging in every combination of home price and interest rate into the PMT calculation. Where would you plug those figures in?

In a simpler version of this mortgage-payment calculation, you might plug the interest-rate figure into cell C22, while the home price goes into C24, the present value cell. That, of course, relies on the figures you plug in there being in the correct format that the PMT formula expects. According to standard financial calculations of monthly payments, the interest rate must be divided by the number of payment periods in one year. Because mortgage payments are made monthly, you must give the PMT function the equivalent of the annual interest rate divided by 12 months. Therefore, if you instruct the Data Table to insert your interest rate values into cell C22, the interest rate values in your table would have to be divided by 12.

I don't know about you, but 0.9167% per month doesn't mean anything to me, whereas its equivalent, 11% per year, sure does. Consequently, I want to type the annual interest rate in my table, but have Excel calculate the monthly interest rate that the PMT function needs.

To do that, I have the Data Table plug my interest rate values into the cell to the right of C22. Then, in cell C22, I put the formula that divides the figures from my table by 12 with the formula:

=D22/12

Similarly, I want to have the total price of the home listed in the home-price column of values in the table. I also want the computer to figure out the down payment and subtract it from the sale price to reach the present value of the loan. Therefore, when I set up the Data Table, I instruct it to place the home-price values into cell D24, which is conveniently next to cell C24 whose formula is:

=D24*((100-down)/100)

This formula performs the following steps:

1   It subtracts the down-payment percentage (retrieved from the Down Payment cell, C3, which I've already named "down") from 100, leaving the percentage of the loan.
2   It divides that dividend by 100 to get the actual percentage figure of the loan amount.
3   It multiplies the percentage of the home price to be mortgaged by the home price values being plugged in from the table, leaving the present value of the loan.

Although I am using cells D22 and D24 as staging cells for the values that the Data Table operation plugs into the calculation, no values ever appear in those cells, even during calculcation. But those cells play an important role in the process.

There is another way I could have done this calculation, in case you're wondering. Instead of setting up those two "dummy" cells in D22 and D24, I could have directed the trial values to cells C22 and C24 and performed the calculations in those two cells instead of in a giant formula solely in cell C25, which would look like:

=ABS(PMT(C22/12,years*12,C24*((100-down)/100)))

But I thought it would be easier to show what's going on the other way.

Before setting up the Data Table, there is one more cell to specify. Cell A5 at the upper-left corner of the table must, according to the design of Excel, contain a reference to the cell on the worksheet that normally would display the outcome of the calculations if you were doing them one at a time. In this case, the outcome appears in cell C25, where the PMT formula is located. To refer to cell C25, all I had to do was place the formula

=C25

in cell A5.

≡ Making the Data Table

Finally, to bring this all together, I selected the range of cells A5:F19 and then called the Table command from the Data menu. A dialog box appeared, asking for the references to the cells that were to be the recipients of the trial values from the top row and left column of the table.

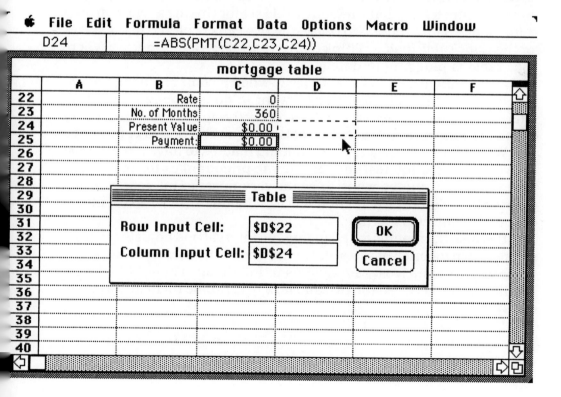

In those boxes, I typed D22 for the top row (interest rate) and D24 for the left columns (home price). After clicking OK, Excel immediately began calculating the payment values for each interest rate and home price listed. But because I had not yet specified a length of the loan, all that happened was that the table filled with 5DIV/O! error messages. Not to worry. The math buried inside the PMT calculation tried to divide by the number of months in cell C23. Because cell C23 multiplied 12 by zero years, the value was zero, throwing the PMT function into disarray. The solution was simple enough: Plug a value into the No. of Years box at the top of the worksheet. Then Excel presented a table of payment values.

When I select one of the cells inside the table, the formula is listed as

{=TABLE(D22,D24)}

The braces indicate that the formula applies to an array, which is of no particular importance in this example. But the TABLE function and its arguments tell us that the Data Table set for this area relies on data being plugged into those two cells—the two cells I entered in the boxes for the Data Table dialog. Think of this formula as a reminder of where your table is plugging in data.

I've mentioned earlier that I'm lazy when it comes to using a worksheet such as this. The last thing I want to do is type in all kinds of interest-rate and home-price values, even though Excel can do a lot of calculation work for me with tools such as the Series command.

Why not use the powers of command macros to have Excel adjust the values in the interest-rate and home-price ranges for me? Moreover, because I might want to see a very specific interest rate not covered in the quarter-percent interval, why not have an Excel macro change the intervals for me?

Because the macros for changing the interval and adjusting values up and down for interest rates and home prices are essentially the same, I'll describe the interest-rate macros in full detail. Then I'll highlight the differences between the two and how to combine them into a coherent system.

≡ Data Table Macro

To do what I want for the interest-rate values, I need a total of six macros:

> rate.interval
> rate 0.01
> rate 0.1
> rate 0.25
> raise rate
> drop rate

Only three of them (rate.interval, raise rate, and drop rate) will be called from the mortgage-table worksheet with the help of Option-Command macro keys. The other three macros will be called, in turn, by one of the macros invoked from the worksheet, depending on the condition of the main worksheet.

The core macros of this system are the ones that control the interval between each cell across the top row of the table. I decided that for maximum flexibility, I'd like to see intervals of 0.01, 0.1, and 0.25 percent. That would allow me to see the effect of relatively large interest-rate steps (1/4 percent) and allow me to examine specific rates that might not be evenly divisible by 1/4 percent, such as 12.11%.

To accomplish the changes in rate intervals, I had to have the macros select the range B5:F5 on the main worksheet and then perform the equivalent of selecting Series from the Data menu, clicking the appropriate radio buttons, and typing in the desired step between items in the series. Fortunately, Command macros in Excel allow calling almost every menu command and making the needed adjustments to the succeeding dialog box, if there is one. Therefore, each of the three macros (for 0.01, 0.1, and 0.25 percent intervals) select the range on the main worksheet (B5:F5) and perform the comparable Series command with the DATA.SERIES macro command.

	B	C	D
	M/mortgage		
1	rate_.01	rate_.1	rate_.25
2	=SELECT(!$B$5:$F$5)	=SELECT(!$B$5:$F$5)	=SELECT(!$B$5:$F$5)
3	=DATA.SERIES(1,1,1,0.0001)	=DATA.SERIES(1,1,1,0.001)	=DATA.SERIES(1,1,1,0.0025)
4	=RETURN()	=RETURN()	=RETURN()
5			
6			
7			
8			

Note that the arguments for the SELECT functions in cells B2, C2, and D2 are preceded by a lone exclamation point instead of a reference to the mortgage-table worksheet. I could have made the reference to the worksheet, but there is little need, for the exclamation point links the reference to whatever worksheet (or macro sheet) is the active window. I'm not likely to invoke this macro from any worksheet other than the mortgage table, so the single exclamation point simplifies the appearance of the formula. Three of the four arguments in the DATA.SERIES formulas control the radio buttons in the dialog box, while the last argument is the value you normally would type into the Step field in the box. The figures here have to be in the number format that the percent format on the worksheet will work with—hence all the numbers are to the right of the decimal.

I could have let these three macros stand as they were and simply called them individually when I wanted a specific interval. But instead, I devised a way for these macros to be called in a cycle—I added a macro, called rate.interval, that cycles through all three intervals. In other words, if the current interval is 0.01, then the next time I call the rate.interval macro, the interval changes to 0.1; the time after that it changes to 0.25. After that, the cycle begins again at 0.01. But to do that, I had to maintain a kind of counter that kept track of which interval was the current one.

In the macro cells B4, C4, and D4, I placed macro functions SET.VALUE.

	B	C	D
		M/mortgage	
	B	**C**	**D**
1	rate_.01	rate_.1	rate_.25
2	=SELECT(!$B$5:$F$5)	=SELECT(!$B$5:$F$5)	=SELECT(!$B$5:$F$5)
3	=DATA.SERIES(1,1,1,0.0001)	=DATA.SERIES(1,1,1,0.001)	=DATA.SERIES(1,1,1,0.0025)
4	=SET.VALUE(record,1)	=SET.VALUE(record,2)	=SET.VALUE(record,3)
5	=RETURN()	=RETURN()	=RETURN()
6			
7	rate record---->	3	
8			

This function places the value of the second argument into a cell with the name of the first argument. To be more specific, in cell B4, the function sticks the value 1 into the cell named "record." To make this all happen, I had to select an unused cell (C7 was convenient) and define its name as "record." From then on, the SET.VALUE (record,X) formulas would place the value of X in that cell, where other formulas could read the current interval setting. To help me remember where the cell was, I placed the title, "rate record—>" in B7 pointing to the named cell.

Oddly enough, the rate.interval command macro that determines which of these three hardworking macros should go to work is rather simple, consisting of only one action-taking formula (besides the RETURN function).

	A
	M/mortgage
	A
1	rate.interval
2	=CHOOSE(record,GOTO(rate_.1),GOTO(rate_.25),GOTO(rate_.01))
3	=RETURN()
4	
5	
6	

It uses a fabulous programming tool, the CHOOSE function—a function that is available to you in worksheets as well as in macros. If you've ever done some BASIC language programming with one of the more powerful dialects, you may recognize the CHOOSE function as a close relative to the ON X GOTO instruction. Here's how it works.

Arguments of the CHOOSE function consist of an index number and one or more values. Each value is assigned a kind of address, starting with the number 1, to identify its location in the sequence of values. The CHOOSE function matches the index argument number against the addresses of the values. When it finds the matching address, the CHOOSE function then displays (or "returns") the value that was sitting at that address.

Here is a more practical example. Let's say that the formula reads:

=CHOOSE(2,"Larry","Moe","Curly")

This means that the three names are stored in locations with "addresses" numbered 1, 2, and 3, with Larry being in number 1. Because the index number in the formula is 2, the formula looks up the value stored at address 2, which happens to be Moe. If you were to put this very formula into a worksheet cell, all you would see in the cell as a result of the formula is "Moe." Try it. Then change the index in the formula to 1, 3, and 5 to see what happens. When you try an index larger than the number of values in the argument, the #VALUE! error message appears because the function tried to find a value in the fifth storage slot but found none.

By itself, the CHOOSE function is pretty worthless, as I just demonstrated. But its power lies in the fact that in place of index and value arguments can go all kinds of things that produce values and, in the case of macros, further macro commands.

For example, in a worksheet, you could have a cell with the CHOOSE formula display a particular message or number depending on the results in a calculated cell somewhere else on the worksheet. In that case, the index in the formula would not be a number but a cell reference. Therefore, the C4 cell formula

=CHOOSE(Q12,"Larry","Moe","Curly)

would display "Curly" if the value in cell Q12 were a three.

Placed inside a macro, the CHOOSE function becomes a powerhouse. Look at how I used it in macro cell A2. The index argument is the contents of the cell named "record," which is the one that records which interval currently is in force on the main worksheet. If the value of record is 1, indicating that the current interval is 0.01 percent, the function looks to see what's in the formula's first address. Instead of a value, however, it finds a macro command instructing macro processing to jump to a macro named rate__.1, the macro that changes the interval to 0.1 percent and updates the record cell to read 2. Next time, the CHOOSE function in A2 finds the index is 2 and sends the macro processing to the macro named rate__.25. And so goes the cycle through the interest-rate intervals. If you try to re-create this macro on your own, the only thing you must remember to do is manually place a value in "record" when you create the macro to prime the pump, so to speak.

Altering the Table Values

The next two macros raise and lower the range of interest rates displayed across the top of the table by one unit, depending on the current interval. In each macro, the procedure is to add or subtract one interval from the number in the "anchor" position of the row, cell B5. I call this the "anchor" cell because it is the one that needs to be filled with the new number on which the DATA.SERIES function will build the series. The next step is to select the range and then pass the Series arguments to the DATA.SERIES function.

To accomplish these feats, I used generous portions of CHOOSE in each macro.

	M/mortgage
	E
1	raise rate
2	=SELECT(!$B$5)
3	=FORMULA(!$B$5+(CHOOSE(record,0.0001,0.001,0.0025)))
4	=SELECT(!$B$5:$F$5)
5	=DATA.SERIES(1,1,1,(CHOOSE(record,0.0001,0.001,0.0025)))
6	=RETURN()
7	
8	

Raising the rate in macro column E started by selecting the anchor cell, B5. Then I used the FORMULA macro function to make cell E3 manipulate data in a cell on the main worksheet. For macro cell E3, the job to be carried out on the main worksheet was the addition of an interval to the original value in B5. The interval to be added is the one specified by the "record" cell and plugged into the formula with the help of the CHOOSE function.

In other words, whatever number comes out of the CHOOSE function in cell E3 is added to the value in cell B5 on the main worksheet. Next, the entire range of the interest rates is selected so that the new Series can be calculated and displayed based on the new value in cell B5. The interval inserted into the Series command is dependent on the current interval and is selected with the CHOOSE function like it was two cells up.

The rates on display are lowered by subtracting one interval from the value in B5, shown in macro drop.rate. Everything else in the macro in column F is the same as the raise.rate macro in column E.

	F
	mortgage
	F
1	drop rate
2	=SELECT(!$B$5)
3	=FORMULA(!$B$5-(CHOOSE(record,0.0001,0.001,0.0025)))
4	=SELECT(!$B$5:$F$5)
5	=DATA.SERIES(1,1,1,(CHOOSE(record,0.0001,0.001,0.0025)))
6	=RETURN()
7	
8	

When I defined the names of all these macros, I was careful not to classify the three internal, interval-changing macros as command macros. To do so would have entered their names on the listing that appears when I call the Run command from the Macro menu. That would only confuse things because the only macros I want to see in that list are the ones that do some real work for me: the one that cycles through the intervals, the one that raises the displayed rates, and the one that lowers the displayed rates. Those last three action macros, however, I defined as Command macros and assigned Option-Command key equivalents to them so I could call them without pulling down that Macro menu and dialog box.

☰ Home-Price Macros

Macros to take care of the home-price column perform the same kind of calculations. The only differences are: the selected cell ranges for formulas involving cell selection; all DATA.SERIES have a 2 as their first argument, for that signifies a Series in a column rather than in a row; and every macro (plus the cell that records the current interval) has different names so they won't be confused with the interest-rate macros.

	I	J	K
1	home .5K	home 1K	home 2.5K
2	=SELECT(!$A$6:$A$18)	=SELECT(!$A$6:$A$18)	=SELECT(!$A$6:$A$18)
3	=DATA.SERIES(2,1,1,500)	=DATA.SERIES(2,1,1,1000)	=DATA.SERIES(2,1,1,2500)
4	=SET.VALUE(cost,1)	=SET.VALUE(cost,2)	=SET.VALUE(cost,3)
5	=RETURN()	=RETURN()	=RETURN()
6			
7	cost recorder----------->3		
8			
9			

mortgage

When all macros were completed, the dialog box listing the command macros showed the six action macros and their Option-Command key equivalents.

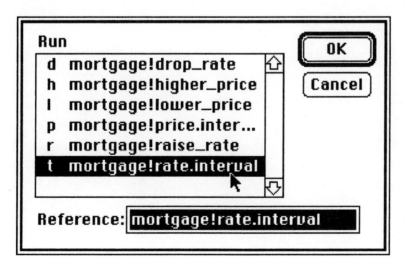

I tried to make the keyboard equivalents both mnemonic and physically segregated in such a way that the interest-rate macros were invoked by keys on the left side of the keyboard, while home-price macros were activated by keys on the right side. This is not always easy, depending on the kinds of macros you design. It also does not help to be restricted to letters of the alphabet, with extra restrictions against using lowercase letter e, u, i, or n.

In Chapter 6 you'll learn about adding custom menus to an Excel worksheet like the mortgage calculator. The menu choices would trigger the macros discussed in this chapter, thereby simplifying the changes in rates and prices.

With these basic strategies in mind, you should be able to create more functional and more powerful spreadsheets. But spreadsheets are only one part of Excel. The program also features a remarkable database environment. Strategies for the database are next.

Chapter 4
DATABASE STRATEGIES

Keep Field Lengths Short
Plan for Optimal Sorting
Preserve Original Data-Entry Order
Use Multiple Windows
Automatic Sort Selection
Create Relational Databases

For years, we've all been told that the five productivity software categories are spreadsheet, database, graphics, word processing, and communications. But with my study of spreadsheet and database "literature" over the years, it is quite clear that the distinction between a spreadsheet and database program is not so carefully defined as you might think.

In Excel, the distinction is no less clear cut. Some of the example models I used in the Spreadsheet Strategies chapter could be constructed on database programs in one form or another. Likewise, some of the examples I'll provide in this database chapter will look suspiciously like a spreadsheet application. About the only thing that makes one application more "databasey" than another is when you call the Set Database, Set Criteria, and Extract commands on the Data menu.

In defense of this lack of distinction, I find having the powers of the spreadsheet functions and macros available to me in my database applications very satisfying. For one thing, because I've learned one command language for the spreadsheet, it's nice to know that I don't have to learn a completely new language to set up a database with another program. Moreover, I might even be encouraged to do more math- and graphics-oriented things with databases in Excel because I have these functions so close at hand. Imagine . . . making a database interesting.

True database fanatics might scoff at the idea of using a spreadsheet program as a database. "If a program does not allow you to input data in a formlike environment," they might say, "then it isn't a true database." Well, as you'll see in Part II, Excel allows you to set up an entry form if you insist. The result is admittedly not so graceful as a dedicated database program or a HyperCard stack might be, but it works well, and it allows you to turn the job of data entry over to someone who has the time and patience for it.

And so, I come to some specific strategies and guidelines you should follow whenever you use Excel for a database chore. The job could be as simple as using the program's sorting capabilities to arrange a list of some kind. Or it could be much more extensive, to include sophisticated invoicing and other financial-transaction records for a small business. And whether you think these applications are more database than spreadsheet or vice versa, the following suggestions should help.

KEEP FIELD LENGTHS SHORT

One of the main benefits of using a spreadsheet environment for database storage is that you can change the width of a field column at any time. Try this with some database programs, and you might literally lose all the data that has been entered up to that point. But the problem with textual database information is that it easily becomes verbose. Because you are limited in Excel to single-line data fields (unlike some databases on the Mac, which allow you to design huge text and picture blocks if you need the space), everything you enter into a given field appears on the line occupied by that record. If the text you typed into a cell is longer than the column width, then the text will spill over into the right adjacent cell, unless there is some other entry in that adjacent cell.

B	C
Primary Customer Contact	

If the adjacent cell is already occupied, the long text you typed in will be "truncated" or cut off at the right edge of the cell.

B	C
Primary Custo	Telephone

The data is intact, but you can't see it unless you select the cell (the text then appears in the formula bar) or widen the column.

My harangue about this is centered on a simple-to-understand, hard-to-follow rule of thumb: Try to keep the contents of any single field to a minimum. The narrower a column can be, the more fields you can display across the screen. The more columns you can see at once, the bigger the picture you have of a particular record.

A corollary to this rule is that titles for very narrow fields, like single- or double-digit numbers, shouldn't be much longer than the width of the data in the fields. It's a great waste to have a skinny field unnecessarily wide only to accommodate a verbose field title at the top of the database.

E
Customer Type
1
1
3
1
0
2
2
0
0
1

Use abbreviations, symbols, and your imagination to shorten such titles.

G
C. Type
1
1
3
1
0
2
2
0
0
1

If you can get one more field on the screen, you'll be better off when it comes time to view records found to match the search criteria.

One other thing about field titles I might mention. To my eye, field titles always should be centered in the column. When they're centered, the database looks more like a professional database report.

	A	B	C	D	E
				Expenses	
7					
8					
9					
10	Date	Expense	Amount	Vendor	
11	1/1/84	overhead	$1,000	A.B. Properties	
12	1/5/84	overhead	$566	Ace Power & Light	
13	1/5/84	overhead	$600	Wheelin's Gas Co.	
14	1/5/84	overhead	$200	Ralph J Cook Garbage	
15	1/5/84	overhead	$440	City of Franklin	
16	1/6/84	inventory	$16,000	SW Wholesale	
17	1/5/84	salary	$1,000	Mary Fuller	

Select the range of cells containing the titles and choose the Alignment command from the Format menu. While the cells are still selected, you might as well place a bottom border under them. On the Excel worksheet display with gridlines, the difference between bordered and unbordered cells is slight, but if you turn off the gridlines or print the database without gridlines (which I highly recommend), the titles will be visually separated from the beginning of the data.

PLAN FOR OPTIMAL SORTING

Designing a practical database takes planning. Sorry, but proceeding without a plan usually ends up in frustration because of data that was either entered improperly or in a form that makes it hard to work with later. Here's what I mean.

In a typical name-and-address kind of database, it is tempting to set up a series of fields for name, street, city, state, and ZIP code. That's fine, until there comes a time when you would like to sort the database alphabetically according to the last names of the entries. If you've been entering name data into the database in a form like Joe Smith, then forget trying to sort by last name.

You can't do it. One alternative is to remember to enter names into a field in the form Smith, Joe. That's not particularly natural, plus it means that you have to insert the comma each time.

A solution that I prefer is to separate the two parts of the name into two separate fields, called First Name and Last Name. In fact, in a database format such as Excel, there's no problem putting the two fields in the natural order of the person's name so that you type the person's first name, press Tab, and then type the last name.

	A	B	C	D	E
				Customer List	
1					
2					
3	Cust. No.	Customer Name	First Name	Last Name	Address
4					
5	101	A.B.Properties	Timothy	Smith	418 Main Street
6	102	Ace Power & Light	Doris	Addams	Box 10
7	103	Andy Lubert	Andy	Lubert	3445 Abercrombie Way
8	104	AR Office	Steve	Jones	400 Wilshire Ave.
9	105	Carol Stansen	Carol	Stansen	9066 114th Street
10	106	City of Franklin	Henry	Champion	45 Washington Street
11	107	James Gregory	James	Gregory	200 Wilshire Ave.
12	108	Jim Parsons	Jim	Parsons	RR 1, Box 22N
13	109	Karen Bush	Karen	Bush	Box 2234
14	110	Lisa La Flamme	Lisa	La Flamme	77 Sunset Street
15	111	Mary Fuller	Mary	Fuller	10 Downing Lane
16	112	Ralph J Cook Garbage	Ralph	Cook	1600 Rhode Island Ave.
17	113	SW Wholesale	Sharon	Wester	919 Michigan Ave.
18	114	Wheelin's Gas Co.	Ralph	Wheelin	333 Fifth Ave.
19					

In sum, the more accurately you can identify the information you intend to record and set each bit of information in its own field, the more flexibility you will have in the future to sort your records by any of the different fields.

Incidentally, if you are entering data in a long database and would like to see the titles of the fields at the top of the window, even when you are entering the 300th record, you should set up your window with a split and frozen pane at the top.

	A	E	F	G	H	I	
						Customer List	
3	Cust. No	Address	City	State	Zip	Phone	
4							
5	101	418 Main Street	Dallas	TX	75544	(214)555-1298	
6	102	Box 10	Houston	TX	79881	(215)834-9384	
7	103	3445 Abercrombie Way	Detroit	MI	34554	(303)221-5455	
8	104	400 Wilshire Ave.	Los Gatos	CA	95223	(408)555-2333	
9	105	9066 114th Street	New York	NY	10003	(212)448-9000	
10	106	45 Washington Street	Smallville	IA	56549	(515)412-8700	
11	107	200 Wilshire Ave.	Los Gatos	CA	95223	(408)555-8101	
12	108	RR 1, Box 22N	Lincoln	NB	62310	(308)499-7676	
13	109	Box 2234	Las Vegas	NV	72773	(702)655-7777	
14	110	77 Sunset Street	Hollywood	CA	90030	(213)555-8922	
15	111	10 Downing Lane	London	ONT	C3T NT2	(402)655-3383	
16	112	1600 Rhode Island Ave.	Washington	DC	20030	(202)344-7474	
17	113	919 Michigan Ave.	Chicago	IL	60621	(312)544-7666	
18	114	333 Fifth Ave.	Lubbock	TX	73000	(806)443-6512	
19							
20							
21							

First, scroll the window so that the titles are in the topmost row displayed in the window. Then drag the split bar down so that it hovers just below the row containing the title. Release the mouse button, and you'll see two sets of titles, one in the top pane and one in the bottom. Choose Freeze Panes from the Options menu. As you scroll, the column titles remain visible, making further data entry much easier. When you next save the file, the status of the window will be saved with it, so you can leave the window in that format for ease of future data entry.

PRESERVE ORIGINAL DATA ENTRY-ORDER

If you've ever worked with dedicated database management programs, you may have recognized that many of them store data in the order originally entered. That is to say, each record is simply tacked onto the bottom of the file. When those records are sorted, the original data is not touched but rather read and organized either in memory or into a separate file.

There is sense to this, because it is sometimes useful to retrace the order in which the data was entered, particularly if the data does not contain a date field to trace its entry data. Even if the date were there, the precise order might not be recoverable if many records were added each day.

In Excel, however, you could use the time of entry to reconstruct the entry order because the date is recorded down to the nearest second. You could, for example, write a command macro that places the precise time of entry in the last column of a record. The simple macro would look like this:

```
┌─────────────────────────────────────┐
│ ▤□▤▤▤▤▤  Macro  ▤▤▤▤▤▤               │
├─────────────────────────────────────┤
│              T                    ⬆  │
├───┬─────────────────────────────┬───┤
│ 1 │ time.stamp                  │   │
│ 2 │ =FORMULA(NOW())             │   │
│ 3 │ =RETURN()                   │   │
│ 4 │                             │   │
│ 5 │                             │ ⬇ │
├───┴─────────────────────────────┴───┤
└─────────────────────────────────────┘
```

Then you will always be able to sort your database according to this field to restore its original order. I prefer another, simpler way of tracing the history of entries—a way that will come in handy if you ever incorporate the database into a relational database in Excel.

The method involves assigning a record number to each entry. A function macro can do this automatically, one entry at a time, but a faster, brute-force way is to simply select a slug of cells down the left-most column of the database range and fill it with a series interval of one. My choice of the leftmost column is not accidental. As you'll see a bit later in this chapter, you can use those serial numbers to hunt for specific records in a relational database arrangement—a very powerful application of multiple windows in Excel.

The drawback to this method, by the way, is that this preset column of record numbers substantially increases the RAM and disk size of the database, even though there is no data filling up all the record numbers. On the other hand, you might say that it is reserving space on the disk for the database when it finally does fill up with data. If you need more record numbers, simply select a further range of cells down the column (beginning with the last number of the previous series) and select Series from the Data menu again.

USE MULTIPLE WINDOWS

While Excel gives you the power to set up the database search criteria and to extract data into a separate list of all records meeting criteria, these features can present some logistical problems on a worksheet. Fortunately, there are ways to work around the problems to give you a relatively streamlined environment for your database.

If you recall the database sample file included with Excel (the one used to demonstrate its powers in Chapter 2 of the tutorial), you'll remember that the designer set up the database region to start on row 10, leaving the top nine rows as a workspace for establishing search criteria and, presumably, for listing database records pulled with the Extract command. Given the size and content of the sample database, this design is not practical for a realistic Extract operation, which performs essentially a report-generating function—you should have an area set aside for an Extract report that is at least as long as the database itself, just in case you set the criteria to generate a list of the entire database in a different order, which Extract lets you do. Or if your extracted reports typically select only a small portion of the database, it is quite possible that you will want to have more than one type of Extract report pulled from the same database. Where will you put them?

The solution lies in arranging the sections of a database in separate windows to the same worksheet so that you can easily find the search criteria range, the extract range, and the actual database range, and then be consistent in this arrangement from one database to another. I also recommend positioning the criteria range just above the extract range in the worksheet, because you can better judge how the report will look in relation to the search criteria you specify.

Here is a schematic of the overall layout of a full database worksheet, complete with criteria and extract ranges.

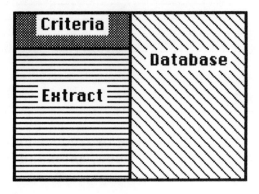

Notice that I have placed the database range to the right of the criteria and extract ranges. The reason for this is that you can find the bottom row of the database much faster in this position when you choose Select Last Cell from the Formula menu. If the database range were against the left edge of the worksheet and the extract range to its right, the last cell is out in space, far to the right of the database. But with the database on the right, the last cell is the rightmost field of the last entry to the database. Another related reason for this database position will be made clear in Part II, when I show you how to add a data-entry form to the top of the worksheet for simplified information entry.

Once you've placed the various sections of the database on the worksheet, I suggest you label them boldly with titles such as "Criteria," "Extract," and "Database." These titles will serve as reminders when you see the ranges in the window.

	A	B	C	D	E
			Customer List		
1			CRITERIA		
2					
3	Cust. No.	Customer Name	First Name	Last Name	Address
4	113				
5					
6					
7					
8					
9					
10					
11					
12					
13			EXTRACT		
14					
15	Cust. No.	Customer Name	First Name	Last Name	Address
16	113	SW Wholesale	Sharon	Wester	919 Michigan Ave.
17					
18					
19					

≡ Window Layout

I also recommend that you then open two more windows to this work-sheet by twice issuing the New Window command from the Window menu.

  File Edit Formula Format Data Options Macro Window

K3		101			

Customer List:3

	A	B	C	D	E	
1			Search Criteria			
2	Cust. No.	Customer Name	First Name	Last Name	Address	C
3	113					
4						

Customer List:2

	A	B	C	D	E	
12			Report Extract			
13	Cust. No.	Customer Name	First Name	Last Name	Address	C
14	113	SW Wholesale	Sharon	Wester	919 Michigan Ave.	
15						
16						

Customer List:1

	K	L	M	N	O	
1			Database			
2	Cust. No.	Customer Name	First Name	Last Name	Address	
3	101	A.B.Properties	Timothy	Smith	418 Main Street	Dal
4	102	Ace Power & Light	Doris	Addams	Box 10	Hou
5	103	Andy Lubert	Andy	Lubert	3445 Abercrombie Way	Det
6	104	AR Office	Steve	Jones	400 Wilshire Ave.	Los

Notice that the title bar of the windows retains the original name of the file, plus a numeric identifier. By carefully sizing and positioning each window, you can have all three ranges in view at once, making it easy to move from one to the other at the click of the mouse. No more scrolling like mad to find a quadrant of the worksheet that contains a particular range. On a 9-inch Macintosh screen, the window arrangement I prefer.leaves four rows of the criteria range, about the same for the extract range, and the balance for the database range. Moreover, I have split the database window into two titles so that the row of column titles always shows, no matter how far down the database I scroll.

Interestingly, when you have multiple windows of a single document open, all inactive windows are automatically updated with the changes made to the active window. Therefore, if you accidentally close a window without saving the changes, the data is still intact in the other windows.

A handy feature of Excel is that these windows, their locations, and sizes are all stored with the worksheet when you save it to the disk. But the safest way to make sure all window parameters are saved is to select Save from the File menu while all windows are open. If you close one window (by clicking the close box), its attributes will not be saved to the disk. But you can select Close All from the File menu and confirm that you want the changes made to each window saved. The next time you open the document, all windows will be restored to their previous locations and proportions.

≡ Restoring Windows

There will come the time, however, when you accidentally close a window before you've had a chance to save the data in the file. If you then try to save the data (it is still OK in the other windows), the location and dimensions of that missing window will not be recorded on the disk. You could re-create the new window, but I recommend you have a safety net macro prepared that will set up your windows at the press of a command macro keystroke.

The macro is a command macro that I initially created strictly with the mouse, using Excel's macro recorder feature.

	A
	DBWindows
1	three.windows
2	=ACTIVATE("Customer List")
3	=SELECT(!$K$3)
4	=SIZE(494,126)
5	=MOVE(10,237)
6	=NEW.WINDOW()
7	=SIZE(494,103)
8	=SELECT(!$A$13)
9	=MOVE(10,147)
10	=NEW.WINDOW()
11	=SIZE(494,98)
12	=MOVE(10,60)
13	=ACTIVATE("Customer List:2")
14	=ACTIVATE("Customer List:1")
15	=RETURN()
16	
17	

To prepare for the macro recording, I split the main database worksheet window so that the first two rows were in their own title displaying the frozen titles. Then, I scrolled the bottom tile just enough so that cell K3 was in the upper-left corner of the lower tile.

	K	L	M	N	O	
1			**Database**			
2	Cust. No.	Customer Name	First Name	Last Name	Address	
3	101	A.B.Properties	Timothy	Smith	418 Main Street	Dal
4	102	Ace Power & Light	Doris	Addams	Box 10	Hou
5	103	Andy Lubert	Andy	Lubert	3445 Abercrombie Way	Det
6	104	AR Office	Steve	Jones	400 Wilshire Ave.	Los
7	105	Carol Stansen	Carol	Stansen	9066 114th Street	New
8	106	City of Franklin	Henry	Champion	45 Washington Street	Sm
9	107	James Gregory	James	Gregory	200 Wilshire Ave.	Los
10	108	Jim Parsons	Jim	Parsons	RR 1, Box 22N	Lin
11	109	Karen Bush	Karen	Bush	Box 2234	Las
12	110	Lisa La Flamme	Lisa	La Flamme	77 Sunset Street	Hol
13	111	Mary Fuller	Mary	Fuller	10 Downing Lane	Lon
14	112	Ralph J Cook Garbage	Ralph	Cook	1600 Rhode Island Ave.	Was
15	113	SW Wholesale	Sharon	Wester	919 Michigan Ave.	Chi
16	114	Wheelin's Gas Co.	Ralph	Wheelin	333 Fifth Ave.	Lub
17						
18						

I selected that cell to indicate to the macro recorder (when it runs) that any commands I give in reference to this window are to apply to the lower tile.

Next, I created a new macro sheet from the File menu. After selecting the entire column A (by clicking the column header), I pulled down the Macro menu and selected Set Recorder. Then I selected Start Recorder. From that instant, and until I selected Stop Recorder, everything I did with the mouse would be converted into macro commands and entered in macro sheet column A. The mouse actions I took and corresponding macro commands automatically inserted into the macro were as follows:

Mouse Action	*Macro Command*
Click the worksheet to make it the current window.	=ACTIVATE ("Customer List")

Issue the Goto Command from the Formula menu and type in M3, the top left cell of the database range.	=FORMULA(GOTO("R3C12"))
Drag the window's size box up so that six rows will show in the window when I release the mouse button.	=SIZE(494,113)
Drag the entire window to the bottom of the screen to make room for the other windows.	=MOVE(10,247)
Select New Window from the Window menu.	=NEW.WINDOW( )
Drag the new window's size box up so that four rows will show when I release the mouse button.	=SIZE(494,98)
Issue the Goto Command from the Formula menu and type in A18, the top left cell of the extract range.	=FORMULA(GOTO("R18C1"))
Drag the entire window down so that the horizontal scroll bar would cover the first window's title bar when I released the mouse button.	=MOVE(10,162)
Select New Window from the Window menu to create the third window.	=NEW.WINDOW( )
Drag the newest window's size box up so that five rows would show when I released the mouse button.	=SIZE(494,111)
Click the middle window to bring its title bar into view.	=ACTIVATE("CustomerList:2")
Click the bottom window to bring its title bar into view.	=ACTIVATE("CustomerList:1")
Select Stop Recorder from the Macro menu.	=RETURN( )

If you study the arguments to the SIZE and MOVE functions in the macro, you'll begin to understand that a window's size and location on the screen are determined by two sets of values: the location of its upper-left corner (the coordinates in the MOVE function) and the number of pixels (picture elements) to the right and below that upper corner (the SIZE parameters).

Therefore, given the location of the upper-left corner and the off-set location of the opposite corner, a window's entire geography is detailed.

To be honest, when I dragged the windows to resize and move them during macro recording, the windows weren't precisely even. Each window was off by a pixel or two, according to the arguments recorded into the functions by the macro recorder. It's a simple feat, though, to go into the macro cells and edit those for fine-tuning. In fact, I also changed two functions almost entirely. I discovered that when I ran the macro, the GOTO command did not scroll the window as I had hoped. But with a little experimentation, I found that the SELECT function did the job the right way, and I made those changes accordingly.

Of course, you don't have to set up your windows in the same order I did. Nor do you need three windows if you only have database and criteria ranges on your worksheet. But if you find a pattern that works well for one database, then it's a snap to adapt this macro to any other database. Simply copy the range of cells from this macro sheet to another macro sheet and change the references to the worksheet names.

To use this macro, you'll first have to close all worksheet windows other than the main one (the one that gets numbered ":1" when multiple windows are on the screen). Make sure that a cell in the lower tile is selected before running the macro. When you do run this macro, stand back. For about ten seconds, it looks like your Mac screen has run amok. Windows appear out of nowhere, resize themselves, move around the screen, and scroll where needed. It looks like something Apple would use in a television commercial to show some exciting things happening on the Macintosh screen. (Incidentally, if you find you don't like this carnival ride of a screen display, add =ECHO(FALSE) at the beginning of the macro; this turns the display off until the macro finishes.)

AUTOMATIC SORT SELECTION

If you've previously used a spreadsheet, such as Multiplan, for sorting, you probably are accustomed to selecting the columns that are to be used as sorting keys. Excel doesn't work quite that way.

Instead, you must select the entire database range if you want all the columns to be sorted together. That is, if you select just a single column and issue the Sort command, Excel sorts only that column, completely disconnecting those fields from the rest of the fields in their respective records—and perhaps destroying the integrity of your database files. Needless to say, that could be dangerous.

Yet, selecting the entire database range can be a laborious task, especially once the database gets to be several hundred records long. One shortcut, provided you've designed your database worksheet as described above, is to select the upper-left corner of the database, then, while holding down the Shift key, choose Select Last Cell in the Formula menu. This action selects the entire database range. Another way is to write a short macro that not only does the database range selection for you, but also calls up the Sort dialog box, ready for you to select the key fields. The macro would look like this:

	C
1	dbottom
2	=SELECT.LAST.CELL()
3	=DEFINE.NAME("dbottom",SELECTION())
4	=SELECT(!dtop:dbottom)
5	=SORT?()
6	=RETURN()
7	

The steps in this macro perform the following tasks:

- The last cell of the worksheet is selected and then assigned the name "dbottom," which in my head means "database bottom."
- The SELECTION() function in the DEFINE.NAME formula tells Excel to assign the name to the cell in the worksheet that is currently selected: the last cell in this case.
- Next, the macro selects the range in the worksheet that consists of all cells between a cell named "dtop" (which I had named separately) and "dbottom," which the macro just named. No matter how many entries you add to the database, each time you run this macro, it makes sure those new records are included in the selection to be sorted.
- Finally, the Sort dialog box is brought to the screen.

Note that if you select this macro function (and other menu functions that produce dialog boxes) from the list in the Paste Function dialog box, there is no entry on the list for the version with the question mark. You must type it into the macro formula. The mark is critical in this case, because it signals the macro to bring up the dialog box rather than to expect a list of arguments in the parentheses following the function.

With this macro attached to every database you sort, you will be assured of selecting all columns of the database for sorting, thus keeping your record rows intact. Keep this one handy.

CREATE RELATIONAL DATABASES

You'd think that because database management is a secondary, if not tertiary, application in Excel, that it would be relatively limited in its abilities to resemble more powerful, dedicated database products. Well, hold onto your hats, because you happen to have the makings of a rather sophisticated relational database on your hands.

What Is a Relational Database?

I suppose I should explain what a relational database is before getting too deeply into how to set one up in Excel. Not every database job needs a relational database, but you might find that your data management tasks can be simplified (and your memory and disk capacities stretched) with one.

In a more traditional database management system, such as a single database on a single Excel worksheet, information storage and retrieval closely resemble the steps you might perform in a noncomputerized database. For example, a Rolodex-type card file on the desk organizes a database of names and addresses. To find a particular address, you twirl the rack of cards until you come to the letter of the alphabet that matches the first letter of the person's name. Gradually, you use your alphabet skills to search through the cards until you have the desired card, with all its information before your eyes. By searching the file with only one criterion, the person's name, you now have access to other fields stored on that card, such as address or telephone.

The computer enhances this kind of database—often called a file management system—because you can search not only by more than one criterion, but you can sort the electronic equivalents of the Rolodex cards according to any field with information on the cards: name, ZIP code, state, and so on. Moreover, most file management programs allow you to select a range of the files and compile a report that contains only those records that meet certain criteria, such as listing all the card files with the last name of Jones in states east of the Mississippi River.

Now suppose that the Rolodex file were actually a customer file, with each customer's basic information listed, including details such as how orders are to be shipped to that customer, what kind of discount the customer gets, and the like. With this information stored in a file management kind of database, the data would have to be retyped into an order form each time an order comes in from that customer. In other words, the information stored in the card file is restricted to that file.

But then, suppose instead that you had a system that allowed you to simply type in the customer number in one blank on the order form and, magically, all relevant information from the customer Rolodex appeared in the appropriate blanks on the order form.

That's what a relational database is all about. It allows one database in the system to share or retrieve information from another database. Often, the database element that does the retrieval merely holds open slots for the shared data and fetches that data every time it needs to display or print a record.

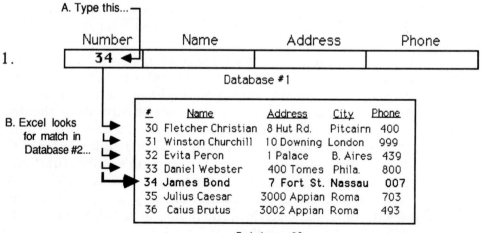

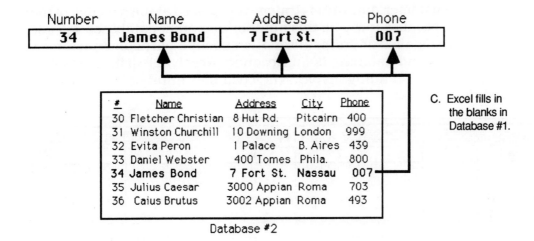

Database #2

C. Excel fills in the blanks in Database #1.

To demonstrate how a relational database is created and used within Excel, I will explain the first part of an extensive relational system that will be completed in Part II. In this part, I will show you how to link together two separate database files to simplify the task of data entry. In Part II, I will expand on this to show you how to link two databases together into a third, which will temporarily take on the guise of a word processor by retrieving data from the two databases and generating an invoice and a form letter.

To begin the first demonstration, I established one database, consisting of fictional customers. The fields for this file consisted of customer number, customer name, the first and last names of a personal contact for each customer, plus the address and phone for each.

	K	L	M	N	O	
			Database			
2	Cust. No.	Customer Name	First Name	Last Name	Address	
3	101	A.B.Properties	Timothy	Smith	418 Main Street	Dal
4	102	Ace Power & Light	Doris	Addams	Box 10	Hou
5	103	Andy Lubert	Andy	Lubert	3445 Abercrombie Way	Det
6	104	AR Office	Steve	Jones	400 Wilshire Ave.	Los
7	105	Carol Stansen	Carol	Stansen	9066 114th Street	New
8	106	City of Franklin	Henry	Champion	45 Washington Street	Sm
9	107	James Gregory	James	Gregory	200 Wilshire Ave.	Los

Customer List

The customer number is strategically placed at the left edge of the database, because it will be this number that other databases will use to retrieve detailed address information about a particular customer.

The second database is an Accounts Receivable list, on which I enter each outstanding invoice, the customer number, amount due, and date due.

	A	B	C	D	E	F
1					Today's Date:	22-Jul-85
2						
3	Invoice No.	Cust. No.	Customer Name	Amount Due	Date Due	Aging (days)
4						
5						
6						
7						

The window title bar reads: **A/R List**

The Customer Name (described more fully below) and Aging fields are calculated on the spot as I enter the other data.

I'll dismiss the Aging field formula by saying that it simply subtracts the contents of the Date Due field from the Today's Date field at the upper-right corner. Because Excel tracks dates and time as numbers in the format date.time, I can have the formula leave only the integer (the value to the left of the decimal), which, in Excel's calculations, is the number of days between those two dates. The formula for the cells F4 and below reads

=INT($F$1-E4)

The action in cell C4, the Customer Name field, takes a bit more explanation, however. My goal was to have Excel automatically fill in the Customer Name when I entered the customer number, thus freeing me of tedious typing. The formula reads:

=IF(B4="","",VLOOKUP(B4,'Customer List'!Database,2))

Here, Excel waits for an entry in cell B4. If nothing is entered in cell B4 (i.e., if the contents of B4 equals a null string), then a null string is entered into cell C4. If I hadn't specified a null string as the TRUE result of the IF test, Excel would have placed a "TRUE" in cell C4. Because this formula will be filled all the way down this database in anticipation of later entries, the column would be filled with TRUEs, not a pretty sight.

The real relational work is performed by that part of the C4 formula that is performed whenever you enter something in B4 (i.e., when B4 is not a null string):

VLOOKUP (B4,'Customer List'!Database,2)

VLOOKUP, and its sister function, HLOOKUP, are standard Excel functions (as distinguished from macro functions), that perform a powerful operation. They literally scan the left column (VLOOKUP) and top row (HLOOKUP) of a database to find a match for the value listed as the first argument on the function. In our example, this means that the function scans the left column of the database range (the range established with the Set Database command) in the file "Customer List" for a match to the contents of cell B4, the customer number. The last argument, number 2 in our example, is the number of the field in the searched database whose contents will be displayed in the cell holding this formula if a match is found.

Tracing our example, then, as soon as I enter the customer number, 114, in cell B4, the formula in C4 sees that I've finally gotten around to entering something. It's time for the formula to take that value I just typed and compare it against the left column of the database range called "Database" in the file "Customer List" (whose window must be open to accomplish the search). When the formula finds a match, it counts two cells to the right and takes a snapshot of the customer name, whisking it back to the Accounts Receivable sheet and displaying the customer name in the cell that contains the formula, C4.

A/R List

	A	B	C	D	E	F
1					Today's Date:	22-Jul-85
2						
3	Invoice No.	Cust. No.	Customer Name	Amount Due	Date Due	Aging (days)
4	3002	114	Wheelin's Gas Co.	$40.00	30-Apr-85	83
5						
6						
7						

Even if you select C4 after the name has been placed there, the name does not appear in the formula bar as the value of that cell. The value of that cell is actually the relation between cell B4 and the other database sheet. The name appears in the Accounts Receivable sheet but for the grace of the Customer List database. If I try to display the Accounts Receivable sheet without the Customer List sheet open at the same time, cell C4 will give the #REF! error indication, because it can't make a connection to the reference to "Customer List." And yet, with the proper files open, you see at a glance the names of the customers for each invoice, even though you only had to enter their numbers.

With this example, you might begin to appreciate the potential power that Excel's relational database capabilities offer you. The further applications in Part II should clinch the deal. In the meantime, think of ways you might apply relational database functions to the information you now store in file folders and desktop card files. After using relational databases for a while, you'll wonder how you ever got along without them.

Chapter 5
GRAPHICS STRATEGIES

Column Charts
Bar Charts
Line Charts
Area Charts
Pie Charts
Combination Charts
Scatter Charts
Customize Charts in MacPaint and MacDraw

If you believe in the old business adage, "Figures lie and liars figure," then add this to your repertoire: Graphics programs are the figures' portrait artists. This is especially true in a program such as Excel, because the charts and graphs appearing on the screen are derived solely from the numbers you put in a worksheet. If you've found a creative way to make your department look good in the numbers, then the graphics will make your department look fantastic. But the reverse is not necessarily true, because it is possible to make bad numbers look not so bad.

One thing you can count on is that whatever message you are trying to communicate with columns and rows of numbers will make their point to an audience much faster and with far longer retention if you state it graphically instead of numerically.

Some years ago, I was a member of a giant, worldwide corporation. Periodically, I'd have to sit through seemingly endless presentations prepared by various product managers and higher-level management. Onto the wall they'd project page after page of historical and forecast numbers—sales projections, advertising expenditures, staffing requirements, and so on. In most cases, the precise figures weren't important to me. What I wanted to see were trends and relative sizes of various categories, such as how much bigger sales will be for a particular product in the third quarter over the second quarter. To derive this information from the numbers took a close study of the figures on the screen.

Every once in a while, a more clever manager in this male-dominated, chauvinist company would have his secretary prepare a summary graph of what the numbers were all about. Those graphs weren't necessarily works of art, but it was far easier for the audience to grasp what was going on in the previous column-and-row transparencies on the screen. I could see the trends and relative changes of quantities in an instant, without any eyestraining scrutiny of bottom-line figures. And if the list of presenters at the meeting included a higher-level manager who had clout with the in-house art department, his transparency graphics were astounding. It was clear that the Top Brass enjoyed the prerequisites of fancy foils and intimidated underlings accordingly.

All in all, this experience taught me that graphics make the point, while the numbers should only be there to back up the graphic conclusions and to survive closer inspection by the budget watchers. In working with a graphics program such as Excel, however, I've also discovered that graphics can be a useful analytical tool. For example, I can look at some expense figures for the year and have a fairly good idea about where my money is going, but a pie chart of the same data makes the percentages of those figures to the total really stand out. Similarly, I can use Excel's statistical functions to evaluate the figures and plot trends that otherwise might not be obvious. So the charting functions of Excel are indeed practical for presentations as well as one-on-one analyses.

Using Excel to graph your numbers properly takes a little knowledge about the different kinds of chart formats available in the Gallery and how they interpret the numbers in your worksheets. Likewise, if you know what a particular chart type does with the numbers in your worksheets, you can better plan your worksheets so that the desired numbers are readily available for selection prior to opening the new chart window. Therefore, an important strategy is to know what each chart type expects from you and what type of chart will best display the meaning you want to give to those numbers.

Chart types in the Gallery menu are listed alphabetically. Unfortunately, this is not a good way to start you off to learn the chart types, so I'll take them in a different order, starting with the chart type that Excel considers the preferred type the first time you use the program, Column Charts.

COLUMN CHARTS

According to traditional graphing terminology, the horizontal axis of a column chart represents the *independent variable* in a graph, while the vertical axis represents the *dependent variable*. Translated into more practical charting terms, an independent variable is most often a measure of time, or rather, points along a continuum of some kind. The dependent variable, then, is the value of a certain item at whatever point in time is specified by the independent variable.

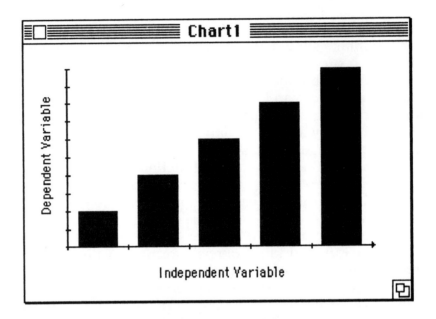

In other words, the values or sequence of values running along the horizontal axis are independent of anything that goes on: The clock keeps ticking, for example, no matter what else goes on at those moments. On the other hand, the measurement you take of a certain item *depends* on the time that you take the measurement—hence the term dependent variable.

In the worksheet below, the income, expense, and profit figures for four quarters and the total year are displayed.

	A	B	C	D	E	F
1						
2						
3						
4		1st Q.	2nd Q.	3rd Q.	4th Q.	Total Year
5	Income	$10,000	$6,000	$13,000	$16,000	$45,000
6	Expenses	$5,500	$6,500	$8,000	$9,000	$29,000
7	Profit/Loss	$4,500	($500)	$5,000	$7,000	$16,000
8						

The relevant figures we might want to graph are the three items—categories—for all four quarters to see graphically how each quarter's figures compare with the others. In terms of dependent and independent variables, the time factor (the quarters) is the independent variable.

At the end of each quarter, we take a snapshot of the three categories and put those numbers in the spreadsheet. Their values depend on the time at which we take the snapshot.

Selecting cells A4:E7, and asking for a new chart from the New dialog box, the default chart type—a column chart—displays the data (I've also added the legend with the Add Legend command in the Chart menu).

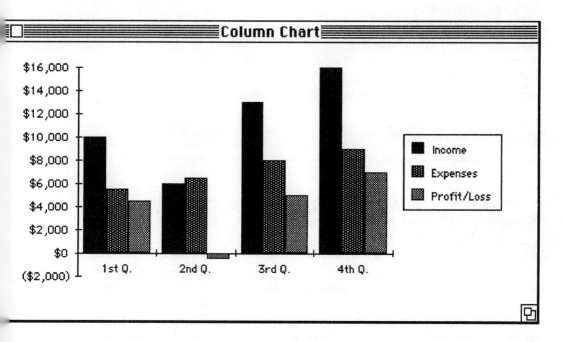

Column Chart

The horizontal axis marks off each quarter, while the vertical axis ticks the dollar values for each category.

Pay particular attention to the way Excel extracts the data from the selected spreadsheet range and assigns the elements to the graph. Excel assumes (sometimes incorrectly) that you always will want the row or column with the fewest items to be the dependent variable. Because in our example there are more quarters than there are items to measure in each quarter, the titles in the top row of the selected area are automatically assigned to labels for the horizontal, independent axis of the chart. This might not be so easy to remember, because you may have instances when you'd like to look at more items in each quarter than you have quarters in the spreadsheet (as shown below). And if there are equal numbers of items in each direction, Excel takes it upon itself to make the horizontal rows the independent values (the quarters in our example).

As to why column charting assigns variables as it does, it could be that the designers figured that there must be better ways of showing data for five dependent items in four or fewer independent values. Or are they suggesting it is in poor taste to design such a graphic? In theory, the column chart is used whenever you want to show values of only one or two items at specific points in time, such as expense values at the end of each quarter. Still, you may want to analyze the data the other way.

To effect this in Excel, you must first open a new chart window. Clear the chart by choosing Select All (Command-A) from the Chart menu and then Clear (Command-B) from the Edit menu. In response to the Clear dialog box, select All. The chart window will empty. Return to the worksheet and select the cell range you want to chart.

	A	B	C	D	E	F
1						
2						
3						
4		1st Q.	2nd Q.	3rd Q.	4th Q.	Total Year
5	Income	$10,000	$6,000	$13,000	$16,000	$45,000
6	Expenses	$5,500	$6,500	$8,000	$9,000	$29,000
7	Profit/Loss	$4,500	($500)	$5,000	$7,000	$16,000
8						

Then choose Copy (Command-C) from the Edit menu. A marquee sizzles around the selection. Return to the empty chart and choose Paste Special from the Edit menu. When the dialog box appears, click the Columns radio button. This plots the values as they are grouped in columns, rather than rows. The result is a chart with a different perspective on the same figures.

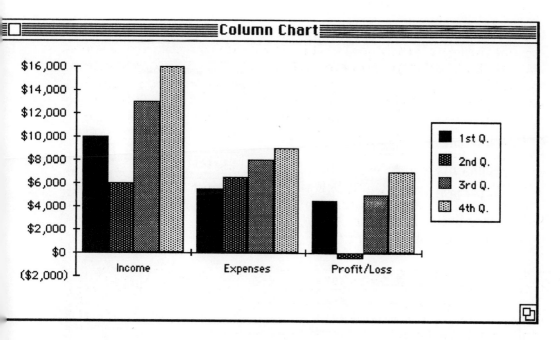

The dependent, vertical axis is fascinating to me. Excel evaluates the range of values and automatically calculates the axis values. You can change many parameters of the axis markings by selecting the axis on the chart (place the pointer anywhere close to the axis and click—two circles at the ends of the axis indicate that the axis is selected) and issuing the Axis command in the Format menu. A dialog box lets you adjust the values, intervals, and relative location of the markings on the axis.

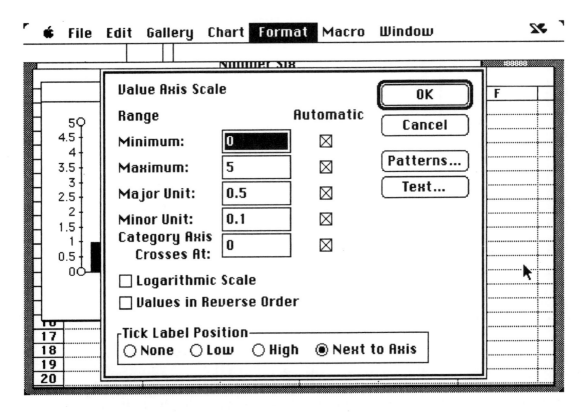

The default settings for most items are "Automatic," as indicated by the column of checkboxes to the right of the range settings. In the hundreds of column charts Excel has created for me, I have yet to find fault with the automatic settings for the vertical axis. One day, however, I won't like what I see, and the program will be ready to accommodate me.

I must caution you about one important element of column chart making (it also applies to many other chart formats in Excel). If, in the worksheet example above, you had selected the cells B5:E7, which contain values only, Excel would have interpreted that as meaning you want no horizontal axis or legend titles in the spreadsheet (you can add them by hand, one at a time, in the chart with the Attach Text command in the Chart menu). Excel is intelligent enough to know that titles must be text values in the spreadsheet, rather than numeric values. That rule goes partially out the window, however, because you can mix text and numeric values in the top row or left column of a selection, and Excel will interpret all items in those cells as text. But if you want numbers only for titles, such as a series of calendar years, you have to type them into TEXT functions (e.g., =TEXT(1985,0), which turns the number 1985 into a text number with a plain number format).

BAR CHARTS

Even though a bar chart looks like nothing more than a column chart laid on its side, there are subtle differences in the kinds of information each is suited for. Traditionally, bar charts are used to display the values of many items at a particular point in time. But first, let's look at the elements of a bar chart compared to the column chart.

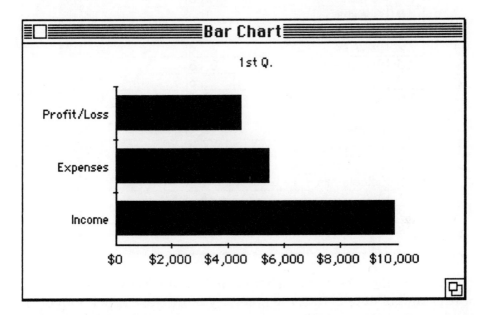

Independent variables are plotted along the vertical axis in a bar chart instead of the horizontal axis as in the column chart. In the case of a bar chart, however, the independent variable usually consists of the item names (Excel calls them *categories*) of the things you are plotting. As such, we need a different series of data to plot.

As an example, I plotted the 1984 and 1985 unit sales of many consumer electronics products (the figures are fictitious but representative of the actual numbers reported by research groups).

	A	B	C
		Worksheet	
24	**Consumer Electronics Sales**		
25		1984	1985
26	Boom Box	6.5	6.9
27	Personal Stere	23	22.1
28	VCR	7.7	10.2
29	Cameras	0.6	0.61
30	Videodisc	0.2	0.18
31	Color TV	15.5	15.6
32	B&W TV	4	4.2
33	Projection TV	0.15	0.23
34	Home PCs	3	3.6
35	Games	2.3	0.9
36	Std. Phones	22	25
37	Cordless	4.3	4.3
38	Answerers	1.4	2.6
39	CD Players	0.2	0.5
40	Calculators	22	24
41			
42			
43			

What makes the bar chart so much better than a column chart for this kind of data is that the category names are much longer than could be crammed into the horizontal axis line. When I first selected the six video products and called up a new chart, the default chart type (column) presented a wholly unreadable chart.

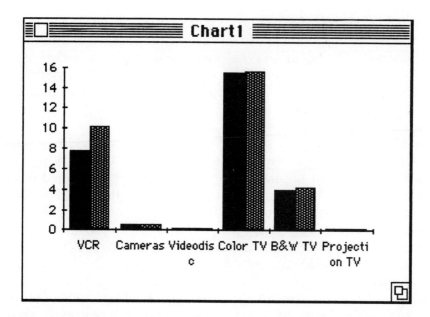

But changing over to a bar chart remedied that problem entirely.

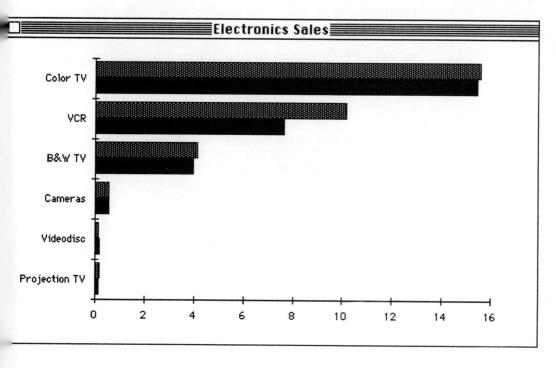

The axes were adjusted to the right to accommodate the long category names. Because some of the values were rather small and difficult to read with any accuracy, I selected the bar chart type that displays the values of each bar at their tips. A few other embellishments, such as boldfaced descriptive text ("Millions of Units") attached to the horizontal axis and a title in Chicago-12 text, would make the chart more presentable.

Incidentally, when I first entered the data for the video products, they were not in the order as they appear the bar chart. When I plotted the values in their haphazard order, the bar chart looked terrible, with long and short bars scattered up and down the axis. To clean up the appearance, I sorted the six video product rows according to the values in column B. The chart was automatically redrawn to reflect the changed order, and the results are shown above, a much better organized chart whose category order tells a story of consumer patterns in itself.

It's easy to get carried away with a bar chart and expect to graph a huge number of items, for you can list a lot of independent variables (like the product names in our example). But don't put too many items in the chart. As you can see from the 1984-only plots of 15 items, things can get pretty jumbled up.

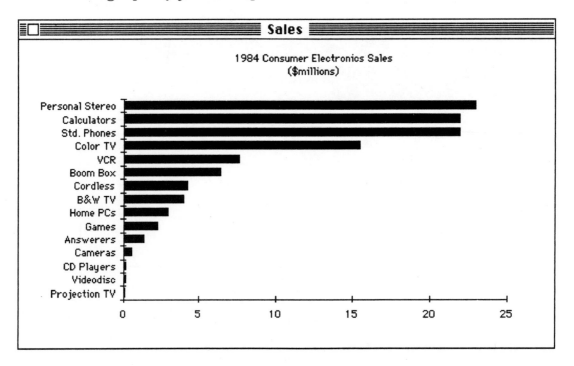

A better approach is to try to separate groups of items and plot them individually. Then, a summary plotting of each group should give a good picture of the entire universe you are tracking.

One problem you may encounter on a bar chart is the bunching up of tick mark labels on the horizontal axis. This is especially true if the values in your spreadsheet are in currency. Be aware that the format of numeric tick mark labels are the same format as the values in the cells being plotted. If the cells are all in the currency format with two digits to the right of the decimal, so will be the labels.

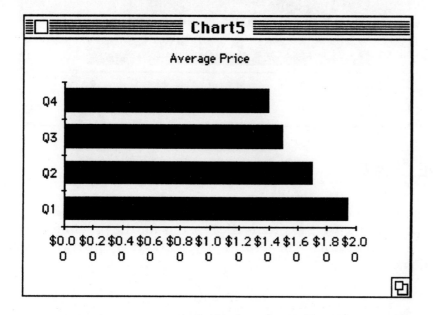

You'll probably find it necessary to select the axis and choose the Axis command from the Format menu and adjust the increments to make room for all the digits. If the values you are charting are currency, you probably will want to scale the figures, reduce the number of increments displayed, and then add a title to the axis explaining that the digits represent hundreds of thousands.

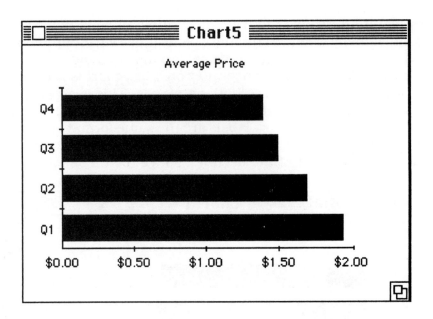

LINE CHARTS

We've all seen cartoons that picture the setting in a boardroom just as the chief executive explains the reasons for the precipitous decline in sales on the chart. The chart aptly portrays a downward slope to the floor.

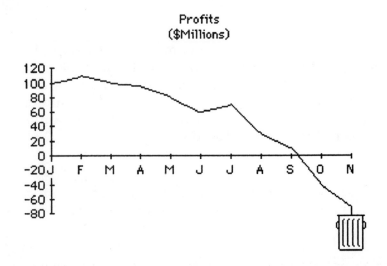

That chart is a line chart, and it is no coincidence that this kind of graphic is an excellent medium for communicating trends, particularly when the trends are based on a lot of data points.

There is something about the appearance of a line chart that gives it a dynamic feeling. As the line angles from data point to data point, you really get the message that a steeply sloping line means some kind of big change, while a flat line indicates a large slice of status quo. I believe it's because your eye tends to follow the line from left to right, giving those data points a flow, almost a kind of life. If that's the kind of message you want to get across with your figures, then the line chart is the ideal candidate.

One problem you probably will encounter with a line chart is that the tick markers for the horizontal axis will be scrunched together because you'll have perhaps 30 or more points to be plotted, each with its own title in the spreadsheet. Select the axis and choose the Axis command from the Format menu. In the succeeding dialog box, increase the number in the second box, "Number of Categories Between Tick Labels," until the labels don't overlap or are wrapped around.

For example, if your spreadsheet labels are spelled-out months of the year, you will be in big trouble when Excel tries to cram 12 or 24 labels on the horizontal axis, especially in the small, default chart size (as you increase the size of the window, Excel readjusts labels to fit the space).

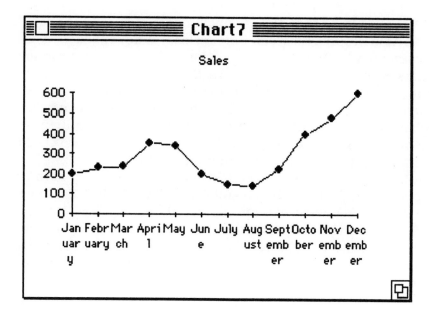

You'd be better off returning to the spreadsheet and renaming the titles to either three-letter abbreviations or, if you are plotting a couple years, simply the first letters of the months. Even then, you'll probably have to increase the number of spaces between tick labels on the horizontal axis in the Axis dialog box.

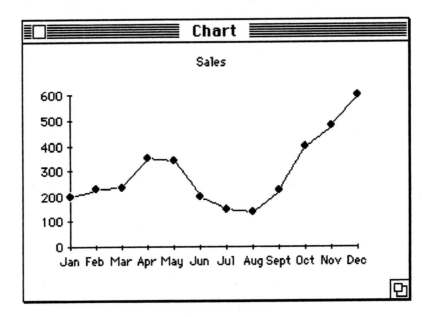

While you're in that dialog box, notice that one of the checkboxes, "Value Axis Crosses Between Categories," is not checked. This selection controls whether the point is plotted at the intersections of tick markers or in between tick markers. Line charts are much more readable if the points are plotted at the intersections, and Excel does this automatically. If you change the line chart to a column chart, however, Excel knows that columns look better when they are drawn between tick labels. In the Axis dialog box of a column chart, the box is checked automatically (of course, you can change it if you like).

A line chart is also an excellent medium to display both the raw data points and the smoothed results of the TREND function on a series of points. I'll have more to demonstrate about the TREND function in Part II, but I'll show you how easy it is to calculate the trend line (also called a regression line) and how well it works on the line chart.

In the worksheet below, I have entered 24 figures, one for each month of a two-year period.

	A	B	C	D	E	F
15						
16						
17		J	F	M	A	M
18	Sales	200	230	235	350	3
19						
20						
21						

When I have Excel plot the figures by themselves, the resulting line chart appears to have a series of seasonal ups and downs, making it difficult to sense a significant trend over the period.

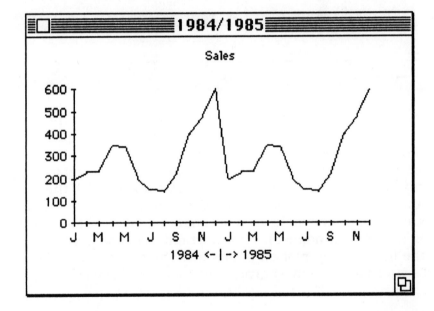

To get an idea of where these figures are going, I select a blank row that has the same number of cells as the row of figures in the original plot. In the leftmost cell of that selection, I type the TREND function as follows:

= TREND(B18:Y18)

The cell range in the formula is the range containing the values that will be calculated into the regression line. Because this formula is ruling over an array (the selected row of cells), I must hold down the Command key while pressing Enter or Return. When I do this, the formula calculates the regression line of all the values in B18:Y18 and places the results in the selected cells.

| | **File** | **Edit** | **Formula** | **Format** | **Data** | **Options** | **Macro** | **Window** | |

| B19 | | =TREND(B18:Y18) | | | |

Worksheet

	A	**B**	**C**	**D**	**E**	**F**
15						
16						
17		J	F	M	A	M
18	Sales	200	230	235	350	340
19		230.5333333	268.2	298.866667	326.4	332.416667
20						
21						

The values are calculated to much higher precision than is indicated in the 10-space-wide columns. These smoothed figures are the ones that will be plotted along the trend line.

Because I already have a line chart with the individual points plotted, I may as well add the trend line to it. To accomplish this, I select the range of trend value, choose Copy from the Edit menu (or Command-C), switch windows to the chart, and choose Paste from the Edit menu (or Command-V). The chart redraws itself, this time with both the individually plotted points and the trend line, giving me a much better idea of how sharply the smoothed growth is going.

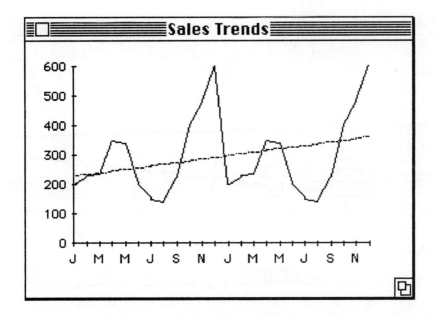

I've discovered that on most line charts, particularly when more than one line is being plotted, the differentiation between the kinds of lines is much less distinct than, say, when columns are filled with different patterns. When the lines of a line chart are going through steep slopes, their consistencies and patterns become difficult to see clearly. Because the chart usually tries to make one strong point, with the rest of the lines backing up the data (such as a trend line backed up by the actual data), I change the weight (thickness) of the important line by choosing Patterns from the Format menu and selecting either the middle or heavy weight in the dialog box.

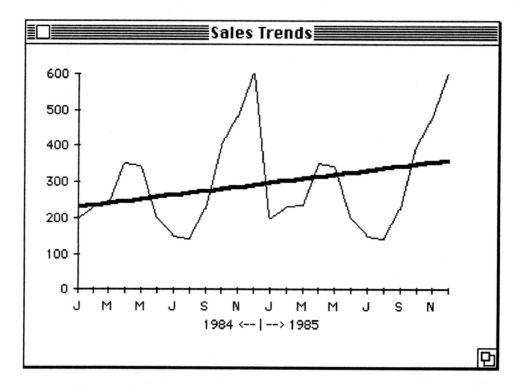

A line chart (or any Excel chart) is capable of plotting up to 1024 data points, a huge number. In the line chart below, for example, a sine curve was plotted from 100 sine values (caution if you want to try this: the SIN function calculates sin values from radians, not degrees).

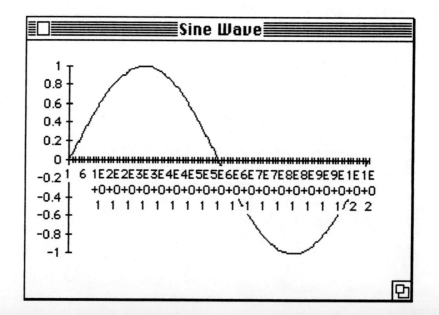

Of course, when you plot that many values, the horizontal axis will be loaded with all 100 tick labels and markers. Removing the labels still leaves an ugly horizontal axis cluttered with short, vertical tick markers. You can remove the axis altogether (via the dialog box you get from choosing Axes in the Format menu) and replace it with an arrow.

To replace it with a simple line, you'll have to fix up the chart in MacPaint (described in more detail later in this chapter). But because the horizontal axis of a line chart usually measures time or other linear, ongoing measure, an arrow pointing to infinity off to the right often is quite appropriate.

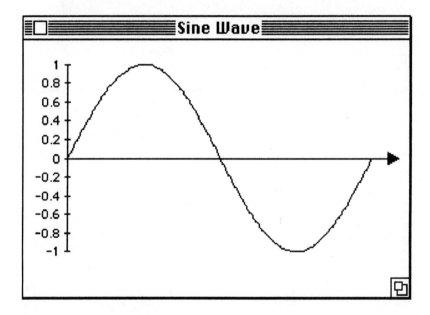

AREA CHARTS

An even more dramatic presentation of line chart ups and downs can be accomplished with an area chart. An area chart is a hybrid of the column and line chart.

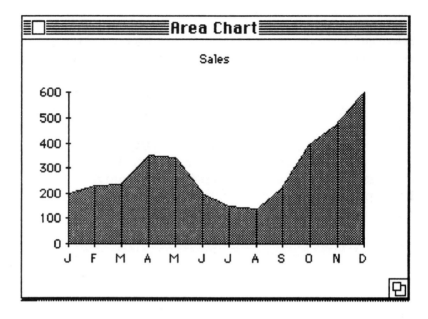

It's like a line chart in that the data points are joined by a line; it's like a column chart because the area beneath the plotted line is filled with a pattern. One significant difference between the Excel area chart and line chart, however, is that the area chart does not display negative number plots. For example, a plot of the sine wave data produces two humps above the horizontal axis.

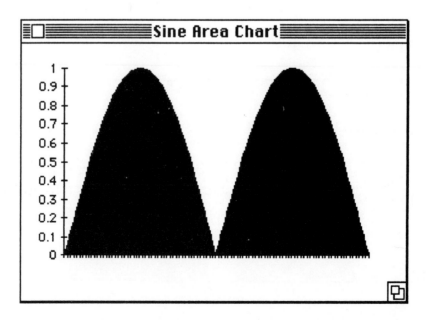

A good strategy for area charts, in my opinion, is choosing Area Gallery choice number five, which places the legend names inside the appropriate area. As long as the areas of each plot have enough room for the words, I prefer this arrangement to a separate legend. Importantly, this choice allows more of the window to be devoted to the chart—which is particularly critical if you are plotting a large number of points.

You must be careful in the way you apply an area chart to multiple plots. Such charts are easy to misinterpret if you aren't fully familiar with the dynamics of area charts. Here's why.

If you plot two series in a line chart, the actual values for each series are plotted individually, with no regard for the values of each other.

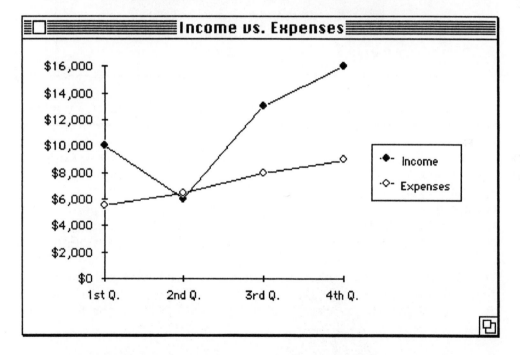

That's not the case with an area chart. When you plot those two sets of figures in an area chart, they are plotted cumulatively: The area of one series is plotted above the area of the other.

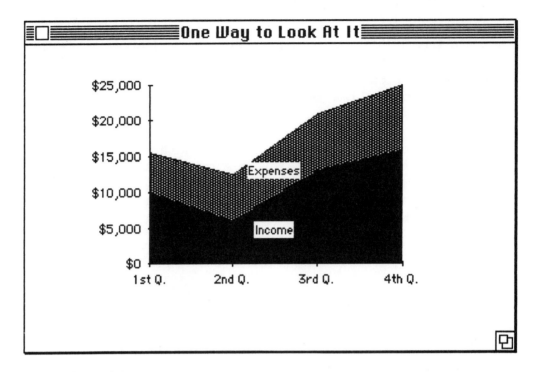

Thus, the plotted values for Income (the black area above) are the true values. Values for Expenses, on the other hand, are plotted with reference to the values for Income. The amount of Income for each plot point is actually the difference between the plot of the Expenses line and the plot of the Income line. Unless you know that the Income area border represents the zero line for the Expense figures, you might not get the true meaning of the upper plot.

Moreover, it's easy to lead your audience down a different path if they're not aware of the dynamics of area charts. You can reverse the order of the above area chart plottings and obtain the following chart:

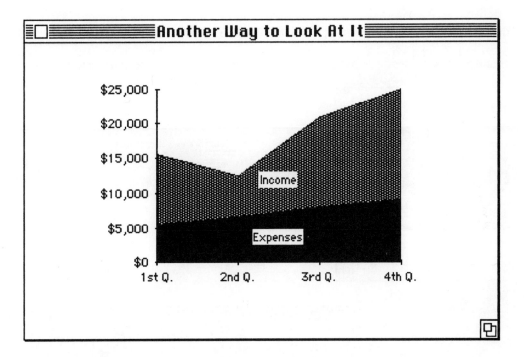

See how easy it is to tailor a chart to your message?

PIE CHARTS

While all the other charts I've discussed so far let you plot more than one series—such as plotting income, expenses, and profit in one chart—the pie chart plots only one series. It is one of the best communications tools to show how much each piece contributes to the whole. While you can stare at a series of percentage figures for several minutes trying to get the relationships of the various parts, a quick glance at a pie chart of those figures gives you an instantaneous appreciation for the relative sizes of each part.

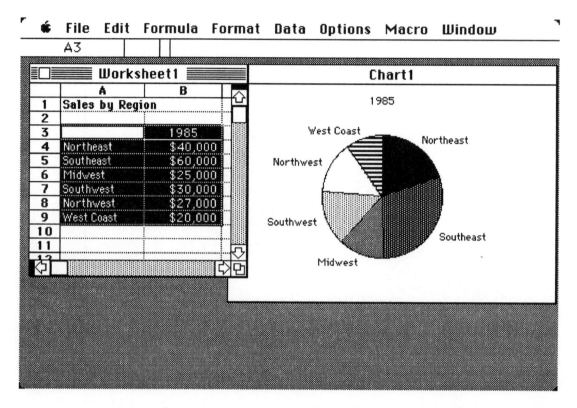

A pie chart data series can be either horizontally or vertically oriented. Excel simply looks at the selection and knows to plot the greater number of items as slices of the pie. The pieces are ordered around the pie (starting at 12 o'clock and working clockwise) according to the order in which they are entered in the spreadsheet. The topmost or leftmost item in a selection is assigned to the first piece of pie clockwise from noon.

Avoid selecting cells in the range that have values of zero. When these values are plotted, they can really mess up the pie chart if you choose the chart type that shows the legend text around the pie.

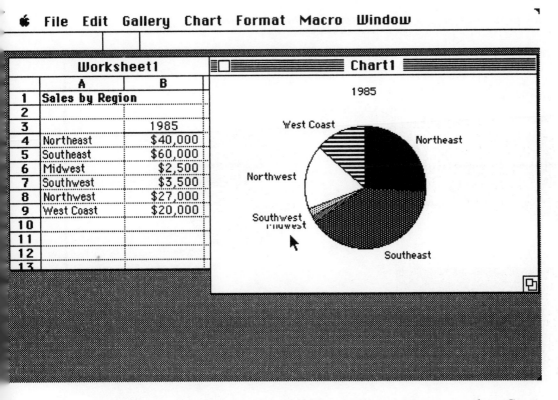

You may easily have legend labels overlapping one another. Similarly, if the size of one or more slices is small enough, there will not be a recognizable pattern visible in the pie. The pattern will show up in the legend box, but you won't be able to see where it is on the pie.

Among the chart types in the pie chart gallery, there are a few that I check out before settling on one. Among my favorites are selections one, five, and six. Selection one is a basic pie chart, with each slice shaded in a different pattern. I prefer this over the exploded pie chart in selection four primarily because the slices in the exploded chart are placed too far away from each other for my taste.

I begin to lose the sense that this is pie when all the pieces are spread far apart. I do, however, like to separate one or more pieces from time to time to highlight a particular slice (and then add some explanatory text nearby). Excel allows me to select and move each slice of pie chart very simply. All I have to do is point to the slice, click the mouse button, and then drag the slice slightly away from the rest of the pack.

 File Edit Gallery Chart Format Macro Window

	Worksheet1	
	A	**B**
1	Sales by Region	
2		
3		1985
4	Northeast	$40,000
5	Southeast	$60,000
6	Midwest	$12,500
7	Southwest	$5,500
8	Northwest	$27,000
9	West Coast	$20,000
10		
11		
12		
13		

Chart1

1985

West Coast — Northeast — Northwest — Southwest — Midwest — Southeast

Pie chart number 5 is the same as number 1, except that the legend text is placed adjacent to each slice of the pie. As noted above, this only works when the slices are sufficiently large so that the titles don't run into one another. The text for each title also must be relatively short. As your title text gets longer, the diameter of the pie decreases slightly. But the main advantage of this chart type is that you don't need a legend box.

Finally, pie chart number 6 automatically calculates the percentage each slice is to the whole and displays the percentage adjacent to the slices.

Incidentally, with chart types five and six, when you grab a slice and drag it away from the rest of the pie, any text automatically attached to the slice is moved along with it, simplifying the customization process.

When you select the worksheet cells to be plotted for a pie chart, be sure to select not only category labels (the quarters, above), but also the value label. That label becomes the title of the pie chart. Although it first appears in a small font size, you can select it and manipulate it into various fonts, sizes, and styles with the Text command choice in the Format menu.

Of course, if the value label does not accurately represent the title of the pie chart, then don't select it with the numbers to be plotted; instead, choose Attach Text from the Chart menu and click OK, signifying that the next text you type will be attached to the place on the chart reserved for the chart title. Then, with the invisible space selected (you see two overlapping white circles), type the title you want. With the title still selected, choose the Text command from the Format menu to adjust font information as desired.

If you accidentally select two data series for plotting a pie chart, Excel will plot the topmost/leftmost series in the worksheet by default. Without closing the chart window and creating a new chart, you can change to the other data series. To do this, select any slice of the pie chart. In the formula bar will be an intimidating, long formula showing the derivation of the data series being plotted.

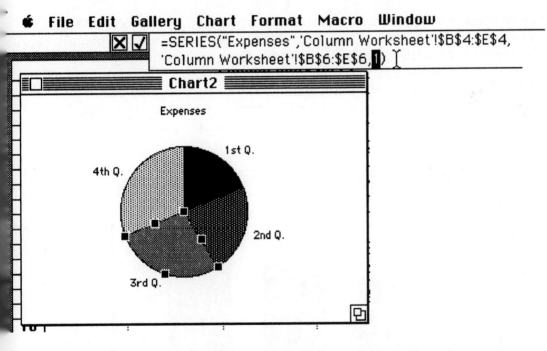

The cell range will be the topmost/leftmost two rows/columns of cells. At the end of the formula, just before the last closed parenthesis, is the number 1, which indicates that the series in the formula is the series that is plotted first. When the pie chart mechanism inside the program sees this figure, it recognizes it as the only series it can plot. Any number other than 1 in this spot is ignored by Excel. What you need to do is change this number 1 to number 2.

This is easier than it sounds because Excel does some automatic adjustments for you. First, select the number 1 at the end of the formula with the text pointer. Then type the number 2 and press Return or Enter. Behind the scenes, Excel automatically swaps the number 1 and 2 in the two series. Then, magically, the other series, now labeled number 1, appears in the formula bar and its data plotted as a pie chart in the window.

Pie charts are fun to work with, perhaps because their circularity and variety of patterns are more interesting to look at than column or other charts. And used with no more than about six data points, they also are extraordinarily effective communication tools.

COMBINATION CHARTS

You may encounter graphics situations in which you want to show the correlation between two different kinds of categories. For example, if you want to show the correlation between fixed costs and the pattern of sales over a certain period, you probably would want to show the costs in snapshot, column chart form, while sales would be best displayed as a line graph because it better conveys the dynamic characteristics of the category. To plot these two factors properly, you could choose a combination chart.

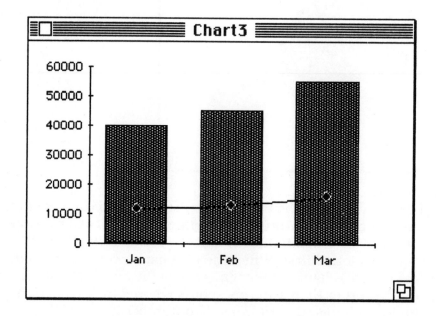

The type of combination chart you select can be of critical importance, particularly if one type can better support your contentions. But by the same token, a combination chart can be a dangerous tool in inexperienced hands.

Of the four combination chart types in Excel, two of them—types two and three—can cause interpretation problems or opportunities, depending on your expertise. These two types not only plot the two series independently, but also create a separate vertical scale for each series. As such, they are ideal if you are trying to show the correlation between two factors that have different measures—displaying how the labor hours relate to the net profit over the period of a month, for example. Such a combination chart would look something like this.

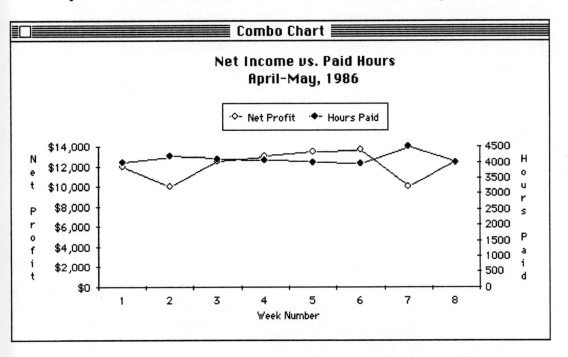

Pay special attention to the two vertical scales. The left one measures over a range of 14,000 dollars, while the right one measures over a range of 4,500 hours. The graph supports the numeric data in the spreadsheet that, as a rule, the net profit increases when labor costs go down and vice versa.

	E	F	G	
23				
24	Week	Net Profit	Hours Paid	
25	1	$12,000	4000	
26	2	$10,000	4200	
27	3	$12,500	4100	
28	4	$13,000	4050	
29	5	$13,450	4000	
30	6	$13,650	3950	
31	7	$10,000	4500	
32	8	$12,500	4000	
33				

Column Worksheet

You would have no way of showing this correlation with any other Excel chart type.

If you try to re-create this chart (and it would be a good exercise to do so), let me give you a few pointers. First of all, the week numbers in the spreadsheet must be entered as TEXT functions. To enter them as numbers only throws Excel off when it comes time to format the dollar figures on the vertical axis. Excel gets a bit confused and displays the labels as plain numbers, despite their formatting in the spreadsheet. Therefore, enter the first week number with the formula

=TEXT(1,0)

As a shortcut, fill down the eight rows with this formula, then tab to each cell and edit the number to the appropriate week number.

Second, Excel does not let you attach text to each of the two vertical axes when you choose Attach Text from the Chart menu. By default, it attaches the text to the left-hand vertical axis only. If you want to title the right-hand vertical axis, simply start typing the appropriate text, press Enter, and then drag the text into position. For each axis title in this chart, you must select the title, choose Text from the Format menu, and click the Vertical Orientation radio button (or double-click it to select it and return to the chart).

Third, it is critical that a combination chart have a legend. Without it, there is no way for the uninitiated chart viewer to know which vertical axis applies to which graphic element. In this example, I found it most visually appealing to place the legend at the top, as selected with the Legend dialog box from the Format menu. When I did this, however, the legend box displayed somewhat off-center, accentuated to that effect because the chart title I had added was on-center. To make the two elements line up with each other, I added some spaces to the left of both lines of title text.

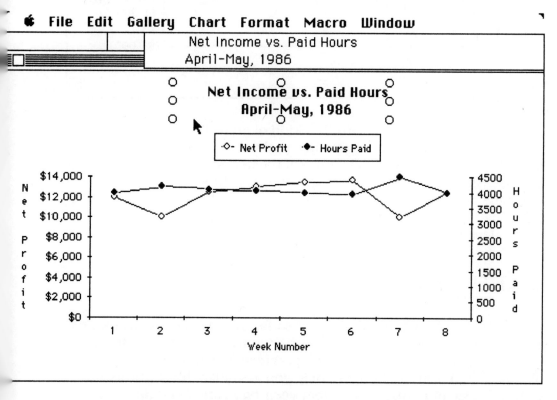

The danger of using combination charts types two and three comes when the two items being graphed are measured in the same units. These chart types automatically create two vertical axes, one for each of the data series. Unless the range of figures in both series are identical—a most unlikely occurrence—the axes will be scaled to meet the range demands of the values in the series. One axis may have a top value of $20,000, for example, while another has a top value of $5,000.

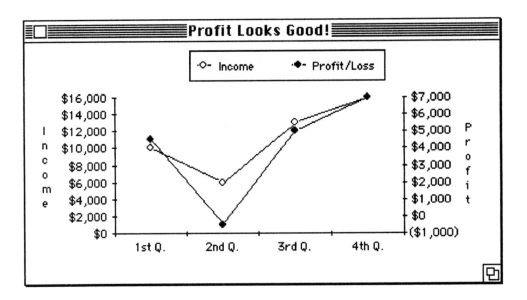

Someone unfamiliar with this kind of chart may easily misinterpret the two charted items to be on equal-value footing, thereby artificially inflating the perceived values of the items on the chart. You can turn this around to your advantage, however, if you want to impress someone with comparative figures, one series of which is embarrassingly low. When the two series are scaled to their own axes, the low series doesn't look quite so bad.

SCATTER CHARTS

While all the chart types discussed so far are excellent communications and presentation tools, the scatter chart is, I believe, better used as an analytical and statistical tool, provided you apply the right kinds of data to it. A scatter chart can help you visualize the relationships—or the degree of relationships—between two series of data.

For example, if you survey people with sedentary jobs and ask them to report their weight and number of calories eaten per day, you could plot the results as a scatter chart. In the chart, you probably would see a substantial grouping of points clustered around a certain spot or perhaps around a sloping line. The more the plotted points coincide with each other, the greater the correlation of the data. In any statistical sampling, of course, you will find individual points that are outside the clusters—someone with an abnormally high metabolism, for example, who can wolf down food like no tomorrow and be as skinny as a rail. But as long as the charted points are clustered in a definite pattern, you could draw a conclusion that there is a significant relationship between the calories consumed and weight of individuals surveyed.

As you might imagine, it helps to have a lot of points plotted before you can draw any viable conclusions from such data, just like a larger statistical sample is more likely to produce more accurate results than a small one. Also, the scatter chart handles only two data series at a time.

Creating an analytical scatter chart in Excel is not quite so easy as creating the other chart types. The reason is that the default styles of scatter charts in Excel more closely resemble a line chart. The program plots two data series against a vertical axis of values and a horizontal axis of incidents of data. To demonstrate the default style and how to correct the problem, let's take a look at a data series that I'd like to analyze to observe the correlation between radio and TV set ownership in 30 European countries.

	A	B	C
	Country	**Radio Sets**	**TV Sets**
45			
46	Albania	210,000	20,500
47	Austria	5,520,000	6,500,000
48	Azores	62,000	1,800
49	Belgium	4,617,037	2,976,383
50	Bulgaria	2,148,811	2,000,000
51	Canary Islands	560,000	182,000
52	Cyprus	400,000	111,000
53	Czechoslovakia	4,550,000	4,300,000
54	Finland	2,515,000	2,200,000
55	France	20,000,000	19,000,000
56	Germany, E.	6,410,000	5,842,000
57	Germany, W.	24,299,855	21,835,778
58	Gibralter	10,000	7,100
59	Greece	4,000,000	1,700,000
60	Greenland	13,000	10,000
61	Hungary	5,500,000	2,810,000
62	Iceland	70,035	62,634
63	Ireland	1,715,000	878,000

Radio/TV Analysis (Europe)

The raw data lists three columns of information about the country, radio sets, and TV sets owned for a particular year (these figures are fictitious, but representative of actual numbers compiled annually by the International Telecommunications Union). I call this the raw data, because later on it will make sense to adjust the scale of these numbers so they plot as shorter numbers on the chart axes.

At first, you might think that to visualize the correlation between the two values for each country, you would select the two columns of figures, create a new chart, and choose one of the scatter chart types. When you do that, this is the result.

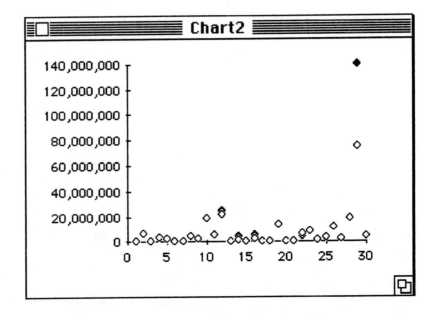

It may not be obvious from this plotting, but Excel actually has made two separate plots, one each for radio sets and TV sets. Look at the right edge of the chart. Notice that there is an open circle plotted near the 80 million mark, while a solid circle appears at the 140 million mark. Looking back at the data in the worksheet, you'd find that the USSR is estimated to have 75 million radios and 140 million TVs.

In other words, this chart is not technically showing the correlation between the two values except for the distance between the two plottings for each instance. Because the values in this table of data cover such a wide range, it is not possible to see with any clarity the relationships between radio and TV set ownership along that bunch of plottings at the bottom of the chart.

The horizontal axis on this default plotting, you'll note, is a simple scale from zero to 30. This scale merely represents the relative number down the table for each country's figures. The big figures for the USSR are shown plotted at point 29; these figures are listed twenty-ninth in the alphabetized data table on the worksheet.

I could help alleviate the problem of the bunched data points by selecting a different scatter chart type. Chart type four features a logarithmic scale for the vertical axis. Log scales are most helpful when the data points you are plotting extend over a wide range, because the scale spreads out lower values while keeping higher values within sight. Selecting this chart type with the radio-TV data, however, doesn't help us too much in our analysis.

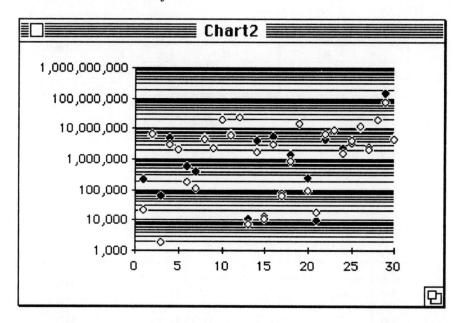

The light and dark circles are so closely spaced in the horizontal direction that there doesn't seem to be any formal relationship among any of the points. Close examination, of course, reveals that many of the twin data points are fairly close to each other, completely overlapping in several cases. But this type of chart looks more like a Jackson Pollock painting than a useful chart.

To get the proper correlation, we have to perform some special operations outside of the usual charting procedure. First of all, I want to adjust the values in the table to be more realistic for plotting purposes. Notice in the log chart above that the scale of the vertical axis ranges up to one billion in order to accommodate the 140 million figure.

Having those big numbers on a scale makes me nervous. And besides, when it comes time to do the kind of scatter chart I want, the horizontal axis will need small numbers, or they'll run into each other. Therefore, I set up a separate area on the worksheet that takes the values from each cell in the original data table and multiplies it by 10E-6. One of the formulas reads:

=B34*0.000001

For the rest of the cells, I first fill right one cell, then fill down the pair of cells for a total of 30 cells. Instantly, the values in the original table shrink to manageable length for the axes scales.

	A	B	C
		Radios(millions)	TVs(millions)
80		0.21	0.0205
81		5.52	6.5
82		0.062	0.0018
83		4.617037	2.976383
84		2.148811	2
85		0.56	0.182
86		0.4	0.111
87		4.55	4.3
88		2.515	2.2
89		20	19
90		6.41	5.842
91		24.299855	21.835778
92		0.01	0.0071
93		4	1.7
94		0.013	0.01
95		5.5	2.81
96		0.070035	0.062634
97		1.315	0.838

Column Worksheet

Next, I created a new, blank chart. Before doing anything with the figures, I changed the chart type to Scatter chart type 5. Then I returned to the worksheet and selected the new calls. After that, I issued the

Copy command to get these values and formats into the Clipboard. Then, I chose Paste Special from the Edit menu. It is important to choose this menu item instead of the plain Paste, because this selection gives me the opportunity to reorder the data so the chart will interpret it the way I want.

In the Paste Special dialog box, I clicked the Columns radio button because the succeeding values to be plotted run down columns. Then I checked the box I labeled, "Categories in First Column." Doing so caused Excel to regard the values in the table's left column as measures for the horizontal category axis. After I clicked OK, the proper scatter chart was plotted.

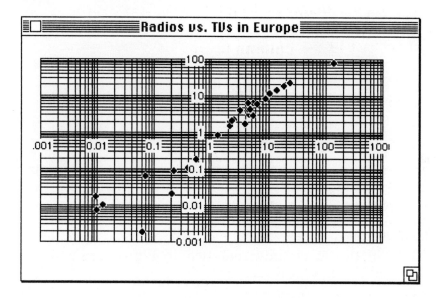

Because the logarithmic chart (this one, with two log scales, is said to have a log-log scale) by default forces the horizontal and vertical axes to cross at the point 1,1, the axis labels cross in the middle of this chart. To fix that, and make the axes more readable, I selected each axis and adjusted the tick label position (with the Axis selection in the Format menu) to Low. This brought the labels to the edges of the chart, although this position also robs the chart of some size. Next, I added text to label the axes and chart, noting that the figures are in millions.

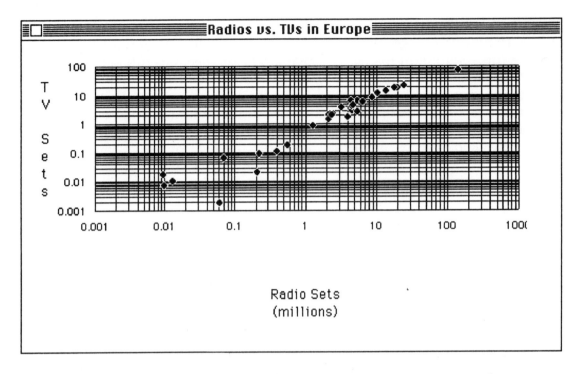

In analyzing the data plotted in this chart, it is now plain to see that there is a close correlation between radio and TV set ownership in most countries. A more subtle indication is that TV and radio ownership also reflects the population of a given country; a certain number of TVs and radios are owned by every X number of people.

All in all, this is a handy analytical tool, provided you know the tricks to get the right kind of chart.

CUSTOMIZE CHARTS IN MACPAINT AND MACDRAW

While the charting capabilities of Excel are almost equal to the dedicated graphics programs such as Microsoft Chart and Cricket Graph, you still are somewhat limited in the amount of embellishment you can add to a graph. Considering that you have a powerful, graphics-oriented computer at your command, you should investigate the possibility of enhancing your Excel charts with MacPaint or MacDraw, two very powerful graphics tools in themselves. Likewise, you are free to use other Macintosh drawing tools that mimic the feature and flexibility of MacPaint and MacDraw. These include Cricket Draw, FullPaint, and SuperPaint.

A word of caution is necessary, however. Too often, I see the results of Mac users who have run amok with the variety of fonts and other graphics powers at their fingertips. What comes out of the printer is juvenile hodgepodge. Flexibility ruled, while taste went out the window. It is vitally important to remember that with an Excel graphic you are more than likely trying to communicate a message.

Don't let the form of the message overpower the message itself. The form is a reflection of your style and ability just like a well-written report or memo reflects an organized, intelligent manager. Therefore embellish only when it contributes meaning to your message, not just because you can add a decoration here and change a font style there.

Your choice of embellishing with MacPaint, MacDraw, or a combination of the two depends on two factors: how you want to modify the Excel chart and on what printer the result will be printed. It also will help if you understand the different ways MacPaint and MacDraw treat graphics.

≡ MacPaint Versus MacDraw

When you draw a rectangle in MacPaint with the help of the rectangle icon, the minute you release the mouse button, the rectangle is no longer a rectangle as far as MacPaint is concerned. It is, instead, a particular collection of dots that happen to be aligned along four lines that meet at the ends. In other words, MacPaint graphics consist solely of a set of dots that you have arranged on the page. Those dots resemble something when you look at them, but MacPaint considers them strictly in terms of the locations of the dots on the screen.

MacDraw, on the other hand, is somewhat more intelligent in this regard, because when you draw a rectangle on the MacDraw screen, the program recognizes that shape as a rectangular object. MacDraw and similar programs are often called *object graphics* programs. In fact, in memory, MacDraw tracks that rectangle by very little information: the coordinates of the top-left and bottom-right corners, the thickness of the lines, and the pattern filling the area, if any. When it's time to produce the rectangle on the screen, MacDraw looks at those few pieces of information and literally draws the shape on the screen for you. In other words, both you and the program know that the rectangle is, indeed, a rectangle.

An important benefit to MacDraw's method of handling graphics objects (besides considerable savings in memory and disk space) is that when you resize an object, you are simply adjusting one of its coordinate points. You do not change the line thickness or the consistency of the pattern inside the box: The lines and fill pattern are redrawn to the new size, but with their old parameters.

That is definitely not the case in MacPaint. If you resize a filled rectangle in MacPaint (by dragging on the selection marquee around it), the program scales the pixels of the image to the new size. For example, if you resize a rectangle so it is twice as wide as the original, every dot will have a new dot placed next to it. Vertical lines that were one pixel wide become two pixels wide, while one-pixel-wide horizontal lines remain intact.

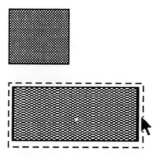

The result is usually a distorted mess, especially if the rectangle is filled with a pattern, because the dots of the pattern are likewise scaled.

When you try to combine the two programs by pasting a piece of MacPaint art into MacDraw, MacDraw treats the imported art as a single object, no matter how many separate elements the MacPaint art may appear to have. This is largely because when MacPaint copies art into the Clipboard, it does so as a collection of dots, not as rectangles, circles, and so on. Thus, MacDraw sees the MacPaint art as a single block. But when you try to stretch this MacPaint-originated block, its contents are scaled, just like they are in MacPaint. Because MacDraw can't recognize an imported shape as a rectangle or some other discrete object, the program must treat it as a block of dots.

☰ MacPaint

Using MacPaint to enhance an Excel chart may cause some problems if you're not prepared. One way to transfer Excel charts to MacPaint files is to make a MacPaint snapshot of the screen. Do so by pressing the Command-Shift-3 keys together. An image of the screen appears as a MacPaint file on your disk.

Each MacPaint screen document (labeled Screen0 through Screen9) can range in size between about 11 and 22K (more with the Mac II). You must have ample disk space or the Macintosh won't be able to record the screen image.

You'll have better luck recording a series of screen images if you own a hard disk drive. If you have a hard disk, then copy the Excel program to a disk volume that has at least 100-200K of empty space. Then, when you've sized a chart that you'd like to fix up, move the pointer out of the way and press Command-Shift-3.

When you have the snapshot(s) you want, quit Excel and start up MacPaint. Open the first screen shot, Screen0. The screen you shot will be located in the upper-left corner of the MacPaint page. It also will display the menu bar and chart window title bar. Choose Show Page from the Goodies menu and drag the image down to near the center of the page to make it easier to work with. Erase those parts of the screen you don't want in your final printout. Then proceed to customize as you wish.

The kinds of enhancements you can make in MacPaint are seemingly endless. You can alter the constitution of the columns in a column chart if the subject of the chart is something that lends itself to graphic interpretation. A good example would be turning the columns of a nuclear arms chart into missiles. Gordon McComb demonstrates this admirably in the May, 1985, issue of *Macworld.* Another approach might be to use a pictograph of tiny people representing the bars in a bar chart.

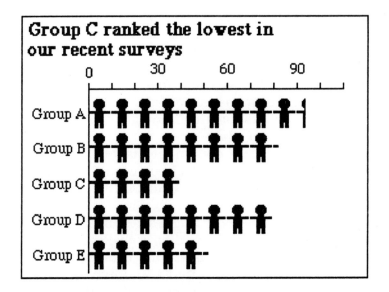

You also can add pictures from the dozens of clip-art disks available for the Mac, provided, of course, that the pictures add to the message rather than junk up an otherwise fine graphic. In the chart below, for example, I copied a truck from a Mac art collection designed by Tom Christopher and available as The Mac Art Dept. (Computer Software Division/Simon & Schuster, Inc.).

The image from the disk was too big to fit into the chart of trucking sales and profits I had copied from Excel, so I shrunk the truck by selecting a rectangle in the chart with the marquee and then pasting the image into it.

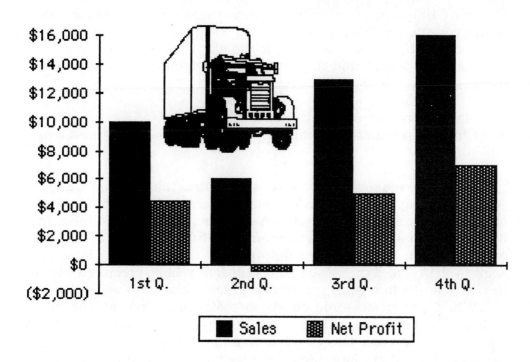

Trucking Sales & Profits

When you preselect a rectangle for the Paste command, the image is scaled to fit into that rectangular area. By having a truck picture on this chart, the viewers would be able to see instantly that the subject is trucking. The picture also may distract viewers from the loss showing in the second quarter.

☰ MacDraw

I actually prefer to enhance my Excel charts in MacDraw or other object graphics program rather than in MacPaint. I still can import MacPaint frills if I need them, yet I have remarkable flexibility in working with an Excel chart in MacDraw.

When I copied my first Excel chart into MacDraw, I expected Mac-Draw to treat the chart as a MacPaint-type object—a block of dots that sits on the screen like a lump of clay. Was I ever wrong and delighted to discover that MacDraw reads the chart as if MacDraw created it.

Almost every element of the chart—each line, piece of text, or block—is a separate MacDraw object. You can group all the pieces together— with the Group command in the Arrange menu—and resize the chart to suit your needs. (NOTE: You should leave text out of the group and position text blocks manually after the graphic has been resized.)

MacDraw knows how to reshape all the elements without scaling them; the exceptions to this are:

- Markers in line and scatter charts.
- Circles of pie charts, adding the possibility of distorting the shapes somewhat.

What also makes MacDraw so appealing is that MacDraw allows you to very simply change the font, size, and style of one or more pieces of text that Excel places into the chart. True, you could do the same in MacPaint, but you'd have to do some careful positioning of new text over the old. In MacDraw, you simply select the axis or tick label you want to change and then issue any of the font-related commands from the menus. It's like getting a second chance after you've left Excel.

When you paste some charts into MacDraw, not all the filled columns, areas, or pie wedges retain their patterns. But that's a little problem, for you can select each area and fill it with one of the Mac-Draw patterns (don't forget to fill the legend boxes if you've copied a legend along with the chart). Despite the slight scaling problem with pie charts, you still can resize them if you're careful to keep the pie round. With MacDraw's Grid feature on, this is simple, for you can adjust the size of the chart in relatively large and uniform steps verti-cally and horizontally.

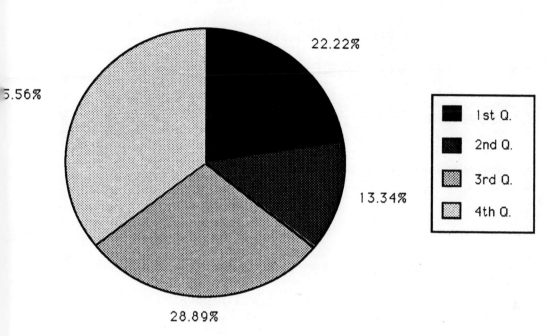

Income

22.22%

5.56%

13.34%

28.89%

Legend:
- 1st Q.
- 2nd Q.
- 3rd Q.
- 4th Q.

Another particularly useful aspect of using MacDraw is that you can easily combine several charts on a single page and put borders around each one not available in Excel. For overhead presentations, for example, I've found that rounded rectangular borders are very appealing. They soften the otherwise cold, angular appearance of most charts. I modified a scatter chart in MacDraw to have not only a rounded rectangular border, but a shaded one at that.

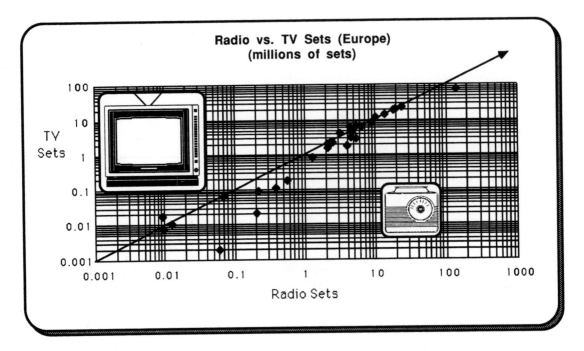

After I drew the first round rectangle, I duplicated it (with Dupli-cate in the Edit menu), adjusted it just a bit upward and to the left (I had to turn off the Grid for this fine adjustment), selected a shaded pat-tern, and then sent it to the back.

I also added some figures from MacPaint to dramatize the relation-ships between the two factors being plotted. Both the TV set and radio art came from Tom Christopher's Mac art collection and were scaled in MacDraw to fit comfortably into the chart. Because the scatter chart is an analytical tool (from which other, more detailed numeric conclu-sions can be charted), the graphics can cover the gridlines. In this case, too, the graphics more clearly show that points falling below the line indicate more radios than TVs and the opposite for points above the line.

≣ Printing

Combining MacDraw and MacPaint graphics into a MacDraw document, however, causes problems if you print out your finished work on the ImageWriter. Unfortunately, the ImageWriter prints out the MacPaint material in lower density than the MacDraw material (when High quality is selected from the Print dialog box). That means that the print quality of a combined document will be uneven. This goes, too, for those charts that have MacPaint elements, such as the plotted point markers in the scatter chart (although pie charts come out fine).

You do get high quality all around if you have access to a LaserWriter. If you do a lot of presentations, it may be worth your while to acquire one or find a local service that will print out your MacDraw disks.

Be aware, however, that graphics created in MacPaint (whether or not actually printed in MacPaint) will not have the high resolution of charts created and printed in Excel or MacDraw. The reason: The LaserWriter attempts to smooth the angular, dotty appearance of MacPaint graphics, but its attempts go only so far.

Overall, be creative with your graphics, but don't go too far. Excel, by itself, produces competent, professional-looking graphics. But in the hands of even a modest MacDraw or MacPaint artist, they can be pure dynamite in a boring business presentation.

Chapter **6**
CUSTOM MENUS AND DIALOG BOXES

Customized menus and dialog boxes allow you to create your own personal miniapplications from within Excel. Let's say you want to create a fully functional double-entry accounting worksheet. This worksheet is designed so that persons with little or no experience with Excel can enter data, calculate results, and print reports. By adding your own commands, menus, and dialog boxes, you provide simple pull-down and pop-up solutions to these tasks. Users can be totally shielded from Excel.

One menu may provide a list of possible entry types: cash, charge, paid-out, and so forth. To make an entry, you need only select the desired entry type from a menu, and Excel prompts for all the right information. A dialog box may provide a list of report types. Clicking on a report type selects all of the currently entered data, formats it in a specific manner, and prints it out.

Your own personalized menus and dialog boxes are created with macros, and, as you found in Chapter 2, you can do just about anything with Excel's rich macro language. In this chapter, you'll learn how to customize Excel with your own commands, menus, and dialog boxes. The techniques are relatively simple and straightforward, but the results can be astounding.

ADDING CUSTOM COMMANDS

You can add a command to any of Excel's existing pull-down menus. Your personal command is added to the bottom of the list. To understand how the technique works, let's first take a look at how Excel's commands and menus are laid out.

Excel uses three menu bars. The first two bars correspond to the Worksheet and Chart applications, the third to the Nil Menu, shown when no documents are open or when the Clipboard or a desk accessory is opened. These menu bars are referred to by number. You will use these numbers later when adding your own commands and menus.

	File	Edit	Formula	Format	Data	Options	Macro	Window		1
	File	Edit	Gallery	Chart	Format	Macro	Window			2
	File	Edit	Window							3

Bar Number	Description
1	Worksheet
2	Chart
3	Nil Menu

Menus also are referenced by number. Menus begin on the far left (excluding the Apple logo menu); the first one is considered menu number 1. The menu to the right of that is menu number 2 and so forth.

1	2	3	4	5	6	7	8

 File   Edit   Formula   Format   Data   Options   Macro   Window

Two macro functions are used to add a command to an existing Excel menu. They are ADD.COMMAND and ENABLE.COMMAND. The ADD.COMMAND function tells Excel you want to add a command to a specific menu. The ENABLE.COMMAND function lets you turn commands on and off. When turned on, the command is accessible to the user; when turned off, the command appears dim and is deactivated. Both functions require specific arguments as follows:

ADD.COMMAND (bar number, menu number, menu reference)

ENABLE.COMMAND (bar number, menu number, command position, enable condition)

In both functions, bar number refers to one of three Excel menu bars, as discussed above. Similarly, menu number refers to the menu in which you want to place the new command.

The menu reference argument tells Excel where to find the actual text for the new command, as well as any macro functions that perform the command. The menu reference can be a single cell or a range.

The command position argument is either a number indicating the position of the command (down the list of menu items) you want enabled or the name of the command as a text string. In most instances, it's easier to use the text-string approach because you can more readily identify the exact command you want to enable.

When using numbers, you must refer to the command you want to enable by counting from the top of the menu. For example, if the command to be enabled is the fourteenth on the list, you enter "14" as the argument.

Finally, the enable condition argument lets you turn command enable on and off. To turn a command on, enter a TRUE or 1; to turn it off, enter a FALSE or 0. Note that you cannot enable and disable Excel's built-in commands using this macro function.

Let's turn theory into practice with a short and simple macro. The following example shows the commands for a macro I've called Add.Command. Cell A1 contains the ADD.COMMAND function, with the required arguments to place a new command in the first menu of menu bar 1 (this corresponds to the File menu of the Worksheet menu bar). The actual command text is indicated by the range A5:C6.

	A	B	C
1	=ADD.COMMAND(1,1,A5:C6)		
2	=ENABLE.COMMAND(1,1,15,TRUE)		
3	=RETURN()		
4			
5	-		
6	Test	Add.Command!Test	
7			
8			
9	Test		
10	=ALERT("This is just a test",2)		
11	=DELETE.COMMAND(1,1,14)		
12	=DELETE.COMMAND(1,1,14)		
13	=RETURN()		

Add.Command

Column A contains the text of the command. In this case, I've used a hyphen to indicate a separation line in the menu. The line helps separate the new command from the existing ones already in the menu. The name of the command is "Test," not an overly creative name but one that indicates its application and usefulness.

Column B contains the macro name for the command. In cell B6 is the notation Add.Command!Test, indicating the name of the macro file (Add.Command) and the macro to run when the Test command is selected.

Column C contains a shortcut equivalent key activating the command from the keyboard. An equivalent key is not used in this demonstration, but Column C is included in the ADD.COMMAND argument range just the same.

Also shown in the example is the macro code for the Test command. The code simply calls up an alert box and displays the text "This is just a test." The separation hyphen and the "Test" command is then deleted from the menu using the DELETE.COMMAND macro function. Arguments for DELETE.COMMAND call for the bar number, menu number, and command position. In the example, you see that the bar number is 1, the menu number is 1, and the command position is 14 (that is, fourteenth from the top of the menu). The DELETE.COMMAND function is issued twice, with the exact same arguments, in order to remove both the separating line and the command text.

```
File

New...          ⌘N
Open...         ⌘O
Links...
Close All
Save            ⌘S
Save As...
Delete...
.......................................
Page Setup...
Print...        ⌘P
Printer Setup...
.......................................
Quit            ⌘Q
.......................................
Test
```

ADDING CUSTOM MENUS

The process is almost the same for adding complete menus as it is for adding just one command. You can create your own menus for one of Excel's three built-in menu bars, or you can attach your own menu to a new menu bar. While you can realistically fit only one more menu to one of Excel's three built-in menu bars, you can add as many as seven or eight custom menus to your own menu bars. Excel lets you define up to 15 menu bars and easily toggle between them.

You add a new menu with the ADD.MENU macro function. The arguments for ADD.MENU are simple:

ADD.MENU (bar number, menu reference)

Bar number can be any of Excel's three built-in menu bars (1, 2, or 3) or a menu bar of your own. Note that you must add a new menu bar—using the macro functions detailed later in this section—before you can attach a menu to it.

The menu reference argument tells Excel where to find the relevant information for the commands contained in the menu. The menu reference is always a range. As you can see in the following figure, the first cell in the range, A6, contains the name of the menu, called New Menu. Next, in cells A7 through A9 are the commands contained in New Menu. They are Custom 1, Custom 2, and Exit This Menu. Cells in column B indicate the macro to be executed when one of the three commands is given.

	A	B	C
	≡≡≡≡≡≡≡≡ **NewMenu** ≡≡≡≡≡≡≡≡		
1	=ADD.MENU(1,A6:C9)		
2	=CHECK.COMMAND(1,9,2,TRUE)		
3	=ENABLE.COMMAND(1,9,A7,TRUE)		
4	=RETURN()		
5			
6	**New Menu**		
7	Custom 1	New Menu!Command_1	
8	Custom 2	New Menu!Command_2	
9	Exit This Menu	New Menu!Exit	E
10	**Exit**		
11	=DELETE.MENU(1,9)		
12	=RETURN()		
13	**Command 1**		
14	=RENAME.COMMAND(1,9,2,"This is a new test.")		
15	=RETURN()		
16	**Command 2**		
17	=CHECK.COMMAND(1,9,2,FALSE)		
18	=RETURN()		

The last command, Exit This Menu, is given a Command key shortcut. The Exit This Menu includes the notation "Command-E" opposite the Exit This Menu command. You can activate this command either from the pull-down menu or by pressing Command-E.

The macro for Command-1 includes a new function, RENAME.COMMAND. This function changes the name of the specified command and is useful when the command changes a state in Excel. The RENAME.COMMAND function uses the arguments:

RENAME.COMMAND (bar number, menu number, command position, new name)

All of the arguments are the same as for ADD.COMMAND, except that the new name argument expects the text for the new command. Surround the text with quote marks. As shown in the example, choosing Command 1 changes the text to the New Command 1.

The macro for Command 2 also includes a new function, CHECK.COMMAND. This function places a check mark beside the command indicated in the argument. The check mark is useful to indicate that a condition or control has been "turned on." CHECK.COMMAND uses the arguments:

> CHECK.COMMAND (bar number, menu number, command position, check condition)

The arguments are the same as for ENABLE.COMMAND. The check condition argument expects a Boolean expression of TRUE (1) or FALSE (0). As you may suspect, a check mark is placed next to the command when you use TRUE; it is removed when you use FALSE.

The Exit This Menu command deletes the entire menu from the bar. You use the DELETE.MENU function to remove any of the menus you've added (Excel's own menus can't be deleted). The function requires you to provide the number of the menu bar and the menu position. Cell A11 contains the macro instruction.

> =DELETE.MENU (1,9)

which means delete the ninth menu from the left in menu bar number 1 (e.g., the Worksheet menu bar, which is the bar number 1 and has eight menus; the custom menu is added as the ninth).

If you want to add a menu to a new bar, you must first preface the ADD.MENU command with the ADD.BAR and SHOW.BAR commands. ADD.BAR expects no argument; SHOW.BAR needs to be told the bar number to use. The bar number can be any one of Excel's built-in menu bars or the number returned by a previously executed ADD.BAR function. The following example shows a sample bar and single menu macro. Here's how it works:

- Cell A2 adds a new bar.

- Cell A3 defines a new menu; the contents of the menu are specified in the range A7:C12.

- Cell A4 contains =SHOW.BAR(A2), which displays the menu bar and menu.

	A	B	C
1	TestMenu		
2	=ADD.BAR()		
3	=ADD.MENU(A2,A7:C12)		
4	=SHOW.BAR(A2)		
5	=RETURN()		
6			
7	Sample Menu		
8	Item 1	TestMenu!Item_1	A
9	Item 2	TestMenu!Item_2	B
10	Item 3	TestMenu!Item_3	C
11	--		
12	Exit This Bar	TestMenu!Exit	D
13			
14	Exit		
15	=ADD.BAR()		
16	=SHOW.BAR(1)		
17	=RETURN()		

For simplicity, only one of the commands is active in this example, the command for Exit This Bar. The Exit macro simply returns to menu bar in the Worksheet menu bar.

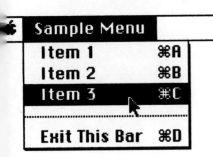

ADDING CUSTOM DIALOG BOXES

Excel uses a number of pop-up dialog boxes that provide you with multiple-choice selections. Dialog boxes are a convenient way to interact with Excel because all of the available choices are directly in front of you, displayed in the box on the screen.

A special macro command, DIALOG.BOX, is used to generate your own dialog boxes. You have full control over the size, content, and appearance of the box. Although the process of making custom dialog boxes is not difficult, you must be sure to follow a rather strict format. Excel expects to see the data for the dialog box in a specific layout.

Anatomy of a Dialog Box Macro

The macro for a custom dialog box is composed of two main segments. The first segment is the actual macro area, which includes the DIALOG.BOX function, as well as any macro commands (such as IF functions) that are initiated when you make a selection from the dialog box. The second segment is the dialog box definition table. This table lists all of the components or "items" that appear in the box, including its size, position, and type. You are limited to a maximum of 64 dialog box items.

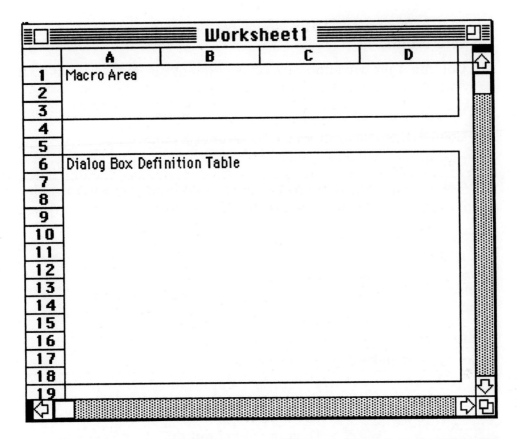

The first item in the dialog box definition is always the size and screen position of the box itself. The remaining items, which include buttons, text entry fields, and checkboxes can be listed in any order. However, if you are using many text entry fields, they should appear in the definition list in the order that you'd like them to be activated in the dialog box. That way, you can go from one entry field to the other in the correct order simply by pressing the Tab key.

The definition list is divided into eight columns.

- Column 1 provides a description of the dialog box item. It is used for reference only and isn't required by Excel, so it's optional. However, you'll find it very helpful to include the description in your dialog box definitions so that when you return to the macro later on, you can more easily figure out what everything is doing.

- Column 2 provides the item number. The item number identifies the dialog box element to Excel. A list of item numbers appears in Table 6-2.

- Column 3 provides the horizontal position of the item in Macintosh screen units.

- Column 4 provides the vertical position of the item in Macintosh screen units.

- Column 5 provides the width of the item in Macintosh screen units.

- Column 6 provides the height of the item in Macintosh screen units.

- Column 7 provides the text included with the item, if any.

- Column 8 provides the initial value for the dialog box item or else its result after you are finished with the box.

The notation "Macintosh screen units" means the pixels or dots that make up the Mac's display. The standard Macintosh screen displays 512 pixels horizontally and 342 pixels vertically. There are 72 pixels per inch, so a dialog box item defined as having a width of "72" is one inch wide.

Table 6-2

Item Type Number	Description
1	Default OK button
2	Cancel button
3	OK button
4	Default cancel button
5	Displayed text
6	Text box
7	Integer box
8	Number box
9	Formula box
10	Reference box
11	Option button group
12	Option button
13	Checkbox
14	Group box
15	List box
16	Linked list box
17	Icon

☰ Using the Dialog Box
Desk Accessory

While you can program your custom dialog boxes by typing the definition manually, an easier approach is to use the dialog box desk accessory, provided with Excel 1.5.

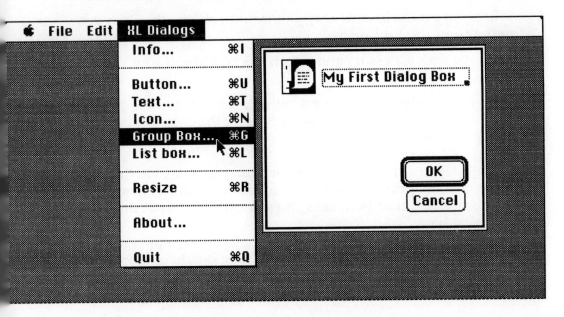

Using the desk accessory is quite simple:

1   Install the desk accessory into your System File, if you haven't already. Use Apple's Font/DA Mover, supplied on your Macintosh system disks, for this task.

2   Open the desk accessory either from within Excel or from the Finder. If you only have 1 megabyte of memory in your Mac, you may not be able to open the accessory from within Excel.

3   When the desk accessory opens, a blank dialog box appears. Grab the "handle" at the lower-left corner and resize it as desired. You can drag the box anywhere you wish with the mouse. The exact size and placement of the box will be recorded within the dialog box definition list.

4   Add items from the selection menu. I find it easier to map out the box first using pencil and paper, then construct the real thing on the Mac using the desk accessory. For best results, start from the upper-right corner of the box and work your way down. Remember that you can add, delete, or change text from within the dialog box desk accessory (use the Text command in the dialog box menu) or in the definition table after it is pasted into a macro sheet.

5   When you get the box the way you want it, choose the Copy command from the Edit menu.

6   Close the desk accessory and return to Excel (if you aren't already there).

7   Open a new macro sheet, select cell B7, and paste in the contents of the Clipboard. You must manually enter the description of each dialog box item.

I suggest you select cell B7 as the starting point for the paste because it not only provides you with an empty column A to write the item descriptions, but it also leaves you some room to write the macro for the dialog box.

A handy macro shown in the following figure sets up a new dialog box macro sheet, formats the columns to make them most readable (yet all visible in one screen width), and enters the column heading for the dialog box items.

	A
1	DiaBoxFormat
2	=NEW(3)
3	=SELECT("R1C1")
4	=MESSAGE(TRUE,"Please wait...")
5	=ECHO(FALSE)
6	=FORMULA("=DIALOG.BOX(#N/A)")
7	=SELECT("R2C1")
8	=FORMULA("=RETURN()")
9	=SELECT("C1")
10	=COLUMN.WIDTH(11)
11	=SELECT("C2:C6")
12	=COLUMN.WIDTH(2)
13	=SELECT("C7")
14	=COLUMN.WIDTH(3)
15	=SELECT("C8")
16	=COLUMN.WIDTH(4)
17	=SELECT("R5C2")
18	=FORMULA("Item")
19	=SELECT("R5C3")
20	=FORMULA("Horiz")
21	=SELECT("R5C4")
22	=FORMULA("Vert")
23	=SELECT("R5C5")
24	=FORMULA("Item")
25	=SELECT("R5C6")
26	=FORMULA("Item")
27	=SELECT("R5C7")
28	=FORMULA("Text")
29	=SELECT("R5C8")
30	=FORMULA("Initial/")
31	=SELECT("R6C2")
32	=FORMULA("Num")
33	=SELECT("R6C3")
34	=FORMULA("Pos")
35	=SELECT("R6C4")
36	=FORMULA("Pos")
37	=SELECT("R6C5")
38	=FORMULA("Width")
39	=SELECT("R6C6")
40	=FORMULA("Height")
41	=SELECT("R6C8")
42	=FORMULA("Result")
43	=FORMULA.GOTO("R1C1")
44	=MESSAGE(FALSE)
45	=FULL(TRUE)
46	=RETURN()

≡ ## Pasting Back Into
the Desk Accessory

The dialog box desk accessory allows two-way copy-and-paste. If you're not satisfied with the way a dialog box looks or works in Excel, copy its definition (leave out the first column of descriptions and any column headings), open the desk accessory, and choose Paste from the Edit menu. The original dialog box appears on the screen. Rework the items as necessary, then copy and paste it back into Excel.

≡ ## Static Versus Dynamic Dialog Box

Excel lets you create two types of dialog boxes, static and dynamic. Though the Macintosh treats each type differently internally, from a user standpoint, the biggest difference is that a dynamic dialog box can be moved around with the mouse and a static box cannot.

You'd select a dynamic dialog box if you feel you (or another user) may need to scoot the box around to see the contents of the screen underneath. A dynamic dialog box also allows you to select cells in the worksheet and have that cell selection appear in an editing field in the box. When the feature of movability and worksheet entry are not required, you may identify the dialog box as static.

The visual appearance of a static and dynamic dialog box may be similar, but if you know what to look for, you can always tell them apart. Dynamic dialog boxes appear with a title bar and title on the top; static boxes do not.

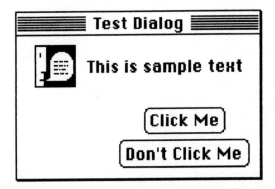

Dynamic

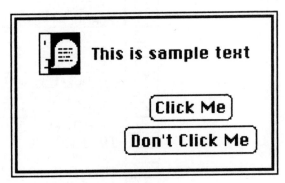

Static

☰ Dialog Box Buttons

Dialog boxes use a variety of buttons. Excel provides four operations buttons, two OKs and two Cancels. You can choose a standard Enter key default for either the OK or Cancel button. The button with the double outline is automatically selected when you press the Enter key.

Note that although the buttons made with the dialog box desk accessory say OK and Cancel, you can edit them so they say anything. You should use only one Cancel button (no matter what you rename it), because it will always return a FALSE to the macro. But you can use any number of renamed OK buttons. Each OK button returns a value corresponding to its item number in the dialog box definition table back to the dialog box macro. The value appears in the DIALOG.BOX formula cell (to actually see the value of the cell, you must turn Formulas off in the Display dialog box, which is accessible under the Options menu). You can then check the value and act upon it accordingly.

☰ Sample Dialog Box Tester

Custom dialog boxes are easiest to learn if you start out short and simple. In the next figure is a basic dialog box definition macro. The macro doesn't really do anything, but it does help teach you the inner workings of custom dialog boxes. You have two button choices, True and False. The True button was originally labeled OK and the False button was originally labeled Cancel. Pressing True displays an alert box that says "That is TRUE," and pressing False displays an alert box that says "That is FALSE."

	A	B	C	D	E	F	G	H
1	=DIALOG.BOX(B8:H10)							
2	=IF(tester,"TRUE","FALSE")							
3	=ALERT("That is "&A2&".",2)							
4								
5	=RETURN()							
6		Item	Horiz	Vert	Item	Item	Text	Initial/
7		Num	Pos	Pos	Width	Height		Result
8			219	122	157	108	Dialog Tester	
9		3	38	25	68	23	TRUE	
10		2	37	52	70	25	FALSE	

Test D.B. Buttons

Here's how the dialog box macro works. Cell A1 contains the DIALOG.BOX function and defines the range of the definition list. Note that the actual definition for the dialog box items is contained in the range B8 to H10. I've given cell A1 a name, "tester," for the use with the next macro formula.

Cell A2 contains the formula

=IF(tester, "TRUE", "FALSE")

This IF conditional test checks which button you press. If you press the True button, the macro passes a positive number (correlating to the item number in the definition list) to cell A1, and the alert box, provided by cell A3, displays "That is TRUE." Conversely, if you press the False button, the macro passes a FALSE to cell A1, and the alter box displays, "That is FALSE." Of course, in a real working macro, you'd construct an IF formula that does a little more work than this. But this shows you the basic operation of custom dialog boxes and the operation of buttons.

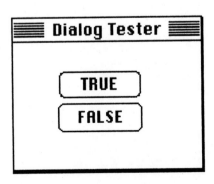

☰ Using the Initial/Result Column

The Initial/Result column is used to pass arguments between the dialog box macro and the dialog box itself. For example, completing a text entry field places the answer in the Initial/Result column for that particular item.

Likewise, you can pass arguments to the dialog box by setting an initial value for a given item. For instance, entering TRUE for a checkbox automatically places a check mark in the box when the dialog box is first opened. You can always click in the box to remove the check.

The order entry definition macro shown below exercises most of the dialog box items that pass data to and from the Initial/Result column. The order entry macro is an engine only; clicking boxes and filling in data doesn't do anything but show the effect on the Initial/Result column.

	A	B	C	D	E	F	G	H
1	=ECHO(FALSE)							
2	=DIALOG.BOX(B9:H41)							
3	=IF(A2=30,RUN('Fig. 6-15'!OrderEntry))							
4	=RETURN()							
5								
6								
7		Item	Horiz	Vert	Item	Item	Text	Initial/
8		Num	Pos	Pos	Width	Height		Result
9	Box Definition		97	47	345	327	Database Entry	
10	First Name Edit Box	6	101	5	206	25		
11	Last Name Edit Box	6	101	32	206	25		
12	Company Edit Box	6	101	59	206	25		
13	Address Edit Box	6	101	86	205	25		
14	City Edit Box	6	101	113	205	25		
15	State Edit Box	6	101	140	42	25		
16	ZIP Code Edit Box	6	213	140	93	25		
17	First Name Static Text	5	9	11	90	18	First Name	
18	Last Name Static Text	5	9	36	89	18	Last Name	
19	Company Static Text	5	9	62	73	18	Company	
20	Address Static Text	5	9	90	64	18	Address	
21	City Static Text	5	9	116	64	18	City	
22	State Static Text	5	9	144	64	18	State	
23	ZIP Code Static Text	5	145	143	65	18	ZIP Code	
24	Item Ordered Box Group	11	11	212	106	111	Item Ordered	#N/A
25	Item 1 Box	13	15	230	73	18	Item 1	TRUE
26	Item 2 Box	13	15	248	73	18	Item 2	
27	Item 3 Box	13	15	266	73	18	Item 3	
28	Item 4 Box	13	15	284	73	18	Item 4	
29	Item 5 Box	13	15	302	73	18	Item 5	
30	Amount Enclosed Static Text	5	9	178	73	18	Amt. Enc.	
31	Amount Enclosed Edit Box	6	82	174	65	25		
32	Payment Type Button Group	11	126	212	122	97	Payment Type	2
33	Cash Button	12	128	234	59	18	Cash	
34	Personal Check Button	12	128	252	107	18	Pers. Check	
35	Compnay Check Button	12	128	270	114	18	Comp. Check	
36	Money Order Button	12	128	288	105	18	Money Ord.	
37	New Customer Static Text	5	169	180	115	18	New Customer	
38	New Customer Check Box	13	284	180	21	18		FALSE
39	OK Button (Default)	1	268	217	60	23	Next	
40	Done Button	3	267	254	60	23	Done	
41	Cancel Button	2	267	285	60	23	Cancel	

At the beginning of the macro, in cell A1, the display is turned off with the =ECHO(FALSE) instruction. I used the ECHO() function because complex dialog boxes (those with more than eight or ten items) tend to slow Excel's operation and are drawn rather sluggishly on the screen.

Cell A2 defines the dialog box definition list (range: B9 to H41). Cell A3 does a quick comparison using an IF function. If the returned value of cell A2 is equal to 30 (corresponding to the default OK button, which is on row 39), the macro is simply repeated and you can reenter data. You'll note that the contents of the previous dialog box are shown again; the Initial/Result column hasn't been cleared between entries. In a real order entry dialog box macro, you'd copy the contents of the Initial/Result column to a database, clear the column, reenter any defaults (such as the TRUE for Item #1 Box), then proceed with the next entry.

Pressing the Done or Cancel button exits the dialog box, where you can visually inspect the changes made to the Initial/Result column. Notice that the editing box items include the text you entered into the entry fields, item boxes that you clicked are shown as TRUE, the number of the radio button you clicked is shown opposite the button group definition, and so forth.

```
┌──────────────────────────────────────────────┐
│ ≣≣≣≣≣≣≣≣≣≣≣≣≣≣ Database Entry ≣≣≣≣≣≣≣≣≣≣≣≣ │
│                                                │
│  First Name  ┌──────────────────────────────┐ │
│              └──────────────────────────────┘ │
│  Last Name   ┌──────────────────────────────┐ │
│              └──────────────────────────────┘ │
│  Company     ┌──────────────────────────────┐ │
│              └──────────────────────────────┘ │
│  Address     ┌──────────────────────────────┐ │
│              └──────────────────────────────┘ │
│  City        ┌──────────────────────────────┐ │
│              └──────────────────────────────┘ │
│  State    ┌────┐ ZIP Code ┌──────────────┐   │
│           └────┘           └──────────────┘   │
│  Amt. Enc. ┌──────┐   New Customer  ☐        │
│            └──────┘                           │
│  ┌Item Ordered┐ ┌Payment Type┐ ┌─────────┐  │
│  │ ☒ Item 1   │ │ ○ Cash     │ │  Next   │  │
│  │ ☐ Item 2   │ │ ◉ Pers. Check│└─────────┘  │
│  │ ☐ Item 3   │ │ ○ Comp. Check│ ┌─────────┐ │
│  │ ☐ Item 4   │ │ ○ Money Ord. │ │  Done   │ │
│  │ ☐ Item 5   │ └────────────┘ └─────────┘  │
│  └────────────┘                ┌─────────┐   │
│                                │ Cancel  │   │
│                                └─────────┘   │
└──────────────────────────────────────────────┘
```

THE WHOLE APPROACH

Custom commands, menus, and dialog boxes can be mixed together to create an Excel miniapplication. For example, you can add a command to one of Excel's existing menus that starts the order entry dialog box shown in the last section. Entire procedures can be included in completely new menus and menu bars. Some of these procedures may call up dialog boxes; others may command Excel to format the data you've provided in the box into a chart; and still others may print the chart on a LaserWriter.

The only requirement is that the macro sheet(s) for your miniapplication system be open and available to Excel. You also can initiate automatic macro playback by using the auto-open function as the first command of your menu/dialog box macro.

It's time to move on to the practical applications and examples of Part II of this book. In the chapters that follow, you'll learn firsthand how to apply the power and versatility of Excel using the tips, tricks, and shortcuts you've learned. The fun is only beginning.

PART
2

ADVANCED
TECHNIQUES
AT
WORK

Chapter **7**
LINKING WORKSHEETS

Sales Forecast
Summary Sheets
Charting Linked Worksheets

Think back to Chapter 2 on spreadsheet strategies. There I heartily recommend breaking up large worksheets into smaller modules and then linking the modules together when you need to see the results of the dependent documents. In this chapter, I'll show you a practical example of such linking and how much flexibility it gives you over the long term.

SALES FORECAST

The scenario of the example in this chapter is a regional sales manager who has four salespeople working the field. As is quite often the case in large sales organizations, salespeople up and down the corporate ladder must prepare forecasts of sales for the upcoming year. Top management ultimately uses these forecasts to schedule production, forecast raw materials requirements, establish overall budgets, and later measure the performance of each salesperson and manager.

Salespeople and management in the mythical company in the following example must prepare forecasts of unit shipments and dollar billings by product for each month of the calendar year. For salespeople, the spreadsheet task is simple enough to accomplish on a single worksheet. The challenge is for the sales manager who must collate the forecasts of four territorial salespeople into one forecast for the entire region.

While it is possible for the manager to combine the values submitted by each salesperson into a giant worksheet, it is advantageous to keep each territory on a separate worksheet and then draw the totals into a summary worksheet—the one that goes to the main office. Additionally, it may be better to separate the summary sheet into "units" and "dollars" sheets, because some folks at headquarters need only the former, while other groups base decisions only on the latter. And even if you want to chart the combined effects of units and sales for the complete line of products, you can create a chart that draws data from the two summary sheets (another example of linking multiple documents). Later I'll show you how to do that.

The structure of the example, then, is shown graphically below.

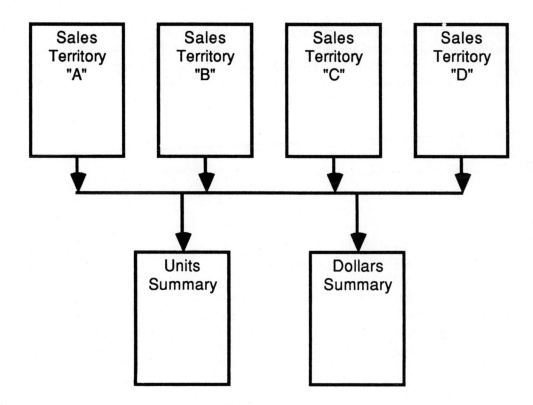

Admittedly, the connections of all these elements look inherently more complex than if they were all contained on one spreadsheet. But by keeping the elements separate, you eventually can build up a considerable library of analytical tools to further massage the numbers from the individual salespeople. You will be able to find a particular cell in the system much faster—such as targeting in on the July Product No. 3 unit forecast for Salesperson B—than on a mammoth worksheet. Moreover, when working solely on entering data into the supporting worksheets, you can recalculate much faster, for recalculation extends no further than the linked documents open at the moment.

≡ Range and Cell Names

Assigning names to ranges and some cells makes a worksheet or macro easier to debug. The examples in this chapter, as well as those chapters that follow, make heavy use of names. Refer to Table 7.1 for cell and range names that I have initially assigned to the worksheets in this chapter. It will help you better visualize the construction of each worksheet (some range names are explained later in Chapter 9).

Table 7.1

Sales A, B, C, and D	
bottom_line	$AA$34:$AB$34
Percent of Plan A	
bottom.line	$AM$34:$AO$34
M/bottomline	
bottom.line.set	$A$11
copy.loop	$C$14
counter	$C$9
ev.other.fill	$C$1
jump	$B$6
location	$B$12
Print_Area	$A$1:$C$19
set.jump	$B$1
view.bottom.line	$A$1

☰ Territory Worksheets

Let's look at the individual territory worksheets—the ones each salesperson will fill out. A manager can prepare a blank template for each salesperson. Once completed, the forms can be telecommunicated to the manager's regional office. As long as the names of the files don't change from the manager's initial setup, the summary worksheets in the manager's Mac will be able to read the supporting worksheets instantly when they come back from the salespeople.

The layout of the territory worksheet should be simple for the salespeople to use, because, as is my experience, few field people are fond of paperwork, even if it's on the computer. Still, the form must elicit the basic information from the salesperson.

As shown in the figure below, the basic structure consists of unit and dollar figures for each product for each month. Here product numbers are a simple data series, but in reality, the product numbers probably would be quite different. They could be listed either in order as Excel would sort them or they could be grouped by product category (e.g., economy models, professional models, accessories).

 File   Edit   Formula   Format   Data   Options   Macro   Window

C13 | =B13*19.35

salesA

	A	B	C	D	E	F
1	Aug-28-85					
2				Salesperson A		
3			1986 Forecast -- Shipments and Billings			
4						
5			January		February	M
6		Units	Dollars	Units	Dollars	Units
7	Product Number	Sales A				
8	1	400	$3,900		$0	
9	2	200	$4,780		$0	
10	3	60	$765		$0	
11	4	45	$898		$0	
12	5	105	$1,360		$0	
13	6	60	$1,161		$0	
14	7	200	$2,490		$0	
15	8	95	$3,795		$0	
16	9	80	$432		$0	
17	10	20	$356		$0	
18	11	110	$1,155		$0	
19	12	25	$688		$0	

Data entry in this form is limited to the number of units for each product. The dollar amount is automatically calculated based on the sales price of each item. In other words, all cells in the Dollars columns are formulas. In cell C13, for example, the dollar value will be the number of units entered into cell B13 multiplied by $19.35, which is the unit cost for Product No. 6. If a sales manager sets up this kind of form for the salespeople, there is no chance that the people filling out the form will get the costs mixed up on the worksheet.

A couple further notes about the territory worksheets are in order. First, notice that because each month consists of two columns of data, the name of the month is spread across both columns. To do this, I entered blank spaces at the beginning of each cell, then entered the name of the month. I was able to perfectly straddle the month between the column boundary simply by adding and removing spaces.

≡ Every Other Fill Macro

While creating this form, I soon found it tedious to copy pairs of cells (Units and Dollars) across the spreadsheet from the January to Totals columns way out in column AB. Filling Right only works with single cells, not multiples. For expediency, a macro was the answer.

First, I created columns for one complete month, including Dollars column formulas and a bottom row of totals in each column. Then, I selected the two columns, Units and Dollars, from the headings row down to the totals row and invoked a simple macro I wrote to do the work of copying the columns, moving the cursor to the right two cells and then pasting the block. Inside the macro, I had Excel repeat this copy-paste sequence 11 times (until it filled out December) and then skip a column before pasting once more for the Totals columns.

I called this macro "ev.other.fill" because it performs essentially a Fill Right function, but with two-column selections.

	M/bottomline — C
1	ev.other.fill
2	=DEFINE.NAME("start",SELECTION())
3	=SET.VALUE(counter,1)
4	copy.loop
5	=SELECT(SELECTION())
6	=COPY()
7	=SELECT(OFFSET(SELECTION(),0,2))
8	=PASTE()
9	=counter+1
10	=IF(counter<12,GOTO(copy.loop))
11	=COPY()
12	=SELECT(OFFSET(SELECTION(),0,4))
13	=PASTE()
14	=SELECT(!start)
15	=DELETE.NAME("start")
16	=RETURN()
17	
18	

One of two preliminary steps in this macro defines the current selection (the January columns, here) with the name "start." When the filling part of this macro is finished, the active cells will be far to the right of the January columns. By defining the January columns, the macro will later be able to reactivate these cells, bringing January back into view for your next action. The second preliminary step is to set the value of a macro cell, called "counter," to zero. This cell, C9 in this macro, will be used as a holding place for a number representing the number of times the main segment of this macro executes.

The meat of the macro is a section called "copy.loop." This is called a loop because it will execute several times, beginning at cell C4 and running through cell C10. Each time through the loop, the number in the cell I had defined as "counter" (with the menu Define Name command) increases by one. In other words, the first time through the loop, cell C9 has a one added to the zero placed there by the SET.VALUE function cell C3; the next time through, a one is added to the one in the cell, making two. This continues until the value reaches 11, at which point the IF test in cell C10 allows execution to break out of the loop, continuing onward to cell C11. As long as the counter is less than 11, execution "loops back" to cell C4.

Inside the loop, the functions are rather simple. First, the macro selects the range of cells selected on the worksheet. Next, it copies the selection. Then it moves the cursor to a location two cells to the right and in the same row as the active cell in the original selection. Finally, it pastes the copied cells into the area selected by the previous formula. In macro cell C9, the formula adds a one to the value of its own cell, and this cell is the one used in the IF test in cell C10.

Once the loop has filled the columns out to December, it does one more, special action, selecting the offset cell three columns to the right. I added this because I prefer to separate the months from the totals columns by at least one blank column. I might return later and reduce the width of the column, but there is extra room between the columns just the same (instructions for selecting the intervening cell and resizing its width also could be placed in the macro).

	W	X	Y	Z	AA	AB	AC
1							
2							
3							
4							
5	mber		Dece mber		Total	Year	
6	Dollars	Units	Dollars		Units	Dollars	
7					Sales A		
8	$0		$0		400	$3,900	
9	$0		$0		200	$4,780	
10	$0		$0		60	$765	
11	$0		$0		45	$898	
12	$0		$0		105	$1,360	
13	$0		$0		60	$1,161	
14	$0		$0		200	$2,490	
15	$0		$0		95	$3,795	
16	$0		$0		80	$432	
17	$0		$0		20	$356	
18	$0		$0		110	$1,155	
19	$0		$0		25	$688	

salesA

To finish the macro, cell C14 selects the original selection in the January columns. Notice that the selection name is preceded by an exclamation mark. This tells the Excel macro to look for cells bearing that name on the active worksheet. If the mark were missing, Excel would look for a cell labeled "start" on the macro worksheet and return an error alert box (unless you had previously defined a cell on the macro with that name). One last bit of housekeeping, I deleted the name "start" from the worksheet. This isn't necessary, but it prevents the accidental buildup of many definitions that aren't used in the course of entering or analyzing data later on.

This macro can be adapted hundreds of ways. You can make it fairly elaborate and even more generic than the one shown here. For example, you could add INPUT functions to prompt the user for the number of cells to skip when filling right and how far to fill—in case you have applications that need this feature on variable-width worksheets. Another INPUT function could ask the user if an extra column should be inserted between the last group of pasted cells and the rest of the bunch.

☰ Tiling Windows

One more touch to simplify data entry on the territory forms would be to divide the window into tiles that freeze the titles.

	A	B	C	D	E	F	
1	Aug-28-85						
2				Salesperson A			
3			1986 Forecast -- Shipments and Billings				
4							
5			January		February		M
6		Units	Dollars	Units	Dollars	Units	
7	Product Number	Sales A					
8	1	400	$3,900		$0		
9	2	200	$4,780		$0		
10	3	60	$765		$0		
11	4	45	$898		$0		
12	5	105	$1,360		$0		
13	6	60	$1,161		$0		
14	7	200	$2,490		$0		
15	8	95	$3,795		$0		
16	9	80	$432		$0		
17	10	20	$356		$0		
18	11	110	$1,155		$0		
19	12	25	$688		$0		

salesA

Then choose Freeze Panes in the Options menu to leave only one set of scroll bars for the salespeople to contend with.

Making a worksheet for each of the salespeople is a snap once you have the first one done. Simply change the name of the salesperson in the title and issue a Save As command from the File menu, giving the file an identifying name for that person or territory.

☰ SUMMARY SHEETS

Creating the summary worksheets (at least the first one) requires some patience, because this is where you'll be making the links among worksheets. Additionally, the structure of the supporting documents—with a pair of columns for each month—causes problems when trying to fill the worksheet, as you'll see.

The first summary worksheet I created was for Units. In many ways it resembles the structure of the supporting worksheets except for the single columns for each month.

	File	**Edit**	**Formula**	**Format**	**Data**	**Options**	**Macro**	**Window**	
	B8			=salesA!B8+salesB!B8+salesC!B8+salesD!B8					

Units Summary

	A	B	C	D	E	F	
1	Aug-28-85						
2				Forecast Summary			
3				Units			
4							
5							
6		January	February	March	April	May	
7	Product Number						
8	1	1035	0	0	0	0	
9	2	645	0	0	0	0	
10	3	340	0	0	0	0	
11	4	370	0	0	0	0	
12	5	615	0	0	0	0	
13	6	60	0	0	0	0	
14	7	200	0	0	0	0	
15	8	95	0	0	0	0	
16	9	80	0	0	0	0	
17	10	220	0	0	0	0	
18	11	110	0	0	0	0	
19	12	25	0	0	0	0	
20	13	85	0	0	0	0	

The months macro from the Create macro worksheet (see Chapter 2, Macro Strategies) simplified the entry of month titles. Product numbers were copied directly from one of the supporting worksheets, for I wanted the summary sheets to be in the same order as the territory worksheets.

Formulas for the data cells consist of simple additions of like cells in the supporting documents. For example, cell B8 in the Units Summary worksheet consists of the formula

=salesA!B8+salesB!B8+salesC!B8+salesD!B8

Notice that I did not use cell names in this case. While the names might make the formula less confusing, you can see that assigning names to each data cell in each of the four supporting worksheets would be a monstrously long procedure. Notice, too, that I entered all cell references as relative references to facilitate filling down the column. Because all January Units cells refer to relative cells in the supporting worksheets, I could complete the rest of the column by Filling Down.

But I could not Fill Right to finish the rest of the Units Summary worksheet, because the cell references would simply increment by one column instead of the two columns I'd need to read the units values for the next month. For example, when the January summary reads unit values from supporting worksheets column B, February's supporting values are in column D, not column C as the Fill Right command expects.

Therefore, I had to manually enter the formula for the first product number of each month. Actually, it's easier to perform a Fill Right command anyway and then edit the formula in the months February through December to reflect the correct columns in the supporting documents. This certainly cuts down on typing. Once the first product's formulas are in place, you can select all of them and Fill Down.

The Dollars Summary worksheet can be easily derived from the Units Summary worksheet. Starting with the Units sheet, I manually adjusted the first row of formulas (Product No. 1) to refer to the appropriate cells on the supporting worksheets. This involved shifting the cell references over one cell. Therefore, the formula in cell B8 changed to

=salesA!C8+salesB!C8+salesC!C8+salesB!C8

When all the first product formulas were adjusted, I Filled Down to make these cell reference changes effective throughout the entire worksheet. Then I changed the worksheet title and selected Save As from the File menu to rename the worksheet to "Dollars Summary."

☰ Linked Expandability

By keeping all these elements separate, I now am free to quickly develop other analytical worksheets, because I need only relevant worksheets open that affect the results I'm after. For example, I created a series of worksheets to calculate how well each sales territory is producing on a month-by-month basis.

 File   Edit   Formula   Format   Data   Options   Macro   Window

| D8 | | =C8/B8 |

Percent of Plan A

	A	B	C	D	E	F
1	Aug-28-85					
2				Salesperson A		
3				Actual vs. Forecast Dollars		
4						
5						
6			January			February
7	Product Number	Forecast	Actual	% of Plan	Forecast	Actual
8	1	$3,900	$4,000	103%	$0	
9	2	$4,780	$3,455	72%	$0	
10	3	$765	$600	78%	$0	
11	4	$898	$483	54%	$0	
12	5	$1,360	$1,200	88%	$0	
13	6	$1,161	$1,439	124%	$0	
14	7	$2,490	$2,809	113%	$0	
15	8	$3,795	$4,002	105%	$0	
16	9	$432	$734	170%	$0	
17	10	$356	$511	144%	$0	
18	11	$1,155	$953	83%	$0	
19	12	$688	$700	102%	$0	
20	13	$2,839	$2,955	104%	$0	

This analyzes each product's dollars forecast with actual dollars shipped in a given month. The worksheet calculates the percentage of the forecast met by the salesperson (a sales manager might use figures such as these to calculate bonuses). Because the Percent of Plan for one territory relies on only one sales forecast worksheet, you won't have to load in large, time-consuming worksheets when you enter the actual sales for that territory.

CHARTING LINKED WORKSHEETS

Even though the overall system of territorial and summary worksheets appears somewhat scattered, it still is possible to join any combination of worksheets into a chart if you need to graph the relationships of data in separate worksheets.

Let's take an example from the system built so far in this chapter. I'll assume that five of the products in the list are in a particular category, such as Deluxe Sprockets. To make a particular point about the participation of each territory to the forecasted unit sales of these five products in the month of January, I want to chart the figures from each of the territory worksheets into a stacked bar chart.

One way to do this would be to create an intermediate worksheet that draws the figures from the four worksheets and in turn becomes the basis for the chart. This seems like an extra step to me, however.

The way I did it was to create the chart directly from the four worksheets. First, I opened the four worksheets. Starting with Salesperson A, I typed an identifying mark, such as "Sales A," in cell B7—a mark that will be used by the charting routine as a legend label. Then I opened a new chart and selected the stacked bar chart (bar chart style number 3) from the Gallery menu.

With only one series charted into the bar chart, the text typed into cell B7 temporarily becomes the title of the chart. That will change in a moment. In each of the succeeding territory worksheets, I labeled cells B7 accordingly, selected cells B7:B12, selected Copy from the Edit menu, switched to the chart window, and selected Paste from the Edit menu. As I pasted each series into the chart, it was added to the stacked chart.

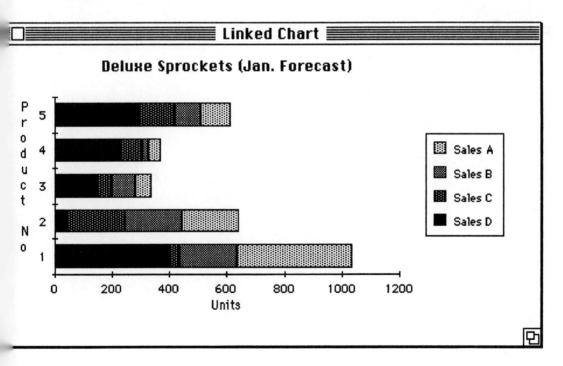

Excel assigns the black pattern to the first series of a plot. In a vertical legend, therefore, the first series appears at the bottom, which might not be the order you expect. For example, by following my directions above, the legend for Sales A would be at the bottom of the legend box. You can select each of the series by clicking on one of the patterns in the chart and editing the last digit in the formula showing in the formula bar. That number indicates the order in which the series is plotted. Change the numbers as you see fit.

Fortunately in Excel, you are not arbitrarily limited in the number of windows you can open at one time. The only limit is available memory. The smaller your files, the more of them you can have open at one time. Additionally, the more unneeded windows you can close, the faster Excel will respond when it recalculates and performs other operations on remaining windows. That's reason enough to pursue worksheet linking whenever possible.

Chapter **8**
DECISION-SUPPORT CALCULATIONS

A relatively new category of personal computer software is surfacing under the category "decision support." Unfortunately, some of the first companies to produce dedicated programs in this genre billed the products as "decision makers," as if trying to convince buyers that the computer, equipped with this new software, was going to do one of the toughest business jobs around: Making a decision. Expecting to find a decision maker on a disk, reviewers and buyers often became disenchanted with the category. Indeed, they saw right through the fact that even computerized decisions still are subjective and cannot be reduced entirely to cold, hard facts.

Still, a decision-support program can be a useful tool particularly for middle managers who must make decisions, such as which investment path to take or to which of several competing vendors should the company commit. The program will not make the decision for the manager, but it will help organize the factors involved with the decision and help everyone, including top management, visualize the process behind making a particular decision. In other words, a decision-support program is more aptly called a *decision-justification* program. With this kind of tool, anyone responsible for making a decision can readily demonstrate the reasons for a particular decision.

As an exercise of several Excel techniques, this chapter demonstrates a decision-support template, which can be used faithfully just like dedicated decision-support programs. It may not have quite the depth, but the principles should be clear enough that you could pursue development of a more sophisticated model if desired. At the end of the chapter, you'll learn about some suggestions for further development.

Among the techniques you'll see include an important one in the macro department. You'll see how command macros can be designed to control the flow of a program. In this case, command macros lead the user from screen to screen in a logical order. You might say that the macros supply the script for an extensive production of a series of screens. At the same time, instructions on the screen prevent the user from forgetting what to do next—something that can happen often in an unplanned template. Putting instructions on the screen is helpful, of course, if someone other than the template creator will be entering data into the worksheet. But sometimes even the creator doesn't work with a template often enough, and the macro commands are easily forgotten. So put those reminders up on the screen for yourself—it will save you time later.

Also in this exercise, you'll see how the TRANSPOSE function can be a critical one when you are trying to convert a table of logically oriented figures into figures that Excel's graphing routine like. And last but not least, the macro printing commands will be given a workout.

HOW DECISION SUPPORT WORKS

The math behind a decision-support process is not so complex as it may seem at first. The underlying calculation is the weighting of the factors that influence a decision. For example, if you are deciding among three stereo systems, the factors you would weigh might be such things as sound quality, cosmetics, expandability for things such as tape decks and compact disc players, speaker size, and cost. Not every factor, of course, is equally important, nor would every shopper place the same emphasis on each of the factors. Someone on a tight budget would place a strong weight on the cost factor; someone in a small apartment might be more concerned with the size of the speakers than the budget; and an audiophile might place sound quality far and above all other factors. Each decision maker, therefore, places different weights on each of the factors that go into the decision process.

Next, the decision maker must rate each of the alternatives (e.g., Sony, Kenwood, McIntosh) and how well each alternative measures up to each factor. In the sound-quality factor, for example, you might rank McIntosh higher than Sony and Kenwood; but for cost, Kenwood might rank much better (less expensive) than the other two. A decision-helping model such as this is very practical because it makes you break a decision into its components, and it applies rankings and weightings (albeit subjectively judged) fairly against each other. There's no question that emotion still can play a role in influencing the outcome of a decision helper model.

And just as with fudging figures in a spreadsheet until the bottom line comes out as you want it, you can play "what-if" with the weights and rankings until the decision flows your way. But in a management situation, if a group can reach a consensus on the weights and rankings, then the calculations will apply those figures fairly.

DECISION-HELPER STRUCTURE

Because the decision helper is a model that will be reused over and over again for each decision applied to it, the original, blank model must be filled in and saved with a different name. In that way, you can start up the decision model each time and not have to worry about clearing away old data. To simplify the entry of data into the decision-helper model, the example procedure is divided into four entry screens.

Cell and Range Names

Table 8.1 shows the cell and range names used in the worksheets and macros in this chapter.

TABLE 8.1

Decision Form	
alt. rank	$B$67:$B$71,$C$67:$C$71, $D$67:$D$71,$E$67:$E$71, $F$67:$F$71
Alternate__1	$C$28
Alternate__2	$C$29
Alternate__3	$C$30
Alternate__4	$C$31
Alternate__5	$C$32
begin	$C$8,$C$8
Compare	$A$107:$F$112
cweight.1	$B$91
cweight.2	$C$91
cweight.3	$D$91
cweight.4	$E$91
cweight.5	$F$91
Decision	$A$99:$B$103
Decision__Name	$C$8
Enter.Weight	$C$47:$C$51,$D$47:$D$51
Factor__1	$C$47
Factor__2	$C$48
Factor__3	$C$49
Factor__4	$C$50
Factor__5	$C$51
Rank1.1	$B$67
Rank1.2	$B$68
Rank1.3	$B$69
Rank1.4	$B$70
Rank1.5	$B$71
Rank2.1	$C$67
Rank2.2	$C$68
Rank2.3	$C$69
Rank2.4	$C$70
Rank2.5	$C$71

Rank3.1	$D$67
Rank3.2	$D$68
Rank3.3	$D$69
Rank3.4	$D$70
Rank3.5	$D$71
Rank4.1	$E$67
Rank4.2	$E$68
Rank4.3	$E$69
Rank4.4	$E$70
Rank4.5	$E$71
Rank5.1	$F$67
Rank5.2	$F$68
Rank5.3	$F$69
Rank5.4	$F$70
Rank5.5	$F$71
sum	$G$91
sum.1	$B$90
sum.2	$C$90
sum.3	$D$90
sum.4	$E$90
sum.5	$F$90
weight__1	$D$47
weight__2	$D$48
weight__3	$D$49
weight__4	$D$50
weight__5	$D$51
M/Decisions	
end	$E$11
loop	$E43
print	$E$1
to.a	$A$1
to.b	$B$1
to.c	$C$1
to.graph	$D$1

☰ Entry Screens

The first screen has only one input area, where the name of the decision is typed.

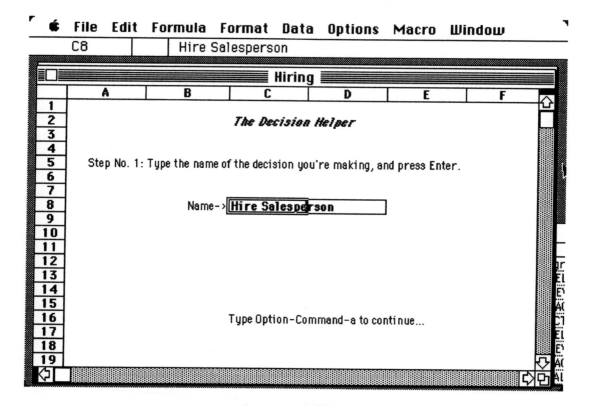

Two adjacent cells are given a border so that the two together look like one double-wide cell. Unfortunately, other pages, below, need the standard column width, so it was not feasible to adjust the column width for this screen. With the leftmost cell of the pair, cell C8, selected, any text that runs over the right edge will automatically bleed into cell D8. Cell C8 is defined as Decision_Name (the default name), because the contents of this cell will be used later in the model.

As the prototype model was tested, I discovered that it's a natural reflect to press the Return key after typing a name into cell C8. When Return is pressed, however, the cell cursor advanced down to cell C9, making the page look odd and sloppily designed. But by selecting cell C8, holding down the Command key, and selecting C8 a second time, the cell cursor will stay on cell C8, even if the Return or Tab keys are pressed after typing a name. By saving the blank model with this selection, the first screen always will behave as planned, provided the macros that operate the flow of the program automatically force you to assign a new name to the model once you enter data into it.

In the second screen, you are prompted for a list of alternatives.

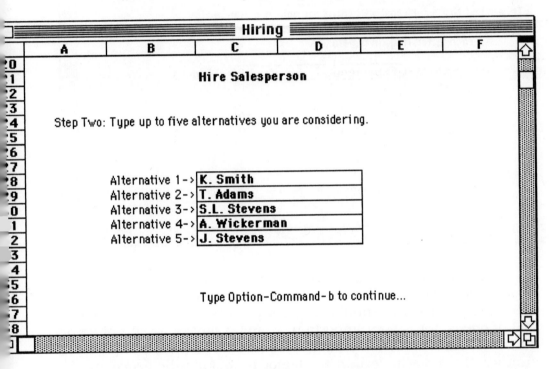

These are the choices you would consider, such as a list of the names of people you're considering for a job. As with all listings in this model, you needn't enter data in every blank. If a particular decision has only three options, leave Alternatives 4 and 5 blank in this screen. As with the name field in the first screen, the alternative fields are comprised of dual fields in columns C and D, although data is entered only into cells in column C.

For convenience later in the model, where these figures will be part of formulas, the individual cells in the range C28 through C32 are defined with the default names in the cells to the left (e.g., Alternative_1). Notice, too, that cell C21 contains a formula (=Decision_Name) that copies the decision name from the first screen.

More data is required in the third screen. Here you enter the factors affecting your decision and their respective weights.

```
┌─────────────────────────────── Hiring ───────────────────────────────┐
│        A          B          C          D          E          F       │
├───┬───────────────────────────────────────────────────────────────────┤
│39 │                                                                   │
│40 │                      Hire Salesperson                             │
│41 │                                                                   │
│42 │                                                                   │
│43 │   Step Three: List the factors that will influence your decision, and │
│44 │              assign a weight (from 1 to 100) to signify the importance │
│45 │              of each factor in your decision.                     │
│46 │                                                                   │
│47 │         Factor 1->│Experience          90│<-Weight 1              │
│48 │         Factor 2->│Age                 60│<-Weight 2              │
│49 │         Factor 3->│Relocation          70│<-Weight 3              │
│50 │         Factor 4->│References          40│<-Weight 4              │
│51 │         Factor 5->│Appearance          45│<-Weight 5              │
│52 │                                                                   │
│53 │                                                                   │
│54 │                                                                   │
│55 │             Type Option-Command-c to continue...                  │
│56 │                                                                   │
│57 │                                                                   │
└───┴───────────────────────────────────────────────────────────────────┘
```

Again, you don't have to fill in all five factors if there are fewer for a particular decision. Values you assign to weights need not add up to 100. In fact, you should consider each factor on a scale of 1 to 100. If one factor is very important, it might have a weight of 85 or 90; if another is moderately important, it could be 50. The higher the number, the more important the factor in making the decision.

The fourth and last input screen asks for the most data.

```
┌─────────────────────── Hiring ───────────────────────┐
│      A    │    B    │    C    │    D    │    E    │    F    │
```

Hire Salesperson

Step Four: On a scale of 1 to 100, rank each alternative's performance
          in each factor.

	Experience	Age	Relocation	References	Appearance
K. Smith	70	60	50	40	50
T. Adams	20	95	100	50	85
S.L. Stevens	45	45	60	80	60
A. Wickerman	85	30	60	95	35
J. Stevens	50	50	20	50	50

Type Option-Command-d to view results...

Formulas in this screen copy the alternative and factor names from the previous screens and build a matrix of cells with these names as headings. Into the data cells go a ranking, again on independent scales of 1 to 100, of how well each alternative measures for a particular factor.

For example, if one of the alternatives in a job-hiring decision has 30 years experience in a similar job, you probably would rank the Experience factor something like 90 or 95; the Age factor, however, might be a 30 or 35 because benefits costs (particularly insurance) will be higher. With so many cells to fill out on this screen, it is important to have the macro select the cells by column so that each press of Enter or Return advances down each column. This makes it easier to establish a consistent ranking of a given factor for all alternatives you're considering.

From the fourth screen, the program flows immediately to the presentation of graphic representations of the results. But there is a lot more to this model that goes on out of sight.

☰ Calculation Areas

In the screen beginning at row 77, most of the weighting and ranking calculations take place. The matrix is organized just like the one in the previous screen, with alternatives down the left column and factors across the top row.

	A	B	C	D	E	F
			Hire Salesperson			
82		Experience	Age	Relocation	References	Appearance
83	K. Smith	20.66	11.80	11.48	5.25	7.38
84	T. Adams	5.90	18.69	22.95	6.56	12.54
85	S.L. Stevens	13.28	8.85	13.77	10.49	8.85
86	A. Wickerman	25.08	5.90	13.77	12.46	5.16
87	J. Stevens	14.75	9.84	4.59	6.56	7.38
90	Rank Totals:	270	280	290	315	280
91	Weight:	29.51	19.67	22.95	13.11	14.75

The math here is a calculation of relative weights of the values with respect to their totals. Look at the formula in cell B83.

=Rank1.1/sum.1*100

To understand what's going on here, you should know that each of the ranking cells in screen 4 is defined as "Rank" plus the relative location in the matrix. Rank1.1 is the definition for the cell in column 1, row 1 of the matrix; Rank2.1 is the cell in the second column, first row; and so on. Sum.1 is the name given to cell B90, whose formula is the sum of all the first column rankings in screen four.

In other words, the formula shown above is dividing the individual ranking for K. Smith's Experience by the total of all Experience rankings and multiplying that result by 100 for convenience in working with larger numbers. What you see in the column of Experience figures, then, is the relative performance of each applicant against the others. These figures will be graphed later.

Another important calculation series in this screen takes place in row 91. To the right of the screen, in cell G91, is a cell, defined as "sum," which is the sum of all weightings of factors in screen 3. A formula in cell B91 performs the same kind of comparative weighting calculation as the rankings above. The formula reads

Weight___1/sum*100

and divides the actual weight assigned to the Experience factor (in screen 3) by the sum of all factor weights.

Across row 91, therefore, you have the comparative weights of each of the factors applicable to this decision. Each of these cells (B91 through F91) is defined by the name "cweightX," where "X" is the number of the factor. Cell B91 is defined as "cweight1."

The final calculations are performed in column G, where the relative weights of each factor are applied to the relative rankings of each alternative.

	File	Edit	Formula	Format	Data	Options	Macro	Window

G83		=SUM(B83:F83)

Hiring

	E	F	G	H	I	J
77						
78						
79						
80						
81						
82	References	Appearance	Total			
83	5.25	7.38	56.56			
84	6.56	12.54	66.64			
85	10.49	8.85	55.25			
86	12.46	5.16	62.38			
87	6.56	7.38	43.11			
88						
89						
90	315	280				
91	13.11	14.75	305			
92						
93						
94						

The formulas look complex, but they simply multiply the rankings (from screen 4) by the weighting (row 91) and add up the results.

▤ TRANSPOSING

But now the trick is to put all this data into a form that Excel can readily graph, especially from as simple a macro as possible. For one graph, all you need is to bring together the alternative names with the final weighted results so they can be selected in one move prior to issuing the command for a new chart. That can be done in the final worksheet.

 ⌘ File   Edit   Formula   Format   Data   Options   Macro   Window

A107		{=TRANSPOSE(A82:F87)}

≡ Hiring ≡

	A	B	C	D	E	F
96						
97						
98	Decision Chart Data:					
99	K. Smith	56.56				
100	T. Adams	66.64				
101	S.L. Stevens	55.25				
102	A. Wickerman	62.38				
103	J. Stevens	43.11				
104						
105						
106	Comparison Chart Data:					
107		K. Smith	T. Adams	S.L. Stevens	A. Wickerman	J. Stevens
108	Experience	20.66	5.90	13.28	25.08	14.75
109	Age	11.80	18.69	8.85	5.90	9.84
110	Relocation	11.48	22.95	13.77	13.77	4.59
111	References	5.25	6.56	10.49	12.46	6.56
112	Appearance	7.38	12.54	8.85	5.16	7.38
113						

These figures will be plotted in a Decision Chart. The specific numbers are not important to the decision process, but their positions relative to each other are.

To plot the comparison data—how much each factor contributes to the results of each alternative—Excel would not correctly plot the figures as presented in the matrix in the previous screen. The rows and columns had to be transposed so that the alternative names are the ones plotted along the horizontal axis.

The most automatic way to accomplish this (that is, other than doing cell-by-cell formulas such as =B91) is to call on Excel's TRANS-POSE function. First select a range of cells (beginning at cell A107) that is the same dimension as the matrix you need to transpose—simple enough in this case because the original and transposed cell ranges are both a six-by-six cell block. Had the original block been seven cells across and six cells deep, the selected range for the transposed block would have had to be six cells wide and seven cells deep.

Next, with cell A107 the active cell in the new range, type the formula

=TRANSPOSE(A82:F87)

which tells Excel to fetch the data in the range A82:F87 and transposes it in the currently selected range. Because this is an array function, hold down the Command key while pressing Enter. In the formula bar, the formula is surrounded by braces. The transposed range is dynamically linked to the original matrix, so any change to the original is instantly updated in the transposed region.

That's all there is to the worksheet part of this model. But it's the macros that bring the creature to life.

DECISION MACROS

You probably noticed that in the Decision-Helper screens requesting input, help lines at the bottom of each screen indicated the macro keystrokes required to continue to the next screen or view the results. The four macros were labeled Option-Command-a, -b, -c, and -d to give some logic to the progression. Let's look closely at each macro.

The first, called "to.a," does more than simply proceed to the next screen. It also performs some necessary housekeeping to keep you on track and prevent you from accidentally destroying the blank Decision-Helper template.

	A
1	to.a
2	=PAGE.SETUP("","",,,,,FALSE,FALSE)
3	=SAVE.AS?()
4	=SELECT(!A24)
5	=SELECT(!C28:C32)
6	=RETURN()
7	

First, the macro issues a page setup command to remove the default page header and page number strings that Excel automatically adds to each new worksheet. A standard page header with the file name is not necessary because each screen contains a boldfaced heading with the name of the decision you type in screen 1.

Default margin settings are fine for these pages, so they are not changed (no values are inserted in the left, right, top, and bottom arguments, but the commas must still be typed into the formula).

Gridlines and row/column numbers need not be printed because I've set up the screens to stand alone without gridlines. Consequently, those arguments in the PAGE.SETUP function are set to FALSE (or zero).

Next, the macro forces the Save As screen to appear, prompting you to assign a new name for the file and save it to disk. By doing this early in the game, you are less likely to press Command-S to save your decision data to the file that should forever remain a blank template.

The last commands in the macro select cell A24 in the main worksheet and then a range of cells in screen 2 comprising the next input series. Selecting cell A24 automatically centers the screen where it should be displayed. It seems that when a macro selects a cell down column A, that cell is positioned at the fourth row from the top. This admittedly crude method of scrolling from screen to screen is used rather than the VPAGE function because you may want to go back to a specific screen by typing the appropriate macro command. If, instead of selecting A24, the macro performed a VPAGE(1)—scrolling the screen vertically one page—then you would not be able to use the macro to jump from screen 4 to screen 2 because the VPAGE function would scroll to the area below screen 4. When the macro selects cell A24, it is highlighted for a brief instant before the input cells are selected.

Macros to.b and to.c are simple extensions of to.a. They select the appropriate cell in the A column, the fourth row from the top of the desired screen, and then select the input cells.

```
┌─────────────────────────────────────┐
│ ▤□▤▤▤ M/Decisions ▤▤▤▤▤              │
├───┬─────────────────────────────┬───┤
│   │            B                │ ⇧ │
├───┼─────────────────────────────┼───┤
│ 1 │ to.b                        │   │
├───┼─────────────────────────────┤   │
│ 2 │ =SELECT(!A43)               │ ■ │
├───┼─────────────────────────────┤   │
│ 3 │ =SELECT(!Factor.Weight)     │   │
├───┼─────────────────────────────┤   │
│ 4 │ =RETURN()                   │   │
├───┼─────────────────────────────┤   │
│ 5 │                             │   │
├───┼─────────────────────────────┤   │
│ 6 │                             │   │
├───┼─────────────────────────────┤   │
│ 7 │                             │   │
├───┼─────────────────────────────┤   │
│ 8 │                             │ ⇩ │
├───┴─────────────────────────────┴───┤
│ ⇦ │     ░░░░░░░░░░░░░░░░░░░  │ ⇨ │ ⬚ │
└─────────────────────────────────────┘
```

Notice that the input cell ranges have been defined by names. For each range, you must define cells in the order that you want the active cursor to move in. For example, in screen 3, it was more logical to type in the names of all the factors before assigning weights to them. Therefore, you should select cells C47:C51, hold down the Command button, and select cells D47:D51 before defining the range with the name Factor.Weight. In this way, the active cell cursor moves down the C column as you enter factor names, then jumps to the top of the range's D column for entry of weights. Similarly, in screen 4, each column was selected while holding down the Command button before defining the range with the name Alt.Rank. Should you find it more convenient to enter the values in a different order, you can reselect the cells in that order and redefine the range with the Define Name command in the Formula menu.

GRAPHING MACROS

The macro that displays the graphic results of the calculations is more involved and presents quite a show on the screen. And yet all it's doing is the kind of operations you normally would do with the mouse to make a couple of charts from the data in the worksheet.

	D
1	to.graph
2	=SELECT(!Decision)
3	=NEW(2)
4	=PAGE.SETUP("","",,,,,)
5	=ACTIVATE.NEXT()
6	=SELECT(!compare)
7	=NEW(2)
8	=PAGE.SETUP("","",,,,,)
9	=GALLERY.COLUMN(3)
10	=LEGEND(1)
11	=MOVE(246,162)
12	=ACTIVATE.PREV()
13	=MESSAGE(1,"Type Option-Command-p to print results")
14	=RETURN()
15	
16	
17	
18	
19	
20	

Here's what's going on in the macro:

- First, it selects the range of cells in the worksheet containing the Decision Chart Data (A99:B103), which was previously defined as "Decision."
- Then it opens a new chart window.
- That window is adjusted by the PAGE.SETUP command to print with all default settings except for blank headers and footers (you can manually adjust this later prior to printing, if you like). This action displays the data as a small column chart at the upper-left corner of the screen.
- Next, the original worksheet is reactivated (ACTIVATE.NEXT), and the transposed range of cells, which had been defined as "compare," is selected.
- A new chart window is opened, and the PAGE.SETUP command is given to this new window to eliminate headers and footers.

For this chart, however, the results should be displayed as a stacked column chart, which is selection 3 in the Column gallery, as performed by the macro in macro cell D9. A legend is added by passing a TRUE or nonzero argument to the LEGEND function in D10. To make the second chart more readily visible on the screen, the macro moves it to the lower-left corner of the screen and then activates the previous window, the first chart. Finally, user instructions on how to print the results are placed in the message bar at the top of the screen. This message will stay there until you invoke the Option-Command-p print macro, at which time, the message argument is reset to FALSE or zero.

At this step in the model, you can view either chart and play "what-if" with any of the values in any previous screen. If you remember the macro command for a particular screen, use it. If not, scroll up to it with the scroll bar. This also would be a good time to save the data in the worksheet. It's not necessary to save the charts unless you go into them and modify them with titles, arrows, and other embellishments for printing later.

PAGE BREAKS

Before printing the results for the first time, it's critical to assign page breaks to this model. You probably will want to print each screen on a separate page to keep the printout organized. Setting page breaks in Excel might not be entirely as intuitive as it is on some other Macintosh spreadsheet programs, but it really isn't all that difficult.

For example, suppose you want to make the first screen a single page. To do that, you need to place a page break between columns F and G and between rows 19 and 20. Select cell G20, which is just below and to the right of the lower-right corner of the desired page. Then choose Set Page Break from the Options menu.

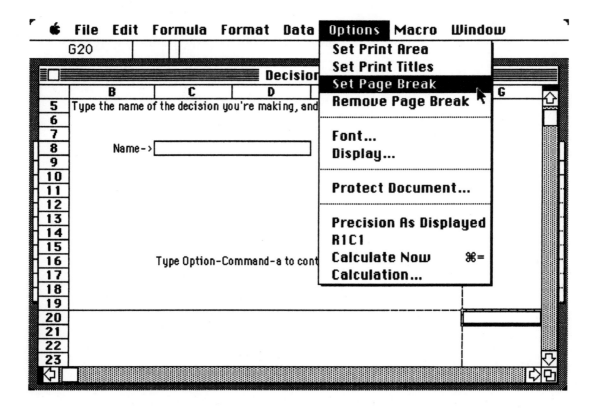

Repeat this for the rest of the pages to be printed.

An alternative to printing each screen in its entirety—which includes the instruction lines—is to create another area on the worksheet that duplicates the important matrixes in an area compact enough to be printed on a single page. For inclusion in a report, this might be a better printout solution.

PRINTING MACRO

All printing is handled by the print macro.

	E
1	print
2	=SET.VALUE(E4,0)
3	loop
4	=E4+1
5	=IF(E4=5,GOTO(end))
6	=INDEX(DOCUMENTS(),E4)
7	=IF(MID(E6,1,2)="M/",GOTO(loop),)
8	=ACTIVATE(E6)
9	=PRINT(2,1,4,1,1)
10	=GOTO(loop)
11	end
12	=MESSAGE(0)
13	=RETURN()
14	

Because the macro needs to print from three different documents—the worksheet and two charts—the macro contains a loop and counter to help it cycle through the available documents and make sure everything that should be printed is, in fact, printed. At the same time, the macro keeps an eye out for the macro sheet so that the macros are not printed out.

The loop counter in the macro is in cell E4. Its value is initially set to zero by the formula in macro cell E2, when the macro starts. At the beginning of the loop, the counter is incremented to one. An IF test in E5 checks to see if the counter has reached five. Because the model creates three windows plus one window for the macros, the loop should be considering no more than four windows for printing. When the counter reaches five, that means that all possible windows have been polled, and the macro should proceed to the part of the macro labeled "end."

When the value of the counter is less than five, the formula in cell E6 performs a critical operation. By combining the INDEX function with the DOCUMENTS function and using the value of the counter in E4, it is possible for this macro cell to represent the name of a currently open document. The way this works is that the DOCUMENTS function stands in for an array consisting of the names of all open documents, just like looking at the list of documents in the Window menu. When the value of the counter in E4 is one, the INDEX function looks at the list of open documents and points to the first one (the order is alphabetical). When the value in E4 equals two, the INDEX function points to the second document and so on. Hereafter, the macro can refer to the name of the document simply by referring to this macro cell number.

And so it happens in cell E7, an IF function performs a little test on the name the INDEX function points to each time through the loop. The MID function was used here to test the starting two characters of the document name. Because I like to start all macro sheets names with "M/", the macro checks for those distinguishing characters. If they're present, then that means that the INDEX is pointing to the macro sheet, and that it is not to be printed. Consequently, the macro shifts back to the beginning of the loop and increments the loop counter once more to look at the next document name.

If the document name is not the macro sheet, however, macro cell E8 activates that document's window, again by reference to the cell containing the INDEX formula. An expanded print command in cell E9 instructs Excel to print only the first four pages of the document. The reason for limiting the printing-page range is that the worksheet would come out to ten pages (half of them with very little readability). And in the case of the charts, because each is only one page, the instruction to print the first four pages is interpreted as printing only the one page, so the formula can apply equally to worksheet and chart printing. When a document is printed, the macro loops back to increment the INDEX counter and test the next candidate to see if it is to be printed.

After all applicable pages have been printed, the formula in E12 turns off the printing-instructions message.

FURTHER ENHANCEMENTS

Dedicated decision-support programs usually have multiple layers or levels of factors. You might, for example, have one major factor labeled Experience, which carries a certain weight. But within that factor might be several contributing factors, such as number of years, performance with other companies, reputation with customers, and so on, each with its own weight. It ends up resembling a numeric version of an outline. Such multiple-level decision procedures can be programmed into Excel, although much care must go into designing the screens to keep everything organized.

Even though the macros in this template automatically null the headers and footers for printed output, you still can manually invoke the Page Setup command from the File menu to type in a consistent header and page-numbering scheme so that the print macro presents a cohesive, consecutively page–numbered report.

This model also can be adapted to other weighting and ranking applications. School grades would be an excellent application, in which tests and assignments throughout the term have different weights affecting the calculations of the final course grade.

Always be on the lookout for ways to apply Excel to any work that you now do with calculator and pencil.

Chapter 9
"BOTTOM-LINE" MACROS

Often, when I'm entering or editing data on a spreadsheet, I like to see how my entries affect the total figures elsewhere on the worksheet. This is particularly true when I'm performing some "what-if" calculations—testing values here and there so the final figure comes to the one that I want. Because the Excel window typically displays no more than six columns by 19 rows (depending on the font chosen), it can be a nuisance to keep scrolling back and forth across the spreadsheet to keep an eye on both the entry points and the final figures.

Of course, Excel gives you the power to both split a worksheet into tiles as well as opening more than one window to a single spreadsheet. But usually, I forget to prepare these things before I realize I want to see the bottom figure. That's why I wrote a macro that displays that bottom-line figure whenever I want it, without any preparation at all.

VIEW.BOTTOM.LINE

The macro is called view.bottom.line, and it automatically performs some simple, but useful, functions.

	A
1	view.bottom.line
2	=SIZE(,260)
3	=NEW.WINDOW()
4	=SIZE(512,55)
5	=MOVE(1,290)
6	=SELECT(!bottom.line)
7	=COPY()
8	=ACTIVATE.NEXT()
9	=RETURN()
10	

First of all, this macro is a generic macro, that is, it can be used on any active worksheet and is not tied to any one worksheet file. Therefore, it can be added to any macro sheet as is, or it can be left as one macro in a sheet of generic macros for data entry and analysis.

Actions in this macro resize the current window to allow room for the bottom-line window to appear at the bottom of the screen. A second window to the current document is created, sized, and moved accordingly, and the cell you had previously defined as "bottom.line" is selected. Control is then restored to the original worksheet for further data entry or editing. Refer to Table 7.1 in Chapter 7 for a list of cell and range names used in the worksheets found in this chapter.

Now for the details (dimensions are given for a 9-inch Macintosh screen).

Macro cell A2 sizes the window so that the lower edge is at 260 pixels below the formula bar. Note that there is only one argument—the y-coordinate—in the SIZE function in cell A2. If you omit the first argument, the current x-coordinate of the lower-right corner is assumed. You can change this, of course, to suit your taste.

In cell A3, I summon a new window. This macro function is the same as choosing the New Window command from the Window menu. It creates a second window to the current document and numbers the windows in series. The next two macro cells size the window to be the full width of the screen and 55 pixels deep and then move it down near the bottom of the screen. Although the screen is only 342 pixels deep, the actual bottom of the new window would be below the bottom edge of the screen. This is intentional. When this second window is active, the horizontal scroll bar will be half hidden below the bottom edge, with just enough showing for easy access with the mouse in case you wish to scroll the window. But at the same time, it lowers the entire window enough so that the "bottom-line" cells will be visible without taking up much room on the screen—leaving the maximum possible for the main window.

After the second window is sized and in position, the cell defined as "bottom.line" is selected. Usually, the selected cell will appear in the second column of the smaller window. If you use this macro, be sure to include the exclamation mark in macro cell A6's reference to the bottom-line cell. This keeps the pointer on the current worksheet, rather than on the macro sheet.

Because it is sometimes hard to tell which cell is precisely the one designated as the bottom-line cell on the strip of cells showing in the second window, I wanted to find a way of highlighting the cell without changing its display parameters (which would be recorded with the worksheet the next time I saved it). To do this, I called upon Excel's habit of encircling a copied cell in a marquee until you perform another operation, such as entering values into a cell or editing existing values. Therefore, in macro cell A7, the macro issues the copy command, even though I have no intention of pasting the value anywhere.

Finally, the macro activates the primary window, from which the smaller window is derived. This function is placed here because my next action will be to edit or enter values in the main worksheet to see how those entries affect the bottom line.

File Edit Formula Format Data Options Macro Window

| B8 | | 400 |

| salesA:1 |

	A	B	C	D	E	F
1	Aug-05-85					
2				Salesperson A		
3			1986 Forecast -- Shipments and Billings			
4						
5			January		February	
6			Units	Dollars	Units	Dollars	Units
7	Product Number	Sales A				
8	1		400	$3,900		$0
9	2		200	$4,780		$0
10	3		60	$765		$0
11	4		45	$898		$0
12	5		105	$1,360		$0
13	6		60	$1,161		$0
14	7		200	$2,490		$0
15	8		95	$3,795		$0
16	9		80	$432		$0

	Y	Z	AA	AB	AC	AD	AE
34	$0		2560	$3,968			
35							

If you have many windows open, however, the ACTIVATE.NEXT formula may bring the wrong window to the forefront or accidently cover up the new, smaller window with an earlier window. You'll have to keep an eye out for this and try to keep only one bottom-line window open at a time.

MOVING BOTTOM LINE

Now it's likely that when you're playing "what-if" on a spreadsheet, you'll want to look at different bottom-line figures at different times.

For example, in the sales forecasts demonstrated in Chapter 7, you may want to view one month's totals while entering the initial forecast unit values, but then watch the annual totals for each product when massaging the figures prior to submitting them to the boss. In these cases, you need to be able to change the cell that becomes the bottom-line cell showing in the bottom-line window at the bottom of the screen. A short macro, called set.bottom.line, does that quite nicely.

	B
1	set.bottom.line
2	=DEFINE.NAME("bottom.line",SELECTION())
3	=RETURN()
4	

All you do to use this macro is to select the cell you wish to be known as "bottom.line" and issue the macro command, perferably from a keyboard equivalent (I use Option-Command-b for this one, and Option-Command-v for view.bottom.line). In one stroke, the cell is defined as "bottom.line," ready to be selected inside the view.bottom.line macro.

QUICK-VIEW MACRO

Another kind of flexibility you may want is a completely variable way of jumping from viewing one cell to another and back again. With the set.jump and jump macros, you can have the same powers with Excel (the long formula in cell B2 is displayed in full in the formula bar).

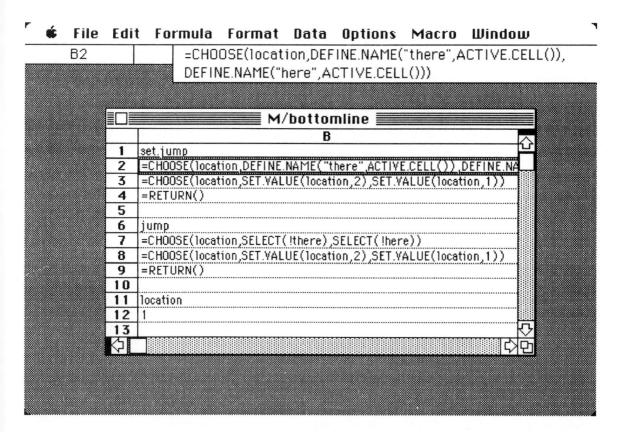

Set.jump alternates between defining cells with the names "here" and "there." In other words, the first time you invoke the set.jump macro, it defines the selected cell as "here." Select another cell and invoke the set.jump macro again, and the second cell is defined as "there." From that point on, the jump macro toggles between cells "here" and "there" each time you issue that macro command. The mechanics of these macros are as follows.

A macro cell at B1 is defined with the name "location." This cell acts as a counter to indicate whether the last invocation of either the jump or set.jump macro was at "here" (the value 1) or "there" (the value 2). In set.jump, the first CHOOSE formula uses the number in "location" to select whether the active cell should be defined as "here" or "there": When the last action had to do with "here," the next cell is defined as "there" and vice versa.

Similarly, the value of "location" is toggled by the second CHOOSE formula in set.jump. When "location" starts out with the value 1, it is changed to the value 2 and vice versa.

In the jump macro, the CHOOSE formulas behave the same way they do in set.jump except that the actions select the cells defined as "here" and "there" depending on the last value set in "location." When "there" is selected, the value of "location" is changed to 2, indicating that "there" was the last cell jumped to.

This probably sounds very confusing. I suggest you type in these macros and try them out. Be sure to define cell B11 as "location" and place the value 2 in that cell before trying the macros. The value there "primes the pump" so the first cell you set will be defined as "here."

To use these macros:

1   Select one cell on a worksheet, issue the set.jump macro.
2   Select another cell and issue set.jump again.
3   Issue the jump macro repeatedly and watch the cell cursor jump between the two cells you set.
4   Set a third cell and watch the cursor jump between the second and third cells you set.

I've found both the bottom-line and jump macros to be valuable tools in data entry and analysis. They are small enough to be added to any generic or specific macro sheets that you keep in the background of your worksheet systems.

Chapter **10**
FORECASTING WITH GRAPHICS

Using the Past
A Forecast Model
Graphing the Future

We'd all love to have a crystal ball to ease the pain of creating forecasts. As much as we'd like Excel or any other software do the detailed forecasting job often required in business, no computer can know all the vagaries of your business or predict when factors outside of mathematical models are going to make mincemeat out of a forecast. But we can use Excel to provide a solid starting point.

USING THE PAST

One popular method of preparing a forecast is to extrapolate the future from historical figures. If history can produce a noticeable trend, then there often is a strong likelihood that under the same conditions, the trend will continue.

One tool that applies this theory is called a trend line (also called a line of regression). A trend line looks at a series of figures and establishes a straight line representing the smoothed figures over the range. Therefore, even if sales for a year experience seasonal ups and downs, a plain trend line analysis will show a straight line. If the line slopes upward (from left to right), then the overall trend through that period is positive, showing growth. If the slope is negative, so is growth.

With this kind of historical trend line, the future can be extrapolated by simply continuing the line further to the right. As you can imagine, there are inherent hazards in this method of forecasting, particularly if you attempt to rely on the trend line forecast to schedule staffing, inventory, production, and so on.

More sophisticated statistical models are available, fortunately, that allow you to account for seasonality in a forecast. That's beyond the scope of this book, so I'll stick with a simple trend line extrapolation. Even though there are pitfalls to this kind of forecast, the trend line can be useful in forecasting the future of certain statistics. Slowly changing numbers, such as a country's census data, offer plenty of history for a reliable trend line, and any forecast drawn from that data won't necessarily have immediate, disruptive impact on the focus of the project you're planning. And yet the data can be an important supportive element to a presentation or thesis.

A FORECAST MODEL

For the demonstration in this chapter, I will be using a manufacturing production example. While I would not use such a model as a reliable forecasting tool to produce a finished forecast, it still could play a role in providing a jumping-off spot for some serious number fudging.

The example takes a year's worth of monthly historical output from a manufacturing plant, from January through December of 1985.

	A	B	C	D	E	F
			Forecast			
1			Production Trends and Forecast--Albuquerque Plant			
2						
3			Factory			
4			Production (units)	Forecast		
5	1985	J	10305			
6		F	11366			
7		M	9440			
8		A	10500			
9		M	12900			
10		J	11620			
11		J	8999			
12		A	10670			
13		S	13800			
14		O	15900			
15		N	15600			
16		D	13570			
17	1986	J		14929.2424		
18		F		15371.3054		
19		M		15813.3683		

Production is listed in units. Months are listed only by their first letters because the final column chart will be displaying historical tick marks for the 12-month history and 6-month forecast, so horizontal space is best served by keeping month indicators to single letters. As you can see from the horizontal production figures, the numbers go up and down with the seasons and vacation periods. Even after graphing these figures by themselves, it may be difficult to perceive a significant trend, much less a factor to use for forecasting the future.

To forecast the first six months of 1986, I used a formula suggested in the Excel manual. In cell D17, the formula reads

$$\{=SUM(LINEST(\$C\$5{:}\$C\$16)*\{13,1\})\}$$

which extrapolates the line of regression from the range of historical cells (C5:C16) and applies the formula to the "thirteenth" month on the line—the first month of the forecast period. Note that the formula is surrounded by braces, indicating that this is an array function and that the Command key must be held down when pressing Enter or clicking the Enter box on the formula bar after typing this formula.

Formulas for each of the remaining five cells are identical except for the number of the extrapolated month, which must relate to the historical series (13th, 14th, etc.). The results are shown below.

	A	B	C	D	E	F
10		J	11620			
11		J	8999			
12		A	10670			
13		S	13800			
14		O	15900			
15		N	15600			
16		D	13570			
17	1986	J		14929.2424		
18		F		15371.3054		
19		M		15813.3683		
20		A		16255.4312		
21		M		16697.4942		
22		J		17139.5571		
23						
24						
25						
26						
27						
28						

Pay particular attention to the organization of the two columns of figures. The history and forecast are entered in two different columns. That's because they must be plotted separately if you want the forecast columns to have a different pattern than the historical columns.

But note also that by setting up the two groups this way, a line chart will be out of the question. When you select the entire range to be charted (B5:D22), the values in the blank cells will be interpreted as being zeros. A line chart will graph those values as zeros, complete with a line running from 13570 in December to 0 in January—a false plot of what the graph is attempting to show. But by graphing as a column chart, the zero values, although plotted, don't show up because they're too small.

GRAPHING THE FUTURE

Selecting the range and calling a new chart brings up the default column chart of the history and forecast values. Adding a legend (from the Chart menu) makes the meaning of the chart clear.

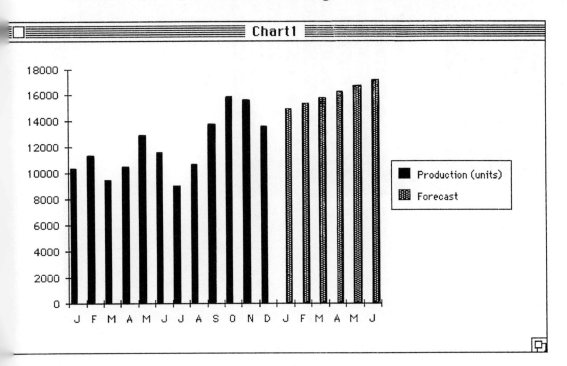

Notice that because this is the default column chart, the historical and forecast columns are off-center. That's because Excel actually is plotting the zero values. They're plotted as zero height columns to the right of the history columns and to the left of the forecast columns. This actually has a nice touch to it in that it further sets history apart from forecast (in addition to the different patterns). But if you want to see broader columns, select the stacked column chart (column gallery selection three) in which the zero values are plotted atop the visible columns.

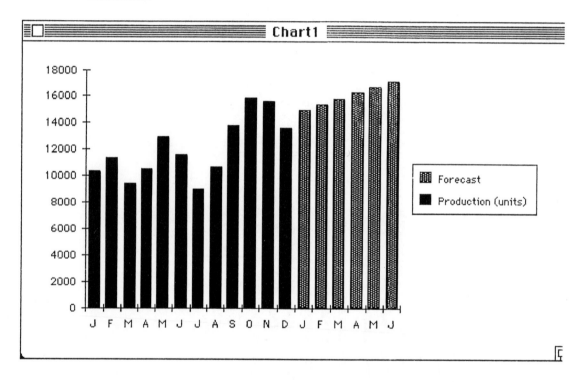

To this chart, you probably would want to add some legend text and title, as well as a possible text comment and arrow somewhere near the forecast columns to drive home a particular point.

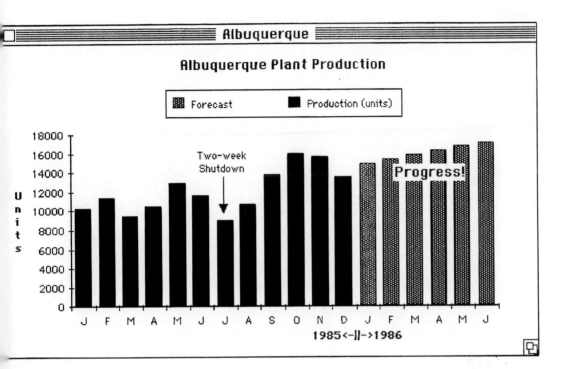

In the next chapter, I'll show you another way to use graphics effectively in calculating and visualizing the break-even point for a product or business.

Chapter **11**
GRAPHIC BREAK-EVEN ANALYSES

The Model
Graphing Matrix
Break-Even Macros

A most helpful number to know when you're in the business of supplying a product is how many units you need to produce in a given period before you start producing a profit. The point at which the product starts making money is called the break-even point.

What makes this calculation not so easy to visualize by a seat-of-the-pants estimate is that the costs attributed to producing a product include both fixed costs (overhead expense items such as rent, utilities, and administrative costs that must be paid even if there are no sales) and variable costs (expenses, such as labor and materials, that increase with the amount shipped to customers).

To establish the proper cost of a product, the fixed and variable costs must be considered jointly. At some point, the gross profit from sales will be greater than the total of fixed and variable costs. The net is net income—the stuff that goes to the bank.

A break-even analysis is most revealing when you plot the lines representing total costs and selling price against a range of product quantities sold. Where the lines cross is your break-even point. That's what I will demonstrate in this chapter. The model is indeed a simplified version, but it can be readily adapted if your business has special cost factors.

THE MODEL

Refer to Table 11.1 for a list of cell and range names used in the models in this chapter. The main screen of the break-even analysis consists of many input cells into which key factors are entered.

Table 11.1

Break-even Form	
Break-Even__Units	$E$4
Fixed	$B$3,$B$4,$B$5,$B$8,$B$9, $B$10,$B$11,$B$12,$B$13, $B$14,$B$15,$B$16,$B$17, $E$8,$E$9,$E$10
percent	$B$4
scale	$B$23:$B$33
selling__price	$B$5
table	$B$22:$B$33
Variable	$E$11

M/Break-even
  cpoint $A$24
  graph.table $A$1
  raw $A$24
  start $B$1
  step $A$21

** File Edit Formula Format Data Options Macro Window**

B3		Boola Boola Hoop			

Breakeven

	A	B	C	D	E	F
1				*Break-Even Analysis*		
2						
3	Product Name	Boola Boola Hoop				
4	% of Total Sales	100%		Break-Even Units->	483	
5	Selling Price	$8.95				
6						
7	Fixed Costs:			Variable Costs:		
8	Rent	$750		Labor	$0.35	
9	Electricity	$90		Materials	$0.75	
0	Gas			Commissions	$0.10	
1	Water	$20		Total	$1.20	
2	Telephone	$105				
3	Insurance	$75				
4	Office Expense	$60				
5	Advertising	$1,490				
6	Admin. Labor	$1,100				
7	Miscellaneous	$50				
8	Total	$3,740				
9				Type Option-Command-g to graph results...		
0						

A cell for the product name is provided. In case the analysis is being performed on one product from a line of several, there is also a cell to input the percentage of the total business one product of a line represents (or should represent in the case of a new company or product). This factor is important because fixed costs should be distributed proportionally to each product in a line of products. The selling price is the amount customers pay for the product. From this number will be subtracted cost factors to arrive at a gross profit figure.

Next in the screen is a long series of fixed cost factors. These are the items that have to be paid regardless of the quantity of products sold. A convenient time frame for these costs is monthly. Whatever time frame you select for these costs, the break-even number will apply to the same time frame. In other words, if you enter monthly fixed costs in these cells, the break-even point will be calculated based on a month's sales.

Variable costs are listed to the right of fixed costs. In this category are expenses that go into each unit sold to a customer. That includes not only labor and materials, but sales commissions if you pay commissions to salespeople. Commissions are variable costs because the dollars increase or decrease with the number of products sold.

To simplify the calculation of the break-even point, I defined each of the key cells with readily identifiable names. Cell B4 is called "percent," while cell B5 is "Selling__Price," which was the default name supplied by Excel when I selected Define Name from the Formula menu (with cell B5 selected). The total fixed-costs cell is called "Fixed" and the total variable-costs cell is "Variable." The formula, then, for the break-even cell, E4, is

$$=(Fixed*percent)/(Selling\_Price-Variable)$$

which is derived from a common business formula for calculating the break-even point.

Even without carrying this model any further, you already have a powerful tool in evaluating the impact on the break-even point of such business decisions as price changes, the increased cost of labor or materials, and the adjustment of any cost factor. You'd be amazed at how much "what-if" playing you'll do with this model if you're concerned with establishing a break-even point.

GRAPHING MATRIX

Below the simple form is the range of cells that gets graphed.

** File Edit Formula Format Data Options Macro Window**

| D23 | | =(Fixed*percent)+(Variable*B23) | | | |

Breakeven

	A	B	C	D	E	F
21						
22			Selling Price	Total Costs		
23		0	$0	$3,740		
24		100	$895	$3,860		
25		200	$1,790	$3,980		
26		300	$2,685	$4,100		
27		400	$3,580	$4,220		
28		500	$4,475	$4,340		
29		600	$5,370	$4,460		
30		700	$6,265	$4,580		
31		800	$7,160	$4,700		
32		900	$8,055	$4,820		
33		1000	$8,950	$4,940		
34						
35						
36						
37						
38						
39						
40						

Because the graph will be charting the relationships of selling price to total costs, I needed to prepare this matrix. Values in the B column of this matrix represent the number of products sold. The range of these numbers, as you'll see in a moment, is calculated by a macro to accommodate a variety of combinations. The selling price at each graph point is simply the selling price (from the Selling__Price cell in the form) multiplied by the number of products in the corresponding B-column cell in the same row. Therefore, the formula in cell C23 is

=Selling__Price*B23

Total costs consist of the fixed costs multiplied by the percent of total sales, plus the variable costs multiplied by the number of products. The formula for cell D23, then, is

=(Fixed*percent)+(Variable*B23)

Both formulas were filled down to include a total of 11 plotting points (zero plus ten points).

≡≡≡ ## BREAK-EVEN MACROS

Two command macros, one large and one small, perform extra work for this model. The small macro is a simple one that selects the input cells of the worksheet in case you deselect them for any reason.

	B
1	select
2	=SELECT(!form)
3	=RETURN()
4	

On the worksheet, I had selected the cells (with the Command key pressed) so that the advance of the active cell cursor proceeds through the ranges B3:B5, B8:B17, and E8:E10. After defining that range as "form," I could invoke the select command macro (defined by the Option-Command-s keyboard equivalent) to select the input cells of the form instantly.

A considerably heftier macro controls the graphing of the break-even results. Not only does it summon a chart, but more importantly the macro establishes the vertical scale of the graph based on the value of the break-even point.

The mechanics of the scale adjuster start at the beginning of the macro.

A cell below the bottom of the macro, defined as "raw" (for the raw, unadjusted increment between tick marks) is set to a value equal to the break-even point from the worksheet divided by five. This will help the macro establish a scale that will display the break-even point as close to the center of the graph as possible.

Another cell below the macro, defined with the name "step," is adjusted in the next seven cells of the macro, depending on the value of "raw." Initially, "step" is given a value of 50 (cell A3), which in this model is the smallest increment possible on the chart.

	A
1	graph.table
2	=SET.VALUE(raw,!BreakEven_Units/5)
3	=SET.VALUE(step,50)
4	=IF(raw>50,SET.VALUE(step,100))
5	=IF(raw>100,SET.VALUE(step,250))
6	=IF(raw>250,SET.VALUE(step,500))
7	=IF(raw>500,SET.VALUE(step,1000))
8	=IF(raw>1000,SET.VALUE(step,2500))
9	=IF(raw>2500,SET.VALUE(step,10000))
10	=SELECT(!scale)
11	=DATA.SERIES(2,1,,step,)
12	=SELECT(!table)
13	=VPAGE(-1)
14	=NEW(2)
15	=GALLERY.LINE(1)
16	=LEGEND(1)
17	=FULL()
18	=RETURN()
19	
20	step
21	50
22	
23	raw
24	48.283333333333
25	

In the next six cells of the macro, however, the value of "raw" is compared against a range of other values. If "raw" is, say, 400, "step" will be adjusted upward with each macro cell until it reaches 500. In the macro IF test after that, "raw" will fail the test of being greater than 500, so "step" will remain at 500 throughout the rest of the IF tests.

In macro cell A10, the column of the Break-even worksheet containing the scale range is selected (it had been previously defined as "scale"). When the worksheet was originally laid out, a zero was consciously placed in the first cell of the "scale" range. That's because the ensuing DATA.SERIES function in the macro requires a starting value be in the topmost cell of the series before it fills according to the function's arguments. The arguments, as shown in macro cell A11, indicate a linear series with the increment as specified in the cell named "step." When the macro runs, you can see the data series fill the range with the new scale.

Now that the graphing matrix is complete, the macro selects the entire range, called "table" (which, again, had been previously defined on the worksheet as the range B22:D33). Before graphing, however, the macro scrolls up one page (VPAGE(-1)) so that the form will be handy after the graphing is done. The entry cells are not selected at this point because the graphing matrix must be selected when the new chart is called, as it is in macro cell A14. A line chart is selected from the gallery, a legend is added, and the graph is blown up to full-screen size, instead of the miniature default graph.

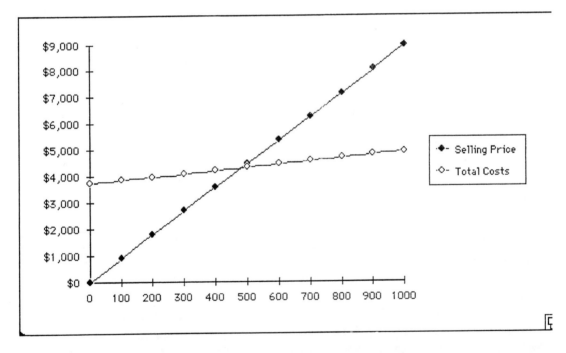

All of this graphing stuff takes a few seconds, and you see every step along the way. If you include an ECHO(FALSE) command at the beginning of the macro, macro execution is faster and you won't be distracted by the light show taking place on the screen.

Once the graph is on the screen, you can manually add final touches such as a chart title and other enhancements to drive home a point, if this chart is to be part of a presentation. To return to the form, type Command-M. You'll be looking at the form you just filled out, but the entry cells won't be selected (the table below the screen is still selected for the chart). Type Option-Command-s to activate the entry cells, using the select macro.

Now that we've done several spreadsheet and graphics models, it's time to move onto some database examples, with demonstrations of Excel's advanced database powers.

Chapter **12**
DATABASE ENTRY FORMS

When you mention database management to an experienced personal computer user, a vision of dedicated database programs such as dBase IV, RBase, or 4th Dimension generally comes to mind. These programs are powerful vehicles to establishing a sophisticated base of data, which you can sort, search, and organize at your whim.

One feature that a database management program has over a simple file management program (such as the basic Excel database function) is the ability to replicate on the screen a paper form with blanks to be filled in by the data-entry person. Well, believe it or not, you can create data-entry forms in Excel and have the data stored in the regular database format. In this chapter we'll be creating a database entry form directly on a worksheet. You can also create the form as a custom Excel dialog box, as described in Chapter 6. The macros and database layout, however, would be identical.

WHY A DATABASE FORM?

A data-entry form has a couple of big advantages over entering data in the standard Excel database format. The most obvious is that you can lay out the various data-entry fields in a single screen, whereas in the standard format you are limited to roughly six fields across the screen (depending on the column width and font selected). With a form, you can set up wide fields for lengthy entries, multiple fields on one line, and two to three times the number of fields on one screen as with the normal format.

A second advantage is that you can set up a database to run on Excel that is easy enough for an inexperienced Excel user to start entering data with very little instruction. The on-screen form metaphor will be much more familiar and easier to learn than the regular Excel database format, with its horizontal scrolling across multiple screens. As you'll also see, the form, when designed as a document separate from the database, can be formatted in a larger font to make the screen easier to read for those unaccustomed to the finely detailed fonts of the Mac (I've witnessed senior citizens having trouble reading anything smaller than Chicago-12).

As an example of a data-entry form used with a database, I've created a hypothetical inventory recordkeeping system for an equally hypothetical office products distributor. The entry form is one document, formatted in Chicago-12, while the actual database that stores the information is a separate document in the normal, Geneva-10, font.

A macro sheet is also part of this system. It contains only two macros, one of which does the work of storing the data from the entry form into the database for future sorting or retrieval. Table 12.1 lists the cell and range names used in the following models.

Table 12.1

Inventory	
item	$P$5:$AE$5
Inventory Entry	
Address__1	$D$3
Address__2	$D$4
City	$D$5
Color	$B$10
Contact	$D$7
Cost__Ea.	$B$12
data	$B$2,$D$2,$D$3,$D$4,$D$5,
	$F$5,$H$5,$D$6,$D$7,
	$B$9,$D$9,$B$10,$B$11
	$B$12,$D$13
EntryTime	$D$13
Item	$D49
Part__No.	$B$9
Phone	$D$6
Reorder__Qty.	$B$13
Size	$B$11
State	$F$5
Vendor	$D$2
Vendor__No.	$B42
ZIP	$H$5
M/Data Entry	
cell	'Inventory Entry'!$D$8
data.enter	$A$1
error.chk	$C$1
select.form	$B$1

The database system I'm about to demonstrate applies a number of Excel techniques that you should watch closely and consider for your applications. You'll see such things as worksheet linking, time- and date-stamping, the application of the Paste Special command, and the powers of Excel macros to do all your dirty work.

≡ PLANNING

A database needs much more preplanning than a spreadsheet, although Excel's database functions are much more forgiving than most dedicated database programs if you change your mind later. The first step in planning an Excel database is to determine the names of fields you'll be using—the same as labeling the blanks on a form. It may be easier to first sketch out on paper what the form should look like, starting with a simple list of field names. Laying out the form probably will be the hardest part of designing an Excel database, because you have practically a clean slate to work with—the possibilities are limitless.

For my inventory entry form, I want to record the following fields:

Vendor Number
Vendor Name
Address Line 1
Address Line 2
City
State
Zip
Telephone
Personal Contact
Part Number
Item Description
Color
Size
Cost Each
Reorder Quantity

The last field, Reorder Quantity, is the number of items in stock at which point the purchasing department should reorder. This order of fields is logical to me as a sequence of entering data, starting with the vendor information followed by the item data, including my company's stock number for the item. No matter what order the data is entered on the form, the fields can be reordered in the database. This is important, because it may be convenient to order fields in a form one way but necessary to order fields in the actual database another way.

ENTRY-FORM DESIGN

The entry-form design is shown below.

```
┌─────────────────────────── Inventory Entry ───────────────────────────┐
│                                                                        ⇧│
│ Vendor No.  ┌─────────┐  Vendor   ┌───────────────────────────┐        ▓│
│             └─────────┘  Address 1 ├───────────────────────────┤        ▓│
│                          Address 2 ├───────────────────────────┤        ▓│
│                          City      ├─────────────────┤State└──┘ZIP└────┘▓│
│                          Phone     ├───────────────────────────┤        ▓│
│                          Contact   └───────────────────────────┘        ▓│
│ ── ── ── ── ── ── ── ── ── ── ── ── ── ── ── ── ── ── ── ── ── ── ── ──│
│ Part No.    ┌─────────┐  Item      ┌───────────────────────────┐        │
│ Color       ├─────────┤                                                 │
│ Size        ├─────────┤                                                 │
│ Cost Ea.    ├─────────┤            ┌───────────────────────────┐        │
│ Reorder Qty.└─────────┘            └───────────────────────────┘       ⇩│
└────────────────────────────────────────────────────────────────────────┘
```

Notice that after I designed the form, I removed the gridlines and the row and column headings (with the Display dialog from the Options menu). Another notable feature of this form design is that the cells that will contain entries have an outline border around them. Additionally, I made sure that all fields were aligned left. In that way, when I type in a zip code or vendor number, Excel won't follow its default alignment and place numbers right-aligned in the cell.

I also made a couple of number-formatting changes. The simplest was to make the cost field a dollars-and-cents field, for it will always be displaying a money figure. The second was a custom format for the telephone field. To simplify the entry of long distance numbers, I created a number format in the Number dialog box that reads

(000)000-0000

This format requires only the typing of the ten phone digits (including area code). Automatically, the numbers are placed into the format, (212)555-1212. If only seven digits are typed, the number displayed would be (000)555-1212. This is just a simple shortcut that Excel makes fun to invent.

To facilitate using the entries later in the transfer of data to the database worksheet, I defined each entry cell with the default name to its left. This can be a somewhat tedious task because you must select each entry cell and then choose Define Name from the Formula menu.

A speedier way to do this is to simply select each cell, press Command-L and immediately press Return without waiting for the dialog box to fill. The name to the left of the selected field will automatically be the name assigned to the selected cell.

Admittedly, the form is not a shining example of design balance. That's where Excel's spreadsheet heritage shows through, for all cells in a column must be the same width. I'll be using some of that blank space later in this chapter and in the next. A dotted line separates areas on the form designated for vendor and item data. Finally, I sized the entry form so that a sliver of space is available at the bottom of the screen for a small window to the database, as you'll see in a moment.

SELECT MACRO

The trick to making this form work smoothly as a data-entry device is preselecting the entry field cells so that a press of the Return or Enter key forces the cell cursor to activate the next logical cell, even if it means skipping to the left or right midway down a column of cells—as in jumping from City to State in the inventory entry form above. Fortunately, Excel makes this easy with the help of a simple macro.

As background to the macro, you may recall that when you select disjointed cells on a worksheet while holding down the Command key, each succeeding cell you select is added to the queue of selected cells. When you press Return, Tab, or Enter with all these cells thus selected, the active cursor follows the order in which you Command-selected the cells, even moving up the worksheet, skipping to opposite corners, or whatever. The job of the macro, then, is to select the cells of the form in the desired order in which the fields are to be filled in by the data-entry operator.

A clean way to do this (and, as it turns out, a convenient tool later) is to Command-select the cells in the appropriate order and then define the selection with a name, such as "data."

```
┌─────────────────────────────────────────────────────────┐
│ ≡≡≡≡≡≡≡≡≡≡≡≡≡≡≡≡≡≡  Define Name  ≡≡≡≡≡≡≡≡≡≡≡≡≡≡≡ │
│ ┌──────────────────────┬─┐              ┌──────────┐ │
│ │ Address_1          ⬆ │              │    OK    │ │
│ │ Address_2            │   Name:       └──────────┘ │
│ │ City               ▒ │              ┌──────────┐ │
│ │ Color              ▒ │   │data│      │ Cancel   │ │
│ │ Contact            ▒ │              └──────────┘ │
│ │ Cost_Ea.           ▒ │   Refers to:  ┌──────────┐ │
│ │ data               ⬇ │              │ Delete   │ │
│ └──────────────────────┴─┘              └──────────┘ │
│         =$B$2,$D$2,$D$3,$D$4,$D$5,$F$5                  │
└─────────────────────────────────────────────────────────┘
```

As you can see in the Define Name dialog box, the cell references to "data" consist of a series of individual cells, starting with cell B2, the Vendor No. entry cell. Follow the procession of cell references as far as you can in the edit window. Notice after cell D5 (city), the selection jumps to the right two cells to F5 (state). What this means is that every time the cell range called "data" is selected, the cells are selected as if they were Command-selected in the order originally prescribed.

Over on the macro sheet, then, the select.form macro simply activates the entry-form window (Inventory Entry) and selects the cell range called "data" on the window. No matter where you might enter a new item to inventory, simply press the Option-Command-key equivalent for the select.form macro (I use lowercase "s") and all the necessary cells will be preset for swift entry.

THE DATABASE

Laying out the actual database entailed placing the field titles at the top of columns dedicated to their respective data fields.

	P	Q	R	S	T	U	
1			Database				
2							
3	Part No.	Description	Color	Size	Cost	Reorder Qty.	
4							
5							
6							
7							
8							
9							
10							
11							
12							

Inventory

Following guidelines outlined in Chapter 4, I set up the database section to start far enough to the right to allow room for a criteria and extract section. The practicality of this arrangement will shine through in Chapter 15, where I discuss a complete database system, along with macros to assist in searching and extracting data from a database.

Also notice that I changed the order of the fields from the order in the entry form. The leftmost field of the database is the Part No. field. The reason for this is that eventually this database may be used as an element of a relational database that other databases will look to for inventory data.

Other databases searching for data, such as cost or vendor number, will link to this inventory listing by part number. Excel has a built-in function that looks down the leftmost column of a database in search of a match for the specified part number. By placing the Part No. as the leftmost database field, I increase the flexibility of expanding this database system in the future.

I also added an extra field that does not appear on the Inventory Entry form—although it's on the form, but invisible most of the time. This extra field is at the far right of the database and is labeled "EntryTime."

As you'll see in a minute, when the data from a form is officially entered into the database, the entry is dated and time-stamped with the NOW( ) function. While the date of entry is not important with regard to the vendor and part information, it is critical if you want to determine the original order of the entries into the database (in case you sort the database later).

Additionally, data-entry errors, once discovered, can be traced to the data-entry operator who was working on the system at the time and date in the Date field.

The physical arrangement of the database window is somewhat important with respect to making the laborious task of data entry easier. First, I split the window so that the top row of the window contains the database column titles. Then I shrink the window vertically so that the titles row and two data rows are visible when the bottom scroll bar is active. The entire window was moved to the very bottom of the screen.

Because the database window will not be the active window when entries are being made to the form, its title bar can overlap with the bottom of the entry form. All that needs to be visible when the entry form is active are the three lines of the database (when the entry form is active, the database scroll bars disappear, revealing one more line of data).

A critical element of this system is the series of formulas that initially go into the first row of the database. These formulas are the primary link between the database and the entry form. They're quite simple, too, because all they do is mimic the data in the entry form. For example, the formulas initially placed into the database cell P4 is

     = 'Inventory Entry'!Part_No.

which says that anything entered into the cell defined as Part_No. in the window labeled Inventory Entry will be duplicated here in cell P4. It is important to note that all cell references in this row of formulas are to defined names in the entry form. You could refer to entry-form cells by cell number, but the minute you start changing the layout of the form, your database formulas will lose track of their cells. But by using defined cell names as references, you have the flexibility of shifting your entry-form cells around at will.

As an extra fail-safe, I recommend that once the formulas are entered into database row 4, you copy them and paste them into an unused row above the database section. In that way, if you accidentally damage the formulas, you'll have a master set from which to retype the formulas.

Let's pause for a moment and see exactly where the system is at this stage of development.

There is an entry form, whose entry fields are selected with the select.form macro. As each field is filled, its value is duplicated in its respective database field in the first available row of the database. What is needed now is a way to permanently transfer those values to the database (i.e., so they are no longer linked to the entry form) and shift the linking formulas down one row to accept data from the next form. Some other chores also are necessary, such as date- and time-stamping the entry and clearing out the data in the entry form to make way for new data. The entry macro does all of this for you.

ENTRY MACRO

I defined the entry macro with the name data.enter because it performs essentially the same operation as pressing the Enter key in a dedicated database.

	A
1	data.enter
2	=SELECT('Inventory Entry'!EntryTime)
3	=FORMULA(NOW())
4	=ACTIVATE("Inventory")
5	=SELECT(!item)
6	=CUT()
7	=SELECT(OFFSET(SELECTION(),1,0))
8	=PASTE()
9	=COPY()
10	=SELECT(OFFSET(SELECTION(),-1,0))
11	=PASTE.SPECIAL(3,1)
12	=FORMAT.NUMBER("#")
13	=ACTIVATE("Inventory Entry")
14	=SELECT(!EntryTime)
15	=CLEAR(3)
16	=SELECT(!data)
17	=CLEAR(3)
18	=RETURN()
19	

The macro listing is longer than most of the ones I've shown you so far, but it really is not too imposing. I'll take it line by line.

The first task the macro performs is the date- and time-stamping of the record. Macro cell A2 selects a cell on the entry form that I had previously defined with the name "EntryTime." No data is normally in that cell (I used cell D13, which is the long cell at the bottom of the form), so it normally displays as completely blank on the form. Only during execution of this macro does anything appear in that cell.

Macro cell A3, using the FORMULA function, performs the equivalent of placing the NOW function in the EntryTime cell. Doing so causes the date and time (counted with Excel's time serial number) to appear in the cell. Although it appears there only for an instant during macro execution, I still formatted the cell in the m/d/yy h:mm format from the Number dialog box so that an operator will recognize it as a date and time entry.

Next, the macro activates the database window, which I labeled "Inventory." In macro cell A5, the previously defined range of cells, called "item," is selected. The cells in this range were defined originally as the row of formulas in the database, the cell range P4:AE4. Because I defined these cells as a single entity, the macro will be able to select, move, and perform quite easily many other operations on the group of cells. Hence, in cell A5, the entire row of formulas—the ones that mimic the entry-form fields—is selected.

The next series of operations are the key ones in this macro and require a bit of background information. With the mimic formulas in the database row, data from the entry form is not really logged into the database.

For example, if I were to Fill Down the cells in the range "item" for a couple rows and then make a change in the entry form, the change would appear in all rows of the database holding those formulas.

In other words, the formulas are simply windows to the current status of the entry form. The values, themselves, are not actually in the database. What the macro needs to do is somehow convert the values in the database windows to real values for permanent storage in the database. That's what macro cells A5 through A11 do.

The formula in cell A5 selects the row of formulas. Next, the row is cut, just like with the Cut operation in the Edit menu. In cell A7, the next row (the row offset down by one row) is selected so the row of formulas can be pasted into the new row by the PASTE function in cell A8. All the macro has done is shifted the row of formulas down one row, leaving the original row blank temporarily.

In cell A9, because the row of formulas in its new location is still selected, the row is copied, just like with the Copy operation in the Edit menu. Now the macro needs to select the row just left blank, the one above the row of formulas, which it does with the SELECT and OFF-SET formula in A10. Now for the trick: In cell A11, instead of just pasting in the copy, which would simply duplicate the formulas in the new row below, the PASTE.SPECIAL function is supplied arguments to paste *only the values.* That means that the values are separated from the mimic formulas and only the values are pasted into the cells of the database. At last, the data is safely in the database.

One last bit of housekeeping is required to make the database look right. Some fields in the entry form will occasionally be left empty. For example, a product that comes in only one color will not have an entry for that field. Down in the database formula that mimics the color data-entry cell, Excel will automatically place a zero in that cell. That doesn't look good and it could lead to confusion sometime later when reviewing the database. Therefore, I needed a way to change those zeros into blanks.

One way I solved the problem was to change the formulas for those cells that mimicked entry-form cells that might be left blank: color, size, address 2, and contact. In place of the straight "equals" formulas, I inserted an IF function that displays a null string in the database formula if no entry is made in the entry form. Therefore, the formula that was originally

    ='Inventory Entry'!Color

was changed to

    =IF('Inventory Entry'!Color="","",'Inventory Entry'!Color)

Now, despite the null string in the cell display, Excel still records the entry as a zero. Therefore, one more step is necessary to assure that the field will be left blank when it is copied and pasted (special) into the database.

That's where the FORMAT.NUMBER("#") formula in macro cell A12 comes to the rescue. This number format is not in the standard library of formats when you get the Number dialog box. But what it does is place a null string in the cell if a zero is the value there. If another value (or text) is present, then that value (or text) is displayed.

So, thus far in the macro, the data in the entry form is now stored in the database, but the data is also displayed on the row below the entries because the formulas still mimic the data in the form. The macro must clear the form to make way for new data entry. Macro cell A13 activates the entry-form window. Then the macro selects the Entry-Time cell to clear it of the date- and time-stamp.

Note that the Clear function in cell A15 uses 3 as an argument. This is important because that argument clears only the formulas from the cells and not the formats. Similarly, cell A16 selects all the data-entry cells, with cell A17 clearing only the formulas (values) from the cells. To specify a different argument would wipe out the formats such as left alignment, the dollar format for the Cost field, and so on.

Now, then, let's follow the entry of a couple of inventory entries and watch what happens.

Invoking the select.form macro, the cells in the form are automatically selected for me, ready to accept data in a logical order.

	B
1	select.form
2	=ACTIVATE("Inventory Entry")
3	=SELECT(!data)
4	=RETURN()
5	

As each field is filled, its mimic in the database (row 4) fills with the same data.

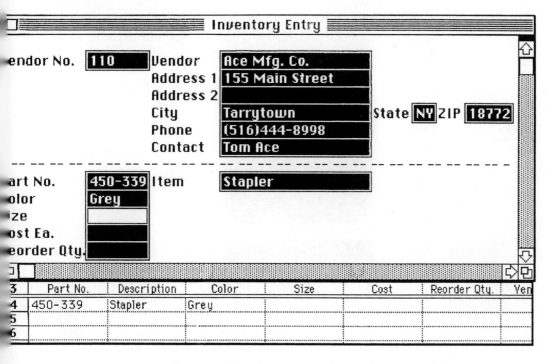

When the form is completed, I issue the data.enter macro. The formulas and data in row 4 are cut and pasted into row 5.

Inventory						
	P	**Q**	**R**	**S**	**T**	**U**
3	Part No.	Description	Color	Size	Cost	Reorder Qty.
4						
5	450-339	Stapler	Grey	Large	5	15

The row 5 cells are copied and pasted special into row 4, leaving only the values in row 4, with the original formulas intact in row 5.

Inventory						
	P	**Q**	**R**	**S**	**T**	**U**
3	Part No.	Description	Color	Size	Cost	Reorder Qty.
4	450-339	Stapler	Grey	Large	4.5	15
5	450-339	Stapler	Grey	Large	5	15

Then the entry form is cleared of its values. As the cells in the form empty out, the formulas in database row 5 mimic the blank cells and stand ready to accept values for the next form.

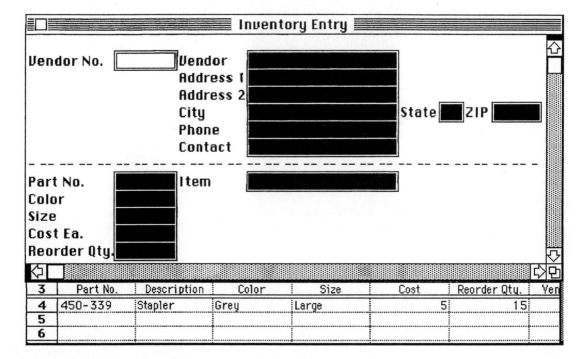

	Part No.	Description	Color	Size	Cost	Reorder Qty.	Ven
3	Part No.	Description	Color	Size	Cost	Reorder Qty.	Ven
4	450-339	Stapler	Grey	Large	5	15	
5							
6							

Notice that the previous entry is visible in the database row above the formulas. As I enter more and more parts to the inventory, the previous entry is always visible in the bottom window while entering the next form. This window to the last entry will help the entry person (it could be you) determine what the last entry was to avoid duplicating entries.

When this style of database loads up with a couple hundred lines of data, the copying and pasting that takes place in the data-entry macro slow down substantially. There is a way to speed this operation up, but you lose the ability to watch data fill in the database cells as you fill out the form.

The basic change you'd make to the database design and macro is to position the database cells that mimic the data-entry cells in a dedicated line of the database (such as above the column labels.) Then, instead of copying and pasting the formulas to push them down the database rows after each entry, merely copy their data and paste it (with Paste Special for values only) to the end of the database. Then clear the values from the line of mimic formulas above the column labels in preparation for the next entries. You'll find that by not copying and pasting the formulas, the operation of transferring data from the form to the database will be much faster.

In the next chapter, I enhance this database system and show you how to apply error-checking routines to help data-entry operators avoid making mistakes while filling in a form.

Chapter **13**
DATA-ENTRY
ERROR-CHECKING

All in a Macro
Error-Checking in Action

Whenever you're in a hurry to enter something into a computer, it's very easy to type in a wrong number of some kind and not realize it until long afterward. Fortunately, you can build in some protection from such errors in Excel by creating function macros that monitor the input of certain fields. If the entries don't measure up to the specifications you establish, then the macro can display an error message right on the form to alert the operator that something is amiss.

Because you're already familiar with the inventory database entry form from the last chapter, I'll use it as an example of how you can build error-checking into a form or worksheet of any kind.

ALL IN A MACRO

If you recall the form, there are four fields into which numbers are entered: vendor no., ZIP code, part no., and cost. A function macro, named error.chk, combines error-checking of all four cells into one macro, although each cell could have its own error-checking routine. I combined them primarily for the sake of demonstrating the possibilities of creating an extensive function macro. In this case, too, a combination of four error-checking routines into one macro allows me to place the error messages for all four checking routines into the same cell—if there is an error message, it will appear in only one place on the form.

You might, however, design a form or spreadsheet in which it is more appropriate to have the error message appear adjacent to the cell containing the entry. In such cases, it will be more efficient—with faster execution—to separate the error-checking routines for each cell.

The link to the error-checking function macro is located in the form, in cell D12.

 File   Edit   Formula   Format   Data   Options   Macro   Window

| D12 | | ='M/data entry'!error.chk(B2,H5,B9,B12) |

=========================== **Inventory Entry** ===========================

Vendor No. [   ]   **Vendor**   [   ]
                          Address 1   [   ]
                          Address 2   [   ]
                          City   [   ]   State [   ] ZIP [   ]
                          Phone
                          Contact   [   ]

- -

Part No. [   ]   **Item**   [   ]
Color   [   ]
Size   [   ]
Cost Ea. [   ]   [   ]
Reorder Qty. [   ]

3	Part No.	Description	Color	Size	Cost	Reorder Qty.	Ven
4	450-339	Stapler	Grey	Large	5	15	
5							
6							

The formula in this cell calls the function macro (called "error check" on the macro sheet labeled M/data entry) each time a value is entered into any one of the four target cells: B2, H5, B9, or B12. If a value is entered into cell H5 (ZIP code), the value is passed as an argument to the macro, more specifically, as the second argument out of a possible list of four arguments.

In the macro, the first four lines acquire the arguments from the formula in entry form cell D12.

	M/data entry
	C
1	error.chk
2	=ARGUMENT("vend.no",2)
3	=ARGUMENT("ZIP",2)
4	=ARGUMENT("part",2)
5	=ARGUMENT("cost",2)
6	=IF(vend.no="",RETURN(""))
7	=IF(LEN(vend.no)<>3,RETURN("Vendor No. must be 3 digits!"))
8	=IF(ZIP="",RETURN(""))
9	=IF(LEN(ZIP)<>5,RETURN("ZIP code must be 5 digits!"))
10	=IF(part="",RETURN(""))
11	=IF(MID(part,4,1)<>"-",RETURN("Part No. must be in XXX-XXX format!"))
12	=IF(LEN(part)<>7,RETURN("Double-check Part Number!"))
13	=IF(cost="",RETURN(""))
14	=IF(cost="0",RETURN("Hey, it's got to cost something!"))
15	=RETURN("")
16	

Whatever value is in form cell B2 (vendor number) is assigned to a variable called "vend.no" by the ARGUMENT function in macro cell C2. The second argument in the ARGUMENT function in macro cell C2 (the number 2) tells the newly assigned name to take only the value from the cell being passed from the form; other argument numbers would pass only the cell reference, for example. Hereafter in this macro, when I need to refer to the vendor-number value entered in the form, I use the name "vend.no."

After the four ARGUMENT formulas comes a series of IF tests, which do the actual error-checking. The first two tests, in macro cells C6 and C7, work with the value assigned to vend.no. If no value is in the cell, then the error message field in the form (D12) is sent a null string. But if the Vendor No. field has a number that is not three digits long, the error message returns.

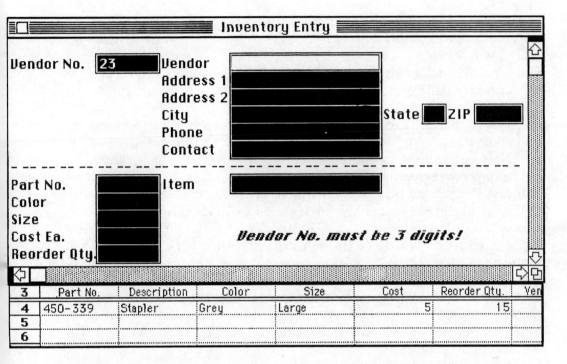

Note that I formatted the error message cell in the form to be bold and italic as a way to draw attention to it while you're busy entering data.

Similar tests are provided for the ZIP code, Part No., and cost fields. The ZIP code, in my form, must be five digits (this can be adapted to accept the new nine-digit codes if you wish). Part numbers for this company consist of two three-digit numbers separated by a hyphen. The first three digits are a code for a product category, while the second three digits are the unique part number in that category.

Notice how the MID function tests the fourth character in the part number to make sure it is a hyphen. A second test, in macro cell C12, is included in case the entry operator gets a hyphen in the right place, but types too few or too many characters afterward. Finally, the cost field is checked to be sure that a cost other than zero has been entered.

ERROR-CHECKING IN ACTION

It's interesting to follow the logic of this macro, because different things happen if you don't see one error message and mistakenly enter another cell that is error-checked.

For example, if you type in an erroneous vendor number, ignore the error message, and then type in a four-digit ZIP code, the function macro will continue to display the vendor-number error message until you repair the problem. That's because the function macro returns to the worksheet after displaying the vendor-number message. But if you then type in a valid vendor number, the macro takes over again (because it checks all four entry cells whenever one of them is changed) and spots the wrong ZIP code format and displays that error message.

Notice, too, that as you enter values into each of the target cells, the macro processes more of its instructions. For example, when you enter a valid vendor number, the macro proceeds to cell C8, where the nonentry in the ZIP code field causes the macro to return to the worksheet. If you then enter a valid ZIP code, the macro starts again at the top and works its way down the column until cell C10, where it returns to the worksheet if nothing is entered into the part-number field. Therefore, by the time you reach the cost field, it may take a second or so for all the IF tests in the long column of macros to process. Fortunately, Excel allows a fast typist to type ahead of the execution without losing keystrokes, so any value typed into the reorder quantity field will be recorded properly.

I strongly urge you to include error-checking macros in as many databases and spreadsheets as you can. Oddly enough, it is the experienced user who needs error-checking more than the novice. I've discovered that the more I get to know a program, the sloppier I get when it comes to operations and procedures I'm familiar with. I'm too ready to press the Return key when I really should be checking my work before committing my work to disk. It's also easy to forget the format of a number if you don't use a worksheet or form for a while. Having the error message remind you of the proper format will instantly refresh your memory.

In the next chapter, I will show you a different database, one you might use on your Mac at home. It demonstrates how you can calculate with time in a worksheet or database.

Chapter **14**
CALCULATING TIME

I'm not about to rehash the material in the Excel manual that describes how Excel records time internally. What I want to demonstrate in this chapter, however, is how you can calculate with time in Excel just like regular numbers. Excel knows that when you reach 60 seconds, it's time to carry the one to the minutes column.

The example I'll use is a database model I created to store data about a record collection. But instead of simply storing information about complete albums, the database contains data about each piece on each record disc, including the timing, when available.

The reason for separating individual pieces is that in case I want to make a cassette tape for the car tape player and need a particular kind of music to fill out approximately three minutes at the end of Side A, I can search the database for a particular kind of music that is between two-and-a-half and three minutes in length.

THE ENTRY FORM

Cell and range names are used in the calculating time models. See Table 14.1 for a list of these names.

Table 14.1

M/Records	
data enter	$A$1
extract	$D$1
leave.enter	$E$1
record.setup	$C$1
search	$D$7
select.form	$B$1
subsequent	$C$8
Record Library	
Artist	$N$7
Composer	$N44
Criteria	$A$2:$G$3
data	$L$4,$L$5,$N44,$N$5,$N$6,
	$N$7,$N$8,$L$9,$L$10,$L$11
Database	$K$14:$S$50
dbend	$S$50
dbtop	$K$14
entry	$K$50:$S$50

extitles	$A$11:$I$11
Format	$L$11
Label	$L$4
Minutes	$L$8
OpusKBWV	$N$6
Recording_Date	$L$10
Record_No.	$L$5
Seconds	$L$9
time	$L$12
Title	$N$5

For this database, I kept the entry form and database on the same worksheet. Because I am the only one likely to enter data, I had no problem working with the Geneva-10 default font on the screen. And because I knew that I would be searching and extracting reports from this database, I structured the worksheet so that the database and form were positioned at the right edge of the active area, leaving plenty of room for the criteria and extract ranges against the left margin of the worksheet (see Chapter 4 for further information regarding database structure).

The data-entry form is a simple one, listing record label and number, information about the piece (I'm a classical music nut, hence the Opus number field), and further data about the recording length, date, and format (Long-Playing Record, Compact Disc, or Cassette).

	K	L	M	N	
			Record Library Form		
1			Record Library Form		
2					
3					
4	Label		Composer		
5	Record No.		Title		
6			Opus/K/BWV		
7			Artist		
8	Minutes				
9	Seconds				
10	Recording Date				
11	Format				

Recording time must be entered as two separate fields—minutes and seconds—because Excel, with all its time functions, does not let you enter a time consisting of only minutes and seconds. Because I'm the lazy type, I'm not fond of having to type zero hours for every entry; nor am I fond of having to type colons between the hours, minutes, and seconds of the approved time-number format. By dividing the minutes and seconds fields into two on the form, all I have to type is the minutes, press Return, and then type the seconds—all in all, a faster procedure.

In a cell out of view of the form is the formula that joins together the data from the minutes and seconds fields into an appropriate time calculation that gets stored into the database. The formula (it's in cell L12 just below the form and just above the database area, as you'll see) is

   = TIME(0,L8,L9)

which assembles a valid time number from the minutes and seconds cells, while assigning a zero to the hours value. It wasn't necessary, but I formatted this cell in the hh:mm:ss format in case I should ever be scrolling down that way and wonder what some strange number (the regular time-serial number) was.

As with the inventory database in Chapter 11, the entry fields will be mimicked in the database section until the values are permanently entered into the database cells. Therefore, I had to define the names of the data-entry cells. Again, the fastest way to do this was to select a data-entry cell, type Command-L (Define Name), and immediately press Return. For each cell this procedure defined the cell with the name of the label of the cell immediately to the left. Only in the case of the complete time cell in L12 did I have to type in a name for the definition, for there is no label adjacent to that cell.

Because the database will be storing only the total time for each musical piece, the minutes and seconds fields don't need to be defined. But it might be a good idea to define them anyway and use them in the formula in cell L12 so that it reads

   = TIME(0,Minutes,Seconds)

just in case you decide to readjust the layout of the form.

THE DATABASE

Because both the form and the database are on the same worksheet, I opened up a second window to the document so I can watch both the database and the form at the same time.

	File	Edit	Formula	Format	Data	Options	Macro	Window

| | L4 | | |

Record Library:1

	K	L	M	N	
1			Record Library Form		
2					
3					
4	Label		Composer		
5	Record No.		Title		
6			Opus/K/BWV		
7			Artist		
8	Minutes				
9	Seconds				
10	Recording Date				
11	Format				

14		Record No.	Label	Composer	Title
47		52DC 436	CBS/Sony	Scriabin	Etude in c#
48		52DC 436	CBS/Sony	Moszkowsky	Etude in Ab
49		52DC 436	CBS/Sony	Schumann	Traumerei from Kinderszenen
50					
51					
52					
53					

For convenience, I split the window into two tiles so that the titles in row 14 will always be showing. The database window is also deep enough for a vertical scroll bar to appear along the right edge of the lower tile. This is important, for I may want to scroll through the database window while the form is on the screen. The order of fields in the database is different from the order of the entry-form fields.

Because there is always the possibility that my Record Library database could become a part of a larger, relational database system, I decided that any such system would look up the data according to record number. That was the field I established as the leftmost field in the database. Other databases will be able to perform a VLOOKUP operation on the database now, using the record number as the "hook" to the rest of the data about a particular album. The order of fields in the database as I established them are: Label, Record No., Composer, Title, Opus No., Artist, Time, and Format. If your record collection is more eclectic—from Byrd to Beatles to Bach—you can substitute a field labeled "Type" for Opus No. and use that field to distinguish jazz from 1960s rock from classical, for example.

DATA-ENTRY MACROS

As with the inventory system in earlier chapters, the record library database has a few macros to perform the data-entry tasks for me. First of all, the database section has a row of formulas that mimic the fields in the entry form. One macro, select.form, selects the data-entry cells on the form. If you followed the inventory example, then this macro should look familiar.

	B
1	select.form
2	=ACTIVATE("Record Library:1")
3	=SELECT(!data)
4	=RETURN()
5	

Likewise, the data.enter macro shifts down the row of mimic formulas and copies the values only (via the PASTE.SPECIAL (3,1) macro formula), following the same format as in the inventory example.

A
1 data.enter
2 =ACTIVATE("Record Library:2")
3 =SELECT(!entry)
4 =CUT()
5 =SELECT(OFFSET(SELECTION(),1,0))
6 =PASTE()
7 =COPY()
8 =SELECT(OFFSET(SELECTION(),-1,0))
9 =PASTE.SPECIAL(3,1)
10 =FORMAT.NUMBER("#")
11 =ACTIVATE("Record Library:1")
12 =SELECT(!data)
13 =CLEAR(3)
14 =RETURN()
15

But I also created a second macro that enters data into the database. The difference in this second one is that it leaves the values in the form in case I need to enter information about a recording that is much like the previous entry. This happens a lot in this database because one record may contain several pieces by the same composer. I could have five recordings to type in, for example, with the only differences in the title, opus number, minutes, and seconds fields. It would be a waste of time to have to retype every field of the record when all that is needed is simple adjustment to four fields.

This second entry macro is called "leave/enter" because it leaves the original data in the form, yet enters the data into the database. There is nothing really special about this macro: It is simply an abbreviated data.enter macro, omitting the formulas that clear out the form.

	E
1	leave/enter
2	=ACTIVATE("Record Library:2")
3	=SELECT(!entry)
4	=CUT()
5	=SELECT(OFFSET(SELECTION(),1,0))
6	=PASTE()
7	=COPY()
8	=SELECT(OFFSET(SELECTION(),-1,0))
9	=PASTE.SPECIAL(3,1)
10	=FORMAT.NUMBER("#")
11	=ACTIVATE("Record Library:1")
12	=SELECT(!data)
13	=RETURN()
14	

Its use might be confusing at first, however, because you expect the fields in the database window below the entry just made to be blank as you fill out the next form. At first it will look like there are two listings for the piece you just entered. But the minute you change the title field in the form, the change will show up in the database window and will be permanently recorded when you issue the next data.enter or leave/enter macro.

I'll show you a little more time calculation in the next chapter, in which I demonstrate macros that perform some wonderful searching and report writing with this database.

Chapter **15**
REPORT-WRITING MACROS

The "reports" I refer to in the title of this chapter are not the kind of reports you write for your boss or instructor. I mean the kinds of reports that database programs usually generate. A report is a printed or on-screen replay of the information stored in a database. Often, the information is sorted or selected according to numerous criteria. For example, in a personal database, you can ask the computer to produce a report that lists all employees who have been with the company for ten years.

OVERVIEW

Excel's report-writing capabilities are to be found in the Extract function. Excel's Extract function works in tandem with the Criteria function. The latter allows you to specify what limits to apply to the search through the entire database so that only records meeting certain criteria are picked. The Extract function then lists those selected records in a worksheet form.

An Extract lists only those fields you want to see. In the personnel database example, for instance, each employee's record probably contains many fields of data that are irrelevant for the purposes of a search—you might not want a person's home address, but you would want the employment starting date if you plan to make an award on the tenth anniversary.

Combining Excel's Extract capabilities with macros makes for some significant automated power. I added three report-generating macros to the Record Library database detailed in the last chapter. One, called report.setup, performs some groundwork to make sure the complete database, including any new additions, has been selected before opening the window to the criteria and extract sections of the document. A second macro performs the Extract equivalent of the Search operation to display individual records inside the database, rather than extracting records.

PRELIMINARY STEPS

It's important to note that prior to setting up these macros, I manually created the Criteria and Extract sections on the worksheet, following the guidelines in Chapter 5.

	A	B	C	D	E	F	G	H
				Search				
1								
2	Record No.	Label	Composer	Title	Opus/K	Artist	Time	Recordin
3								
4								
5								
6								
7								
8								
9								
10	Total Time:	0:00:00		Extract Report				
11	Record No.	Label	Composer	Title	Opus/K	Artist	Time	Recordin
12								
13								
14								
15								
16								
17								
18								
19								
20								

Titles for both the criteria and extract ranges were copied from the database. One extra touch I place in the Extract region was a Total Time field. Because the report might be used to extract a series of recorded pieces for recording on tape, I thought it would be handy to have Excel calculate the totals of all recordings extracted and present the total at the top of the extract range. The formula in cell B2 is

$$=SUM(G12:G37)$$

and is based on the assumption that no criteria selection I'll make will be more than 25 pieces long. That may prove incorrect once the database grows to a hefty size, so the formula may need to be adjusted to extend further down the G column. Finally, that cell was formatted in the hh:mm:ss number format to be easy to interpret.

SETUP MACRO

Report.setup is a kind of preconditioning macro that gets everything ready for you to input your search criteria before extracting or searching a database for the records you want to view.

	C
1	report.setup
2	=IF(ISERROR(INDEX(WINDOWS(),0,4)),,GOTO(subsequent))
3	=ACTIVATE("Record Library:2")
4	=SELECT.LAST.CELL()
5	=SELECT(ACTIVE.CELL():!dbtop)
6	=SET.DATABASE()
7	=NEW.WINDOW()
8	subsequent
9	=ACTIVATE("Record Library:3")
10	=SELECT(!A1)
11	=SELECT(!A3)
12	=ALERT("Enter your Search Criteria in cells A3 through I3.",2)
13	=MESSAGE(TRUE,"Opt-Cmd-E to Extract/Opt-Cmd-S to Search")
14	=RETURN()
15	

The macro is divided into two sections. The first, from cells C2 to C7, checks if the extract window (the third window to the database document) is already open. If it is not, then the actual database area is set (the same as selecting the database range and then issuing the Set Database command from the Data menu) and the third window to the document is opened. If, on the other hand, the third window is already open (if you have previously performed a search or extract), then that window is selected and an alert box advises you where to type in your search criteria. Let's look at the macro one step at a time.

It was important, when developing this macro, to include a formula that would test for the presence of the third window to the database document. If such a test were not made, then the macro would continually open a new window to the document each time it was executed. I could wind up with several Criteria/Extract windows if I switched several times between making searches and entering data into a form.

I believe in keeping the screen as clutterfree as possible, so I wanted to limit the open database windows to three: 1) the entry form, 2) the database, and 3) the Criteria/Extract section. But I also couldn't forget in the test that there would always be one other window open—the macro window.

To test for the presence of the windows, I employed the macro function that creates an array consisting of the names of the windows currently open. I wasn't interested in the names (they are placed in the array in alphabetical order, just as they appear in the Window menu), but just in the number of windows. Assuming that I would have no more than four windows open at a time, I made a test to see if the array created by the WINDOW function contained four items. The vehicle to making this test was the INDEX function.

Arguments to the INDEX() function consisted of the array created by the WINDOWS() function and the location within that array of four rows down the single column of the array. Whenever the INDEX() function expects a value to be in the array and finds none (as when only three windows are open) it "returns" an error message. The surrounding IF test in macro cell C2 tests for the presence of an error message:

- If there is an error (i.e., there are not four windows open), then macro execution continues to the next cell.
- If there is no error (i.e., there are four windows open), then execution jumps down to cell C8, which has been defined with the name "subsequent."

Going back to cell C3, which executes when four windows are *not* open, the database window is activated. Prior to running this macro, I had defined the top left cell of the database with the name "dbtop" as a reference point. Now the macro can select the last cell of the worksheet, which is also the rightmost, bottom cell of the database (and why the database section should always go at the rightmost section of the worksheet). Then, by selecting the range between dbtop and the last cell (performed by the formula in macro cell C5), the entire database range is selected and ripe for the SET.DATABASE macro function in cell C6. Finally, a new window to the database document is opened in cell C7.

At this point, the macro continues to the formulas that are executed every time this macro is started. The first job is to activate the new window, the one that will be used for typing in the search criteria and the extract report. In cell C10, the macro selects the new database window cell A1 to make sure the window displays the worksheet which selects the new window's A3 cell, which is convenient for tabbing to the cells for entry of search criteria.

At macro cell C12, an alert box is brought to the screen. The text in the alert box reminds me where to type in search criteria. I selected alert box type 2, which is simply a "note" type, for it is the least menacing of the three types. Still, it beeps when it appears.

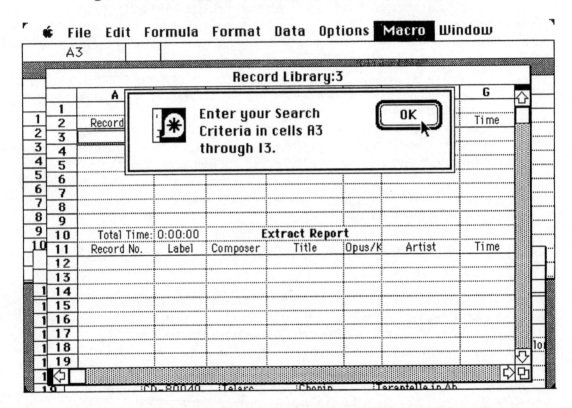

This would be a good spot for a custom Excel dialog box. The box would offer text fields in which to enter search criteria. A macro would then copy the criteria to the criteria range of the worksheet and then perform the extract.

The next macro formula places further help on the screen in the form of a message that appears just below the formula bar. This message reminds me of the macro commands that perform an Extract or Search (Opt-Command-E and Opt-Command-S, respectively).

 File   Edit   Formula   Format   Data   Options   Macro   Window

		Opt-Cmd-E to Extract/Opt-Cmd-S to Search						
A3								

Record Library:3

		A	B	C	D	E	F	G
1	1				Search			
2	2	Record No.	Label	Composer	Title	Opus/K	Artist	Time
3	3							
4	4							
5	5							
6	6							
7	7							
8	8							
9	9							
10	10	Total Time:	0:00:00		Extract Report			
	11	Record No.	Label	Composer	Title	Opus/K	Artist	Time
	12							
1	13							
1	14							
1	15							
1	16							
1	17							
1	18							
1	19							

This message will stay on the screen until another macro function turns it off, as will happen in a moment.

EXTRACT AND SEARCH MACROS

In column D of the macro sheet I placed two macros that do a lot of work for me, even though they are short ones.

```
▤▢▦═══════ M/Records ═══════▤
              D                    ⇧
 1   extract
 2   =SELECT(lextitles)
 3   =EXTRACT(0)
 4   =MESSAGE(0)
 5   =RETURN()
 6
 7   search
 8   =DATA.FIND(1)
 9   =MESSAGE(0)
10   =RETURN()
11
◁▢░░░░░░░░░░░░░░░░░░░░░░░░▷▣
```

The first, called extract, simply selects the titles of the Extract section of the window, performs the Extract operations, and turns off the message. If you recall the way you would manually extract a group of records, you first type in the search criteria in the criteria range, select all relevant titles at the head of an extract section on the worksheet, and then issue the Extract command from the Data menu. In the case of this database, I have elected to extract every field from the database, although I could have just as easily limited the extract fields to a few key ones. When I set up the extract titles, I defined the range of cells holding those titles with the name "extitles." That is the range selected in macro cell D2.

The macro named "search" is even simpler. This one performs the equivalent of selecting Find from the Data menu once you have typed in one or more search criteria. The display shifts to the database section while the first record meeting the search criteria is highlighted. At that time, the message is turned off, and you can continue your search using the database's usual search methods. Typing Command-F advances to the next record meeting the search criteria.

To exit the search mode, you can select Exit Find from the Data menu, but that leaves your view into the database section. Better still, invoke the report.setup macro. This both exits the search mode and returns your view in window 3 to the criteria segment for further criteria selection if you like.

A SAMPLE EXTRACT

To show you these macros in action, I'll perform a search of my record library for a Chopin piece that plays for under five minutes. When I invoke the report.setup macro (Option-Command-R on my system), the alert box reminds me when cells control the search criteria. Then I type "Chopin" under the Composer title and the desired time under the Time title.

**   File   Edit   Formula   Format   Data   Options   Macro   Window**

G3		<0:5:00

Record Library:3

		A	B	C	D	E	F	G
1	1				Search			
2	2	Record No.	Label	Composer	Title	Opus/K	Artist	Time
3	3			Chopin				<0:5:00
4	4							
5	5							
6	6							
7	7							
8	8							
9	9							
0	10	Total Time:	0:00:00		Extract Report			
	11	Record No.	Label	Composer	Title	Opus/K	Artist	Time
	12							
1	13							
1	14							
1	15							
1	16							
1	17							
1	18							
1	19							

Note that because I've formatted cell G3 to be in the hh:mm:ss number format, I must enter time with a leading zero in the hours digits, even though it's unlikely any search criteria will ever extend beyond an hour. The "less than" symbol in front of the time indicates that the extraction should list all Chopin pieces with a recording time of less than five minutes. A message above the formula bar reminds me of the keyboard macro equivalents for the two possible operations I'm likely to make once search criteria are established.

When I type Option-Command-E, Excel picks out all recordings meeting the search criteria.

			É File Edit Formula Format Data Options Macro Window					
		A11		Record No.				

Record Library:3

		A	B	C	D	E	F	G
1	1				Search			
2	2	Record No.	Label	Composer	Title	Opus/K	Artist	Time
3	3			Chopin				<0:5:00
4	4							
5	5							
6	6							
7	7							
8	8							
9	9							
10	10	Total Time:	0:23:58		Extract Report			
	11	Record No.	Label	Composer	Title	Opus/K	Artist	Time
	12	CD-80040	Telarc	Chopin	Mazurkas	6	Malcolm Frage	0:01:39
	13	CD-80040	Telarc	Chopin	Tarantelle in A	43	Malcolm Frage	0:02:49
	14	RCD 14585	RCA	Chopin	Waltz in Ab	69/1	Horowitz	0:03:32
	15	38C37-7050	Denon	Chopin	Valse Brillante	34/1	Jean-Yves Thi	0:04:59
	16	38C37-7050	Denon	Chopin	Valse Brillante	34/3	Jean-Yves Thi	0:02:03
	17	38C37-7050	Denon	Chopin	Valse in A	posth.	Jean-Yves Thi	0:02:13
	18	52DC 436	CBS/Sony	Chopin	Mazurka in c#	30/4	Horowitz	0:04:00
	19	52DC 436	CBS/Sony	Chopin	Etude in F	10/8	Horowitz	0:02:43

They are listed in the order in which they were found in the database. Had I presorted the database according to length, then the extract report would be likewise ordered. But because they're not in this case, I can manually select the extract range and sort according to the Time column.

At this point, if I change my mind and want to view Scarlatti selections with the same time criterion, I can type Option-Command-R for the report.setup macro again. Then I would change the search criteria under Composer to read "Scarlatti" instead of "Chopin." Typing Option-Command-E for the extract report would first clear the worksheet of the previous extract values and then report the findings of the new search.

 File   Edit   Formula   Format   Data   Options   Macro   Window

| D4 | | Record No. | | | | | |

Record Library:3

		A	B	C	D	E	F	G
1	1				Search			
2	2	Record No.	Label	Composer	Title	Opus/K	Artist	Time
3	3			Scarlatti				<0:5:00
4	4							
5	5							
6	6							
7	7							
8	8							
9	9							
10	10	Total Time:	0:15:17		Extract Report			
11	11	Record No.	Label	Composer	Title	Opus/K	Artist	Time
12	12	RCD 14585	RCA	Scarlatti	Sonata in Ab	186	Horowitz	0:02:33
13	13	RCD 14585	RCA	Scarlatti	Sonata in f	118	Horowitz	0:03:22
14	14	RCD 14585	RCA	Scarlatti	Sonata in f	189	Horowitz	0:02:40
15	15	RCD 14585	RCA	Scarlatti	Sonata in A	494	Horowitz	0:04:20
16	16	RCD 14585	RCA	Scarlatti	Sonata in E	224	Horowitz	0:02:22
17	17							
18	18							
19	19							

Our next step is to investigate the ultimate in database systems, the relational database. In the next two chapters, you'll see some techniques that dedicated database programs can't even reproduce.

Chapter **16**
ADVANCED RELATIONAL DATABASES

In Chapter 4, I demonstrated how two databases can be linked together to form what is essentially a relational database system. The example I used was a customer list linked to an accounts-receivable listing. As I entered the customer number in the accounts-receivable list, an Excel function automatically looked up the customer's name in the customer list and displayed the name in a cell adjacent to the customer number.

▤ OVERVIEW

In this chapter, I will take this relational business much further, showing you a way to build an invoicing system based on a similar customer list and accounts-receivable log. A macro will take information from both files and print an invoice—actually a batch of invoices so you can set the machine in motion and leave it unattended, provided your invoices are on continuous-form paper. Cell and range names used in the worksheets of this chapter are shown in Table 16.1.

Table 16.1

A/R List		
	agebot	$F$22
	agetop	$F$6
	Database	$A$5:$F$22
	dbbot	$F$22
	dbtop	$A$5
Customer List		
	Criteria	$A$2:$A$3
	Database	$K$2:$S$16
	dtop	$K$3
Invoice		
	inv.no	$B$6
	invoice	$A$1:$F$21
	Print__Area	$A$1:$F$21
Late Letter		
	invno	$D$21
	Print__Area	$A$1:$F$40

M/Inv

advance	$C$18
counter	$B$12
date.paste	$A$1
end	$C$12
late.letter	$C$1
letter	$C$23
loop	$C$10
print.invoice	$B$1
Print__Area	$C$1:$C$31
start	$B$6
top.count	$B$16

As a reminder, the customer-list worksheet looks like this:

 File   Edit   Formula   Format   Data   Options   Macro   Window

K3		101				

Customer List

	K	L	M	N	O	
1			**Database**			
2	Cust. No.	Customer Name	First Name	Last Name	Address	
3	101	A.B.Properties	Timothy	Smith	418 Main Street	Dal
4	102	Ace Power & Light	Doris	Addams	Box 10	Hou
5	103	Andy Lubert	Andy	Lubert	3445 Abercrombie Way	Det
6	104	AR Office	Steve	Jones	400 Wilshire Ave.	Los
7	105	Carol Stansen	Carol	Stansen	9066 114th Street	New
8	106	City of Franklin	Henry	Champion	45 Washington Street	Sma
9	107	James Gregory	James	Gregory	200 Wilshire Ave.	Los
10	108	Jim Parsons	Jim	Parsons	RR 1, Box 22N	Lin
11	109	Karen Bush	Karen	Bush	Box 2234	Las
12	110	Lisa La Flamme	Lisa	La Flamme	77 Sunset Street	Hol
13	111	Mary Fuller	Mary	Fuller	10 Downing Lane	Lon
14	112	Ralph J Cook Garbage	Ralph	Cook	1600 Rhode Island Ave.	Was
15	113	SW Wholesale	Sharon	Wester	919 Michigan Ave.	Chi
16	114	Wheelin's Gas Co.	Ralph	Wheelin	333 Fifth Ave.	Lub
17						
18						

I've modified slightly the accounts-receivable worksheet so that in place of the customer name is a cell where a description of the work done can be entered.

This description information will be transferred to the invoice so the customer knows what the bill is for.

Two elements—the invoice form and a macro called print.invoice—work together to make the job of invoicing as automatic as possible. The job is split so that the form does the relational work and the macro does the batch processing and printing work. While formulas in the invoice form may seem complex at first, you will readily see a pattern that can be adapted easily to many applications.

THE INVOICE FORM

I'll show you first a sample invoice form in the standard font and with gridlines showing so you can get a feel for the geography of the form.

É **File** **Edit** **Formula** **Format** **Data** **Options** **Macro** **Window**

| D8 | | =IF(B6<>"",VLOOKUP(B6,'A/R List'!Database,2),"") |

≣≣≣≣≣≣≣≣≣≣≣≣≣≣≣≣≣≣ **Invoice** ≣≣≣≣≣≣≣≣≣≣≣≣≣≣≣≣≣

	A	B	C	D	E	F	
1		INVOICE					
2							
3							
4							
5	Date	8/28/85					
6	Invoice #						
7							
8	To:						
9							
10							
11							
12							
13							
14		Description			Amount		
15							
16							
17							
18							
19		Payment Due	------>				

The mechanics of assembling data on the invoice form start with the invoice number. From this number the rest of the data on the form is derived automatically by formulas in each of the information cells. As an overview, the sequence works like this:

1. The customer number cell (D8) uses the invoice number as a pathway to the invoice record in the accounts-receivable worksheet.
2. The customer number on the accounts-receivable worksheet is retrieved and inserted into the invoice form in cell D8.
3. Invoice form formulas in the customer-data (name, address, city, state, and ZIP) cells B8, B9, B10, C10, and C11 use the customer number in D8 as a pointer to the customer record on the customer-list worksheet.
4. Information about the description, invoice amount, and date due use the invoice number in cell B6 as a pointer to the respective data cells in the accounts-receivable worksheet.

Notice, especially, that information for the invoice form is drawn from two distinct worksheets, yet everything hinges around the invoice number. From the invoice number is derived the customer number, from which is derived the customer data—like a thread running through all the open worksheets.

If it sounds like a lot of lookup procedures are being performed each time an invoice is created, you're right. Fortunately, Excel handles it all so quickly that you aren't conscious of all the work going on behind the scenes.

Let's look at the construction of this form in detail to see how all this looking up is being performed. Be prepared to flip back to the illustrations of the customer list and accounts-receivable worksheets because I'll be referring to them.

First of all, the formula in cell B5 consists of the NOW function. Unless you plan to postdate or predate invoices, it's always a good idea to have Excel automatically date your output.

Cell B6 has no formula in it. This is where either a human operator or a macro inserts the number of an invoice to be printed. Many other formulas in this form look to this cell for direction.

One such formula is the one in cell D8, which displays the customer number. Its formula is

=IF(B6<>"",VLOOKUP(B6,'A/R List'!Database,2),"")

The IF test is simply there to display a null string if no invoice number is entered into cell B6. Without specifically ordering a null string, cell D8 would display a zero when no invoice number is present.

The real workhorse of this formula, however, is the VLOOKUP function and its three arguments. The function uses the value in cell B6 as an index number to match against the leftmost column of the selection called 'A/R List'!Database, which is the entire database selection on the accounts-receivable worksheet. That's why I originally placed the invoice numbers in the left column of the database: I knew I would have another worksheet perform a VLOOKUP operation to search for a particular invoice number. Finally, the third argument, "2," tells the VLOOKUP function to retrieve the value from the second column of the database record after it finds a matching invoice number.

If you check the accounts-receivable database, you'll see that the second column is the customer number. Thus, when invoice number 3002 is entered into invoice cell B6, the VLOOKUP function checks the accounts-receivable database for a match; finding one in row 6, the function displays the second column value, or 114, which is the number of the customer to be billed.

Now that the customer number is available on the invoice form, other formulas that rely on that number can use it for their VLOOKUP procedures to find the customer's name and address data. Therefore, the formula in cell B8 is

=IF (D8<>"",VLOOKUP(D8,'Customer List'!Database,2),"")

Its VLOOKUP formula uses the value in D8 (the customer number) to look in the database range of worksheet Customer List. When it finds a match, it then displays the value in the second column of that database—the customer name. Similarly, the formula in the address cell, B9, reads

=IF (D8<>"",VLOOKUP(D8,'Customer List'!Database,5),"")

The only difference between this formula and the last one is the number of the column from which the value is to be retrieved and displayed on the invoice form. Formulas in invoice form cells B10, C10, and D10 likewise look up their data in Customer List columns 6, 7, and 8, respectively.

To retrieve description, invoice amount, and payment due date information, the VLOOKUP formulas in those cells use the invoice number in cell B6 and the index to look up their data in the accounts-receivable worksheet. For example, the formula in cell B15 is

=IF(B6<>"",VLOOKUP(B6,'A/R List'!Database,3),"")

which is identical to that in the customer number cell (D8) except that the column of the database used to return a value is the third column ("Description") instead of the second ("Cust. No.").

To prepare the invoice for printing, I removed the gridlines and headings and then bumped up the font to Chicago-12 so it will fill out a paper invoice form better.

File   Edit   Formula   Format   Data   Options   Macro   Window

| D8 | =IF(B6<>"",VLOOKUP(B6,'A/R List'!Database,2),"") |

```
═══════════════════════ Invoice ═══════════════════════
                        INVOICE

        Date 8/28/85
    Invoice #

        To:                            ┌──────────┐
                                       └──────────┘



                 Description                    Amount
        _____        _____
```

A few more preliminary chores are necessary to make the invoice printing a smooth-running operation.

- The invoice number cell, B6, must be defined with a name (I used "inv.no"), because the macro will be selecting this cell to insert numbers of invoices to print.
- The cells comprising the invoice form must be set as a print area by selecting the entire form and choosing Set Print Area from the Options menu.
- The macro won't be able to select the print quality for invoice printing, nor would it be convenient to have the macro present the print dialog box prior to printing each invoice. You'll have to make sure the print quality is the one you desire prior to setting the invoice printing macro in motion. You can reset the quality with the printer turned off by clicking the appropriate button and then the OK button. As soon as the small status box appears in the middle of the screen, press Command-period to cancel printing. The changes you made to the print dialog box will now be recorded and won't change until you change them again.

PRINT INVOICE MACRO

With the invoice form doing so much of the relational database work, the macro that prints the invoices is relatively simple.

	M/Inv
	B
1	print.invoice
2	=SET.VALUE(counter,INPUT("Select starting Invoice No. to print:",1,"Print Invoice Info"))
3	=SET.VALUE(topcount,INPUT("Select ending Invoice No. to print:",1,"Print Invoice Info"))
4	=OPEN("Invoice")
5	=PAGE.SETUP("","",1,0.75,1,0.75,0,0)
6	start
7	=SELECT(!inv.no)
8	=FORMULA(counter)
9	=SELECT(!invoice)
10	=SET.PRINT.AREA()
11	=PRINT()
12	=counter+1
13	=IF(counter<>topcount+1,GOTO(start))
14	=CLOSE()
15	=RETURN()
16	3006
17	
18	
19	
20	

This macro is divided into two sections. The first prompts the user for the range of invoice numbers to print, while the second section does the actual printing of the invoices.

In macro cells B2 and B3, an INPUT dialog box is created to prompt for the starting and ending invoice number of a series to print. Those numbers are assigned to variables that track how many times the print routine below should be executed. When an INPUT dialog box appears on the screen, the user does not actually have to type in the invoice number. Excel allows you to click the cell on the desired worksheet to input the data from that cell.

 É File Edit Formula Format Data Options Macro Window

| A8 | | 3002 |

A/R List

	A	B	C	D	E	F
1						
2						
3					Today's Date:	28-Aug-85
4						
5	Invoice No.	Cust. No.	Description	Amount Due	Date Due	Aging (days)
6	3002	114	Radio Ad Copy	$40.00	30-Apr-85	120
7	3003	111	Newspaper Release	$25.00	31-Aug-85	-3
8	3004					-3
9	300					-3
10	3006					-3
11						
12						
13						
14						
15						
16						
17						
18						

Print Invoice Info

Select starting Invoice No. to print:

[OK]

[Cancel]

=$A$8

Therefore, when the dialog box requests the starting invoice number, you can click cell A8, for example, to do the equivalent of typing 3004 into the input dialog box. The starting invoice value is plugged into a cell defined below as "counter" (macro cell 10); the ending value is plugged into "topcount" (macro cell B16). I'll show you how these values are employed in a moment.

In the rest of the first section, the macro opens the Invoice form document and establishes a page setup configuration. Arguments in this function give you the power to essentially fill out the extensive Page Setup dialog box, including header/footer data (I've elected null strings for printing of this invoice form), margins (I'm sticking with the standard margin settings, but you can change them), and whether the output should print gridlines and row/column headings (not for this particular output).

Section two, labeled "start," is a loop that executes as many times as there are invoices to print. Its first step is to select the invoice form cell I previously defined as "inv.no." Into that invoice form cell, the macro places the contents of the macro cell defined as "counter," which also happens to be the starting invoice number (at least the first time through the loop).

When the invoice number is inserted into the form, all the relational formulas scattered throughout the form retrieve their data. Then the macro continues to its next instruction, PRINT.

After the first invoice prints, the value of "counter" in macro cell B12 increments itself by one. In macro cell B13, an IF formula tests to see if the value in counter is yet equivalent to the value of "topcount." Because the value of "counter" reads one more than the number of the last invoice printed, the IF test must test the actual invoice number (counter minus one) against the value of topcount. If the values are not equal, then the printing loop starts over. As soon as the value of counter-1 and topcount are the same, that means that all selected invoices have been printed. The Invoice worksheet is closed and control returns to the user.

I can think of several practical variations on this system. One worth exploring is having the macro insert a "flag," like a one into a cell at the right of the accounts-receivable database when the invoice prints. Then the macro can test for the presence of flags when selecting invoices to print—those without them will automatically be printed and flagged, thus eliminating the step of specifying which invoices are to be printed.

In the next chapter, I take this relational business one step further. Watch as Excel becomes a mail-merging machine.

Chapter **17**
MAIL MERGING

In the last chapter, I showed a relational database that printed batches of invoices, drawing data from two different worksheets along the way. Now, chances are good that no business has every customer on account paying bills on time. That's one of the reasons I placed an aging column in the accounts-receivable worksheet, so I know how many days late the deadbeats are. This is valuable data to a business, so why not make use of it and have Excel generate a dunning letter by assembling customer and invoice data into a form letter? That's precisely what I'll show you in this chapter.

Before you get too excited, I am in no way intimating that Excel is a word processor. I'd no sooner use Excel to generate a business letter or report than use a Ferrari to pull a semitrailer. But with relatively careful planning, you can at least merge the data in your databases into usable output that resembles word-processing output.

THE MERGE SYSTEM

As with the invoice form in the last chapter, the dunning letter is loaded with formulas that retrieve data from the customer list and accounts-receivable worksheets. The letter in its gridline and heading form looks like this:

	A	B	C	D	E	F
1						
2						
3						
4	30-Aug-85					
5						
6						
7	Wheelin's Gas Co.		#	114		
8	333 Fifth Ave.					
9	Lubbock		TX	73000		
10						
11	ATTN:		Ralph	Wheelin		
12						
13						
14	Good Day...					
15						
16	In reviewing our Accounts Receivables records, we find that one of your					
17	invoices is still unpaid after		122	days. The invoice in question is		
18	detailed below:					
19						
20		Invoice Date		Invoice No.	Amount Due	
21		3/31/85		3002	$40.00	
22						
23	Please remit the above amount to us as soon as possible so that we may					
24	keep your credit line open for further business with us.					
25						
26	Thank you for your prompt attention.					
27						
28						
29	Sincerely,					
30						
31						
32	Priscilla Morton					
33	Accounts Receivable Manager					
34						

I've increased the font size to Geneva-12, because that size prints better in a letter format. Formulas behave in this form as they do in the invoice form, with the invoice number being the one piece of data that sets up the chain reaction of VLOOKUP operations in many other cells. I've added the first and last name of the customer contact in cells B11 and C1, right-aligning the first name and left-aligning the last name. Notice, too, that the columns were arranged so that the number of days past due (cell C17) mixes in right with the rest of the text.

Text for each full line of the letter is entered in the leftmost cell of the row. Therefore, the first line of the letter is in cell A16. Because no values are entered into other cells in that row, the full line spills over across several columns of the row. In row 17, the next line is broken into two parts, one in cell A17 and the other in cell D17. When you print this worksheet without gridlines and headings, it could pass easily for a MacWrite or Microsoft Word document.

▤ THE PRINTING MACRO

Selecting invoices from the accounts-receivable worksheet to print is a different proposition than printing a contiguous range of records for printing purposes. The macro must evaluate each record and print only those that are past due (in this hypothetical business, "past due" means one day past the due date stated on the invoice). Because the macro will be evaluating the aging column of the accounts-receivable document, I defined the top cell of that range as "agetop" (see the following Table for a list of all cell and range names used in the mail-merge models). The bottom of the range will be continually changing with the number of records in this document, so I leave the naming of the range bottom to the macro.

The macro that prints the dunning letters is called late.letter and resides on the same macro sheet as the invoice generator, so only one macro document needs to be maintained for all accounts-receivable work.

	C
1	late.letter
2	=OPEN("Late Letter")
3	=PAGE.SETUP("","",1,0.75,1,0.75,0,0)
4	=ACTIVATE("A/R List")
5	=SELECT.LAST.CELL()
6	=DEFINE.NAME("dbbot",ACTIVE.CELL())
7	=SELECT(!dbtop:!dbbot)
8	=SET.DATABASE()
9	=SELECT(OFFSET(!dbtop,1,0))
10	loop
11	=IF(ACTIVE.CELL()<>"",GOTO(advance),GOTO(end))
12	end
13	=ACTIVATE("Late Letter")
14	=CLOSE()
15	=ACTIVATE("A/R List")
16	=RETURN()
17	
18	advance
19	=IF(OFFSET(ACTIVE.CELL(),0,5)>30,letter())
20	=SELECT(OFFSET(ACTIVE.CELL(),1,0))
21	=GOTO(loop)
22	
23	letter
24	=SELECT(ACTIVE.CELL())
25	=COPY()
26	=ACTIVATE("Late Letter")
27	=SELECT(!invno)
28	=PASTE.SPECIAL(3,1)
29	=PRINT()
30	=ACTIVATE("A/R List")
31	=RETURN()
32	

The macro is divided into five sections. The first section does preliminary work such as opening the letter document and setting the database range. The second section qualifies each row of the database to make sure it contains a record. It also branches to either the third section (which cleans up the screen prior to ending the macro) or the fourth section (which checks each record for ones that are past due). If a record indicates a past-due account, the fifth section plugs the invoice number into the letter template and does the actual printing.

Macro cell C2 opens the letter template file, followed by a formula that establishes the page setup specifications for the letter when it prints. In cell C4, the accounts-receivable worksheet is activated so that the next five formulas can: 1) define the last cell of the worksheet as "dbbot," for it is also the bottom cell of the database; 2) select the entire database region, from the previously defined cell, "dbtop," to "dbbot"; 3) set the database region; and 4) select the first invoice number cell, which is offset one row from dbtop.

In the one-line macro section labeled loop, Excel tests the invoice number cell in a row to make sure a number is entered. If not, it means that there are no more invoices, and the macro should end. But if there is a value in the cell, then execution branches to the section labeled advance.

The advance macro first inspects the aging column of the current row (offset 5 columns to the right) to see if the value there is greater than 30. If the value is less than 30, then execution continues to macro cell C20, which advances the active cell pointer down one row for another test in the "loop" section.

But if the value in the aging active cell is more than 30, then execution jumps temporarily to the macro section labeled letter at cell C23. This macro copies the invoice number from the active cell (i.e., the invoice number cell). Then the letter template is activated, the invoice number cell in it selected, and the invoice number value in the Clipboard pasted into the letter. At that instant, the VLOOKUP formulas in the letter template go to work retrieving the specifics about the invoice and customer. When they're done, the macro continues and prints the letter as just filled in. And after printing, execution returns to the point in the advance section where the active cell pointer is moved down one line before returning to the loop section for another test.

Once all the records in the database have been tested in loop, the macro proceeds to the end section. Here, the letter template worksheet is activated so it can be closed—there's no sense cluttering up your Excel workspace with unnecessary documents. The accounts-receivable worksheet is made the active window, and the macro returns control to you.

Despite what seems to be a lengthy list of macro commands and VLOOKUP formulas in the letter template, this system operates so quickly that you'll have to watch closely to see what goes on as the macro tests the aging column for deadbeats. The best part, however, is that you don't have to watch. If you have continuous-form letterhead, you can set this macro into motion and walk about as the letters are printed out unattended. You can also use single–sheet-fed paper, if you like, but be sure to change the Paper parameter in the Print dialog box before starting this macro. Excel will pause after the printing of each letter and beep at you to put a new sheet of paper into the printer. This is a handy system and one that can be adapted to many applications.

WHAT NOW?

If you've been following the tips and examples in this book, you should be well equipped to tackle all sorts of applications. You also will agree that although Macintosh software for specific applications—medical, real estate, banking, manufacturing—is not abundant today, Excel is flexible enough and powerful enough to fill that gap quickly. Some Excel experts may even find new careers in supplying quick, custom applications for clients wanting to adopt Macs in their workplaces.

Be forever on the lookout for ways to make Excel lighten your workload. Think of ways to let macros make your Excel work more automatically. And in the best spirit of personal computing, share your discoveries with other Excel users. Chances are you'll learn other practical shortcuts, strategies, and techniques.

APPENDICES

APPENDIX A
PASTING DOCUMENTS INTO
MACWRITE AND WORD

A popular feature of the Macintosh is its ability to copy sections of one kind of document and paste them into other kinds of documents. On other computers, notably the IBM PC, this often is impossible unless the programs are completely compatible with one another or share a particular environment, such as windows. Even then, you're not necessarily guaranteed a happy mixture of documents. But with the Mac, if you can copy something to the Clipboard, you can import it into a MacWrite or Microsoft Word document.

Excel makes it quite easy to import graphs or pieces of a spreadsheet into a MacWrite or Word document. But with this flexibility comes the added responsibility of understanding the principles of certain techniques that may affect your printed output, particularly if you print your word-processing output on a LaserWriter.

Graphic Transfers

Because moving a chart into a word-processing document is the simplest, I'll start with that. When you have a chart as the active document on the Excel screen, you have a special option in the Edit menu called Copy Chart. Choosing this item brings a small dialog box that asks whether you wish to copy the chart in the size in which it would normally print or in the exact size of the current window.

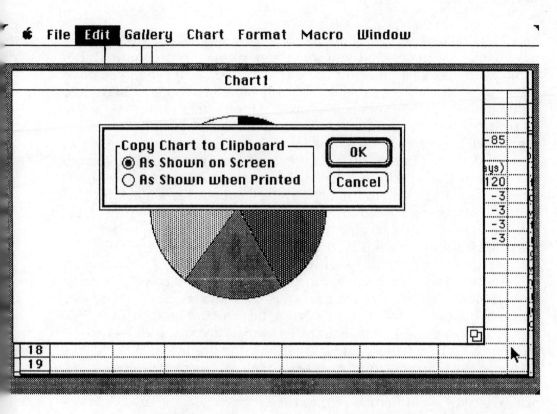

As mentioned in Part I, an Excel chart can be most easily customized in MacDraw because each element of an Excel chart retains its independence when copied to MacDraw. If you are concerned about the appearance of a chart in an important report, then I suggest you spiff up the chart in MacDraw and then import the finished chart from MacDraw into your word-processing program.

☰ Worksheets the Easy Way

Excel offers a clever way of importing worksheets into a word-processing document that you may have missed in the manual. It's by way of a special menu command that appears only when you have a worksheet as the active document and hold down the Shift key while pulling down the Edit menu. The special menu item is labeled "Copy Picture." What this option does (again, it's only when the Shift key is pressed) is take a kind of snapshot of the selected area on the worksheet and store it in the Clipboard. From there, you can change over to your word processor and paste the segment into a document.

Because the segment is stored in the Clipboard as a MacPaintlike picture, the pasted spreadsheet is likewise treated as a picture. That means that you won't be able to change any of the text in the section. All you'll be able to do is adjust its centering and depth. But, just like a picture, if you stretch the picture vertically, the contents will distort.

Another important caution applies to those who run their word-processing output through the LaserWriter. The section of spreadsheet that is in picture form does not address the printer's built-in fonts, but is printed as a graphic image. In other words, if you use Helvetica-10 for your Excel worksheet and copy it as a picture into a Word document, all the Word document sees in that spot is a picture consisting of a bunch of dots.

When the document is sent to the LaserWriter, the printer interprets the spreadsheet segment only as a bit-mapped picture, not with the same very high-resolution text characters that the rest of the document will have. The difference will be noticeable mostly to someone who is accustomed to checking typeface quality, because the LaserWriter does its best to smooth bit-mapped graphics. Still, the Excel paste won't be of exactly the same resolution as surrounding text—something that may influence a decision to offset-print a document from LaserWriter masters.

≡ Worksheet Text Transfers

If the print quality or consistent typeface is important to your finished report, then you probably should import figures from a spreadsheet the old-fashioned way by simply selecting the range of cells and choosing Copy from the Edit menu. This places only the numbers—without any text-character formatting—into the Clipboard.

Changing over to the word processor and pasting the figures into a document may be a shock at first. If you do nothing to change the default tab setting in MacWrite or Microsoft Word, the columns and rows of figures will appear to be scattered all over the screen. What's happening, however, is that when Excel saves columns of text to the Clipboard, it precedes each character with invisible tab characters corresponding to the number of columns in from the left edge of the selection copied into the Clipboard. With the MacWrite default tab way out at 55, the original columns are all jumbled.

To remedy the situation, simply add tabs to the ruler line above the pasted text. You'll need as many tabs as there are columns of text in the selection. Remember, too, that the original text was created in a relatively small font, Geneva-10 (unless you changed the font). In the process of copying and pasting, the font characteristics are stripped away. The text takes on the current font of the word-processing document. Even after adjusting the tab markers, you may have to select all the text and change the font to a smaller size to squeeze all the columns into the width of a MacWrite or Word document.

≡≡≡ # APPENDIX B
USING EXCEL WITH EXPANDED MEMORY

It's amazing how quickly several key software products appeared for the Mac that tax even the 512K of memory of the so-called Fat Mac. The latest incarnation of Excel, version 1.5, is likewise a memory hog, making it unsuitable for use on a Macintosh with anything less than one megabyte of memory. Therefore, Excel cannot be used on the 128K or 512K Macintosh. If you have one of these older machines, you'll need to outfit it with at least one megabyte of RAM or else buy another Macintosh.

Even if you have one megabyte of RAM in your computer, Excel feels cramped. You will find little room (less than about 50K) if you use Excel with MultiFinder. If you are in the habit of creating worksheets of any size, you'll need to use the regular Finder when operating Excel on a one-megabyte Mac. Obviously, you won't be able to run Excel under MultiFinder with another program unless you have more than one megabyte of memory.

If you find you need more memory to construct even the simplest worksheets—especially if you are using MultiFinder—try reducing the size of the Macintosh system. This includes removing unnecessary fonts and desk accessories using the Font/DA Mover utility. Additionally, special system resources such as QuicKeys and Control Panel icons should be removed if not needed. These system resources are located as separate files in the System Folder and are removed simply by locating them in another folder. You always can put them back if you need them later.

Many owners of the Macintosh SE and II have more than one megabyte of RAM. If you are one of the fortunate people who are gifted with excess RAM, you can use it for more than just creating huge worksheets.

One approach is to create a RAM disk with the extra memory and place the Excel program in it. RAM disk software—available commercially as stand-alone products or as public domain or shareware programs—fools the computer into thinking it has an extra disk drive attached to it. Therefore, even though you see an icon on the desktop for a disk, all storage is in a special section of memory reserved for that purpose.

CAUTION: A RAM disk disappears when you turn off the power, so don't store any documents there in case the power goes out before you have a chance to copy them to floppies.

RAM disks on the Mac are best used for program and System file storage. Placing these items on a RAM disk speeds up the operation of the Mac by many times. The first time you witness a RAM disk in action, you won't believe your eyes.

Excel is a large program as Macintosh programs go and requires a RAM disk of upwards of 600K. You'll need an extra 400K if you want to include the System and Finder files on the RAM disk, for a total of one megabyte.

If you have 2.5 megabytes in your Mac, for example, creating a one-megabyte RAM disk leaves 1.5 megabytes for application space. With MultiFinder and Excel loaded at the same time, the remaining free memory is around 500K, enough for a fairly large worksheet or another moderate-size application. Note that with MultiFinder, you can have Excel operate in the "background" while you go off to do another task. While you are working on another application, Excel can be calculating an extremely complex worksheet.

INDEX